WALKING THROUGH
DARKNESS:

a Memoir of Recovery

Marilyn Shelton

WALKING THROUGH DARKNESS:
a Memoir of Recovery

Copyright © 2018 by Marilyn R. Shelton
ISBN-13: 978-1539109105
ISBN-10: 1539109100

Cover design by Graphixity
Interior layout and print design by Laura Shinn Designs
http://laurashinn.yolasite.com

ACKNOWLEDGEMENTS

I would like to thank Laura Shinn and C. Milton Neeley for their beautiful design work, as well as the Graphixity team. Thanks to Aileen Hampton for your critical editorial eye. What would I have done without you? I would like to express gratitude to my family for making me the person I am today. Mom, Dad, Carmen, Jesse, Jackie, Hayden and my cousins, thank you. Thanks to: Kelsey, Aileen, Paula, Bradi, Lusiana, Kassandra, Elham, Lois and Helena for your friendship. Luxury Cat, you have a special place in my heart. And an acknowledgements page wouldn't be complete without a tribute to my miniature pinschers Chloe and Goose, and the memory of Stella.

PREFACE

I felt a need to share my inspirational story of recovery from psychiatric drug addiction, as well as from the field of *psychiatry itself*, so that others can benefit from my experiences. When one thinks of vices one must cease to indulge in, psychiatry and the avoidance of psychiatrists aren't usually among them. Gambling, food addiction, and street drugs more commonly come to mind as bad habits to stop. But the psychiatric system and psychiatric drugs were just as damaging, if not more damaging, to me, than any other addictions I might have had.

Psychiatrist William Glasser, a contrarian in his field with an alternative viewpoint, warns of the hazards of erroneous labeling and a forced identification as permanently ill which can occur while obtaining psychiatric treatment. He lists those hazards as:

1.) Being diagnosed mentally ill when you're not.

2.) Treatment for nonexistent illness, often with harmful brain drugs; and worst of all,

3.) being told that there is nothing you can do for yourself.

(*Warning: Psychiatry can be Hazardous to Your Mental Health* 2003)

For while seeking help for insomnia, I witnessed personally and observed other patients mocked by clinicians, saw their refusal to be taken seriously, forced drugging and a forced identification as permanently ill that was encouraged by medical staff.

At this point, *recovered* is a label I wear proudly. I found traditional psychiatric medications harsh and personality blunting, and they therefore made me less likely to recover and to want to engage with others. You might find the process of how I healed without prescription pills, making it through the perils of the psychiatric system, helpful to you, and that is why I decided to write this memoir. I hope that someone, somewhere, can benefit from my experiences so that they don't have to go through the trials I did. If you must endure anyway, well, then at least maybe you can glean something from my story that speaks to you. And if not afflicted by a mood or sleep disorder yourself, then perhaps you know a friend, sibling, or coworker who can gain from this knowledge. The printing of my experiences, I hope, can shed light on the issue of patient rights as well as helping to end abuses by the psychiatric system. In the end, my specific diagnosis doesn't matter. I am me, and you are you, and we are individuals. We all have a different chemical makeup and background and should receive treatments tailored to those makeups.

Traditional psychiatry never spoke of recovery, but sound nutrition and a restful night's sleep were steps in an overall process that helped me to heal. Best of all, these methods do not come with the risks of permanent movement disorders, dulled cognition, and thyroid disorders that conventional psychiatric methods carry.

I chose the title *Walking through Darkness* for this research-based memoir, because I used walking exercise to increase brain endorphins and to improve my mood during a dark period in my life. Exercise helps to balance one's cortisol secretion, which reduces stress and anxiety. In keeping with the hopeful, optimistic theme of this book, I wanted to convey an image of walking *toward* something, such as moving toward more natural treatments and *away* from the dark days when I took conventional psychiatric drugs which only made me feel worse. That is why I chose this title.

I hope that the state of wellness I find myself in is more than mere coincidence or a fluke. I hope that I am not just in remission or simply riding the crest of a wave or experiencing a high point. I hope that I do not fall into a valley and become ill again. But that I have maintained a state of wellness for a long period of time is a good indication that the state is permanent, and the more time that passes, the more it seems likely that I will continue to do well without psychiatric drugs.

I now am able to sleep a full eight hours a night, to manage a productive job and social life without drugs, and no longer need hospitalization. Traditional psychiatrists told me I would be dependent on psychiatric drugs for the rest of my life, but ironically, I only seemed to recover once I had stopped taking the harsh, damaging pills.

My story began with sleep. Specifically, it began with sleep deprivation. Take away a basic need like food or sleep, and you can separate the sane from the insane based on the lack of sleep alone. Doing without sleep can make a sane person insane. Each of us are just a few days from wild anarchy if such an important basic factor as sleep is removed from our lives.

The consequences of sleep deprivation are severe. That's something we know without thinking, but just how bad are the effects? A Medscape study that attempted to demonstrate the consequences of insomnia cited: After 24 hours of wakefulness, the subjects' performance was equivalent to that seen in persons who are legally intoxicated. My complaints weren't mild ones. When I don't sleep, my bones ache. I feel old, achy and ancient. There's good reason for this, as during sleep the body releases growth hormones and replenishes neurotransmitters that help the brain perceive pain. A sleep deprived person behaves much the same way someone with fibromyalgia or arthritis does. One precipitates the other—those with insomnia are more likely to feel depressed, due to exhaustion and frazzled brain chemicals.

Yet, today I have managed to cure my insomnia with less harmful treatments than the drugs it was suggested I would need for the rest of my life—a prediction that did not turn out to be true. I keep a regular schedule, avoid caffeine, get plenty of exercise, and expose myself to morning daylight. I avoid viewing electronic devices before bedtime to synchronize my body clock with the natural rhythms of the earth. I wish I had resorted to doing these things from the beginning; but live a little, learn a little, and with time comes wisdom. Here is my story.

WALKING THROUGH
DARKNESS:

a Memoir of Recovery

CHAPTER 1

A Crack in the Armor

After spending hours in front of the mirror, I tap my head and hear a satisfactory crunch. My immobile hair is just the way I like it. I am ready for work. I have picked and prodded and aligned each strand to perfection. So what if my head feels like it's set in concrete?

I am twenty-three years old and employed as a preschool teacher and I am under a lot of work-related stress. Occupational anxiety led to severe insomnia which led to sleepless exhaustion, which led me to darken a prescriber's door. But the antidepressant I received to help me sleep amplified my underlying obsessive tendencies, rendering the tablet completely ineffective and even *worsening* my problems. Where before I suffered only from insomnia, the antidepressant caused me to develop a fixation with my hair. Also, my sleep was sparser and more interrupted than before I began taking the tablets. The pills had a primary undesired effect—they increased my energy levels to frenetic proportions and provided me with a small, narrowly focused world view. On the antidepressants, what was not a problem before was suddenly magnified tenfold. You'd think that one pill would have been considered sufficient and that *two* would have been considered overkill for my zealous prescriber. But who is to say what she was thinking before putting pen to pad?

Although I feel I cannot control the environment in which I work, I can control one aspect of my life—my appearance. Behind my obsessive grooming is the motivation to monopolize the circumstances of my life, which of course, just isn't possible. But control of my hair gives me the illusion that my life is in order. At the preschool, I imagine pupils' parents shunning me and rejecting my classroom curriculum, which involved teaching colors and shapes and was not particularly enriching, nor complex.

What occurred to me was a statistically common happening in the psychiatric world. I complained of insomnia and was given sedating antidepressants. At least the chemicals in the drug were *supposed* to sedate me. But they did not achieve what they were designed for; quite the opposite. The antidepressants transformed my insomnia into something monstrous and caused a switchover into a manic state. Antidepressants can act as stimulants in those susceptible and cause a switch toward mania in approximately 8.2 percent of people, particularly in children and adolescents. This sort of antidepressant-induced frenzy can occur even in people who aren't predisposed to mood disorders, particularly in the young. Indeed, the rate of becoming manic on antidepressants is *four times higher* for youth than it is for adults, according to the *Psychiatric Times*. I was just twenty-three years old at the time my crisis began.

In 2004, the FDA called for a black box warning to be placed on antidepressants warning of suicidal behavior in children and adolescents, stating clear legal warnings, but I knew nothing of these statements before my horror descended. In 2007, the FDA extended the age range to include a warning on antidepressants for young adults up to age 24. I hadn't read them. The warning came shortly after the FDA completed a study which concluded that the rate of suicide was higher for those taking antidepressants than those on placebo. The black box warning on antidepressants is the most severe warning an agency can place on a drug or product, short of an outright ban. The black box warning is much like the surgeon general's warning on a pack of cigarettes. Warning: May cause harm or death. I would soon realize that the drug I was taking was the cause of my problem. Some aren't so lucky and end up killing themselves, unaware that their medication is creating their symptoms. Some become homicidal. If psychiatric drugs are so helpful, why are there currently over 35 documented cases of school shootings committed by people either on or having taken psychiatric drugs? Columbine High School shooter Eric Harris was on the antidepressant Luvox at the time of the shooting.

Luckily, I did not choose to commit suicide, have never had any thoughts of hurting others, and avoided becoming a statistic. Though I think psychiatric drugs do help some manage their moods and for some can be the difference between being functional or not, I believe doctors should take more time to explain the potential risks of the drugs to their patients.

On the prescribed antidepressant, I also developed restless legs syndrome. The chances of developing this syndrome is more common in women than men. *Drug Watch* states that antidepressants are linked to akathisia, which is an inability to sit still, and also that akathisia is sometimes misdiagnosed as worsening mental illness, necessitating a dosage increase—an occurrence that happened to me. It was only after I stopped taking all psychiatric drugs that my bizarre leg movements ceased. As if following a tired, deceptive formula, upon observation of the new symptoms caused by the drug, my clinician felt it necessary to institute an increase in dosage, which only compounded the problem as I wasn't suited to the drug in the first place. Receiving *more* of it was disastrous. I felt bombarded by pills at this point and demonstrated zero improvement to advocate for their instatement and continued use. After observation of the new behavior I displayed on the additional antidepressant, I was then given an additional *diagnosis* as well. A diagnosis of manic depression, even though the *DSM-IV* (the Diagnostic and Statistical Manual of Mental Disorders) clearly states:

"Manic-like episodes that are clearly *caused* by somatic antidepressant treatment (e.g., medication, electroconvulsive therapy) *should not count* toward a diagnosis of Bipolar I Disorder."

(First 1994)

Hence what came to be a diagnosis of "manic depression" should have been a diagnosis of "antidepressant-induced mania with primary underlying insomnia." For six years after my introduction to psychiatry, I failed to ever get "manic" again without the help of stimulant drugs. Nor was I driven to extreme behavior such as spending sprees, like many manic-depressive individuals. The only time I felt suicidal in my life, was while I was on psychiatric drugs. My misdiagnosis was so obvious to later psychiatrists that they found the incompetency of the previous doctor's diagnoses humorous when they discussed my records. I found nothing funny about the whole situation and my long period of suffering. Misdiagnosis or not, suffering is suffering. Nor was I ever asked for a current list of medications before being prescribed an additional antidepressant, polypharmacy at its best.

The drugs used to treat manic depression by conventional psychiatry can be very harsh. With my new misdiagnoses, I became subject to them in the effort to treat me—a guinea pig test subject. Lithium is an elemental salt prescribed to treat the condition. As a salt, lithium acts upon the thyroid. But lithium carbonate produces memory loss in 32.5 percent of those taking it, and comes with a six-fold increase in rates of hypothyroidism. A slowed thyroid could make one sluggish and *more depressed* over the state of one's sloth-like condition—ironically undoing the desired effects of the drug. Furthermore, due to the high amount of elemental lithium delivered in lithium carbonate, toxicity can easily occur. Blood levels of lithium must be monitored closely to prevent convulsions, coma, brain damage and death. These risky and even fatal consequences can occur when simply trying to obtain psychiatric treatment. Withdrawal from lithium may lead to a manic episode as the brain can become excitatory in response to its formerly dampened-down state.

(Marohn 2011)

Drugs such as Depakote and Lamictal, originally created for use in epilepsy, are also used to treat manic depression and have demonstrated efficacy in calming the brain. Antiepileptic drugs do not come without a cost to the user, however. Trembling hands, dulled cognition, and more may result from taking these drugs.

Depakote, in particular, depletes the body of folic acid needed for proper fetal development and can cause birth defects. Therefore, Depakote is a particularly devastating drug for women of childbearing age. Depakote can induce polycystic ovarian syndrome due to its influence on female hormones. It raises levels of androgens such as testosterone in the female body, which may be responsible for male-like hair growth or baldness in women using Depakote. A post-Depakote peek at the beard I could have grown, thanks to the drug, would have undone all the drug's purported usefulness, had this happened to me.

A study by Dr. Hadine Joffe at Massachusetts General Hospital looked at the rates for polycystic ovarian syndrome in women taking psychiatric drugs and found that Depakote produced menstrual irregularities in 10.5 percent of women (86 were studied), compared with 1.4 percent of women on lithium or anticonvulsants other than Depakote.

(Health 2007)

Yet there may be more natural, safer ways of calming excitable brains. High levels of glutamate found in overactive brains were found to be calmed by calcium and magnesium, which worked the same way anticonvulsants do with their effect on nerve cell transmission, slowing it, without severe side effects. Calcium and magnesium can reduce anxiety and induce calm. In studies by Chouinard and Giannini, some people with psychiatric complaints had lowered amounts of magnesium in their blood. When magnesium was added to their diet, rates of manic cycling slowed. Calcium and magnesium can also help reduce muscle twitching and restlessness and improve sleep, also due to their effect on nerve cell transmission.

(al. 1990)

Treatments aside, there is no reason to despair over the outcomes for mood and sleep disorders. Even *without treatment*, optimism is higher than previously thought. Although conventional medicine would have you think otherwise, even in those with *schizophrenia*, a more severe diagnosis than the one I was given, outcomes for recovery are more hopeful than one would think. Here are some statistics demonstrating that spontaneous recovery is possible:

- A quarter of all schizophrenics recover completely within the first two years of illness, no matter what type of treatment (or lack of it) they receive. Such patients may be considered to have recovered spontaneously. In such cases, they may have been experiencing a short-term life crisis.

- Another quarter, when maintained on neuroleptics, live relatively independently and can usually work, but relapse without drugs and so must continue taking them indefinitely. This may be due to a supersensitivity psychosis (an extreme dopamine sensitivity effect induced by the drugs) or the underlying original psychosis.

- A third quarter remain ill and can just barely sustain themselves outside of the hospital. They tend toward negative symptoms, such as poverty of thought and anhedonia. They are frequently isolated and unable to maintain friendships, or to undertake the kind of work they used to engage in, if they can work at all. They need support to survive and may occasionally need to be re-hospitalized. These people are termed "improved."

- Fifteen percent become chronically schizophrenic and are hospitalized frequently, if not continually.
- Ten percent kill themselves, usually within the first ten years of illness.

  The last two groups are not considered "recovered."

  (Edelman n.d.)

Here are more hopeful statistics concerning recovery from mood disorders. In 1952, Dr. Hans Eysenck performed a study which demonstrated that two-thirds of "neurotic" patients recovered from their illness within two years of onset, whether they received psychotherapy or not. (Mitchell 1992)

This could be because mood and sleep disorders are cyclical, weaving in and out, present sometimes, and allowing you to be symptom free in others. Insomnia is your enemy some nights, and other nights you will sleep like a baby. The true nature of mood and sleep disorders is that they vary as does the weather. Moods can rage like storms or you can be as calm as the sea. A 2002 study in the Netherlands found that the median duration of major-depressive episodes was three months for those who had no professional care, 4.5 months for those who sought primary care, and six months for those who entered the mental health care system. (http://asserttrue.blogspot.com/2013/04/spontaneous-recovery-from-depression.html# 2013)

CHAPTER 2

Teacher Creature

Not long after ingesting the *second* antidepressant, my hair became my sole focus. Hair, of all body parts to agonize over. If one pill worsened my insomnia, two caused me to go off the deep end. What a foolish thing to worry about, *hair*, something that just "exists" on your head, a benign object that grows quietly and in tiny increments while you sleep. Keratin, that's all it is, hair. Keratin, a fibrous protein that makes up your mane. Yet my hair had become a huge problem, one to spend wasteful hours pondering and arranging.

I dreamt up termination scenarios at night when I went home. I was afraid of being socially abandoned and made frantic, nonsensical efforts to avoid being alone, thinking that being fired would be the ultimate abandonment. A job that might only be moderately stressful for others, or not at all to some, was nerve-wracking to me. The observations by school administrators, meeting the demands of children who seemed to go twenty discombobulated ways at once, their crying and screaming fits, dealing with parental concerns—these responsibilities were all too much for me.

My fears sparked irrational, self-soothing behavior. I would measure with my fingers the exact distance that my hair took up on my face and the way it fell, and then attempt to arrange the slightest flyaway strands into a subjective navigation point that I labeled "organization." Not a true hair-plucking sufferer of trichotillomania, I felt no need to actually *rip* my hair out. I became an obsessive who craved tactile control and enjoyed varying textures and sensations.

I attempted to smooth what I thought was a disheveled appearance, but I probably looked rather ordinary to others. I spent endless time staring at myself in the mirror. I made up a set of rules for myself to follow, religiously. My logic all made sense to me in a sick, twisted way, but my instructions were legible only to me. I made sure my hair was properly held back and stiffly stapled down, until my hair felt sanitary to myself, which was what I was going for. Loaded with exactly seventy-five bobby pins a day, I would carefully count them out, making sure that not even a single hair was out of place. Continuing the antidepressants, wanting to be compliant with my prescriber's instructions, I developed irrational fears and became more and more obsessive. My hair was not allowed to touch my face, ever! What if my hair scraped my eye, causing a corneal abrasion? My solution? I wore ponytails to work. Every single day. But then I felt ashamed of wearing a ponytail because I thought ponytails were a style reserved for gym teachers and Casual Fridays. I was worried I would look too sporty, that staff members would notice the perpetual ponytail and secretly mock it, and that I would be fired due to a violation of the dress code. The ponytail was the only way to go before making the drastic movement of chopping it all off, and I loved my long, dark brown hair with its natural auburn highlights. Random strangers so loved my hair, as well, that they would stop me in stores to ask what kind of shampoo I used.

One day, after downing a couple tablets, I stood in front of the mirror and began to look for a solution to my hair issue. I armed myself with "treatments" in the form of hair accessories. That was when I came up with the bobby pin solution. An army of bobby pins. *Far* too many of them. The excessive pins would fall out on the classroom floor, in the hallway of the school, on the lunch tables, with a sharp, metallic *ping*. I would arrive at work the next day and find, embarrassingly, that the bobby pins were still there on the carpet and that the janitor hadn't vacuumed them up. The myriad pins were a testament to my oddness, a trail of hair accessories spread like breadcrumbs by Hansel and Gretel that, if followed, could lead to the weirdo. At age twenty-three, and without ever having to become a bag lady, I would be known as "The Bobby Pin Girl," with a virtual bird's nest of metal living in my hair. At least that was what I assumed would happen, as I always assumed the worst. My hair must have looked overly neat and stuffy in the pompous, old- fashioned hairdo I settled on. If one hair was out of place, I felt I would freak.

The antidepressant would fill in my cracks, solving all my problems, I thought, influenced by an oversimplified version of a return-to-wellness in drug commercials. My insomnia was a simple case of faulty chemistry. Errant synapses would need to be sent the proper neuronal message, which would be relayed there by the drug, I thought. After that, I would go back to sleeping like a baby.

Oops. This theory was a miscalculation.

I ingest the drug about the time my mom and brother are getting ready to leave on a fishing trip. I am home from teaching, on summer vacation. At least that's how I can gauge the time period by memory. I felt they were abandoning me that day. Thus, they are acting out my worst fears. My family members pack up their tackle boxes and their gear while avoiding eye contact. This must have be due to my disheveled appearance, bloodshot eyes and frantic pacing back and forth, all effects of the drug. I don't blame them. I'm not pleasant to look at nor talk to, nor did I seem particularly stable. My family members avert their eyes and pretend as if they are in a hurry to leave when we all knew the beach wasn't going anywhere anytime soon, neither is high tide encroaching. There is an obvious squeamishness in their actions. They quicken their pace and pretend as if I were an object and not a person, as they hurriedly stuff food into a picnic basket.

They may have said something like, "Just stay home and stop being a nuisance," yet I perceive their words as rejection. Not just rejection, but a complete rejection of everything I am and everything I stand for. They don't want me. The impaired state the drug creates, in combination with lack of sleep, lead me to believe they are abandoning me forever, though they are scheduled to return in a few hours.

I just want to accompany them on the fishing trip. I think that the cool, undulating waves and soft breeze would rock me to sleep. My insomnia is worse than ever. I haven't slept for days. I pace around the yard dressed in my pajamas as my mom and brother continue packing their fishing gear, while I fail to assist them in the carrying of a cooler or the storing of a pole. I am a sideshow spectacle to them. I am so agitated that if I could have escaped my body, I would have opted to. The nervous pacing does not relieve my restless energy, but I feel if I do not stay on the move, I will explode. So I pace all day like a tiger in a cage, barefoot. Shoes feel restricting. There is no relief. I don't know that my brain is being flooded with synthetic dopamine and serotonin.

In my mind, I blow up the perceived fishing trip abandonment to catastrophic proportions, assigning it my own meaning. What if they never came back? My wild pacing and odd behavior had surely scared them away forever. They had terminated all lines of communication. That had to be why they left. I howled, tears rolling down my face.

At the school where I worked, I had recently become nonfunctional. I made forced cheery conversation with parents. About their children, about their health, their specific allergies. Most parents were just delighted to see their kids, to scoop them up in their arms after a long day at work, but others went on and on with lists of required adherences to fad diets, medication dosages, likes and dislikes, their child's habits, and all manner of pickiness. I felt as if the pupils' parents would peek past my neurotic front and discover that I wasn't sane and was consuming a wide variety of psychoactive substances, besides. Or that I would forget their requirements and would feed Little Johnny a food he was allergic to, causing him to go into anaphylactic shock. I must have held it together well enough, because my boss gave me an award, "Employee of the Month," and bestowed upon me the honor of having a set of keys to open the place. Exactly the sort of responsibility that was above me at the time, I felt.

The drug did work... at first. It worked a little too well. Several weeks after the chemical had a chance to accumulate in my body, I was suffering from insomnia more severe than I ever had before. I never slept but was somehow still too exhausted to sleep, if such a thing was possible. My heart began to race. I could feel it pounding in my chest.

On my twenty-fourth birthday my brother gave me a card with Robert Pattinson on the cover, knowing I was a fan of the *Twilight* series. The card had a digital song box in it, and when you opened the cover, it played a haunting vampire tune reminiscent of a bygone era. I opened and reopened the card repetitively, until the worn song device broke, exhausted. The song triggered in me sad memories and an awareness of the passage of time. I was twenty-four now, childhood was gone and I was somehow *old*, *now*. My mind, like an image reflected in a fun house mirror—thanks to the psychotropic drugs I was on—convinced me of warped ideas. Twenty-four, by any means, isn't old by society's measures, but that was what my mind told me. I was ancient now, though no one else would agree. I felt a sense of loss. I seemed to myself to have passed some marker where childhood's last remnants were stored, forever certain I would never retrieve my youth.

I called my dad on the Fourth of July, the holiday shortly after my birthday. Ignoring the fireworks, I got right down to business. I told him that something didn't seem right. In fact, something seemed *very* wrong.

"Dad, I'm depressed." Then, more urgently, "Daddy, I wish I was dead." The antidepressants I was on gave me suicidal tendencies, though I didn't know what was causing me to feel the way I did. Flooded by synthetic serotonin, my brain had stopped producing its own supply and had downgraded its production output.

"Don't say that!" he said, concerned.

But my dad couldn't reach me. No one could. I was drugged and living in outer space. Days would go by and I would never feel tired. I showed up for work feeling that there was something very unusual about not sleeping. Didn't most people go home and sleep at night as a general rule, and as a way of restoring themselves? Isn't that what we all went home to do—to recharge our batteries? I asked my fellow teachers if they slept *every single* night and they gave me strange looks. Of course they did! We'd help the children finger-paint and play with blocks. We'd clean up the colorful stains on the walls, then I'd drag myself home in a zombie-like state after another draining, stressful day. I experienced little joy, pleasure or delight at the prospect of molding young minds, nor did I notice the playful glee the children expressed. I was a robot.

There were still some bright spots of cheer in my dismal life. I adored Ralph, a fat, blond two-year-old at the preschool where I went after I'd finished with my job as a reading teacher at the elementary school. (Working two jobs couldn't have helped my stress levels much.) Ralph had two buck teeth and spiky hair, styled by his parents, no doubt. I would have been very impressed had he been able to tame his coiffure that way on his own merits. If he had, he probably would have used mashed potatoes as styling gel. He was two years old, what other hair products were accessible to him? Sweet little Ralph. Ralph was happy and lively and toddled around pointing at everything with one finger and affixing a label of "this" to every object whose name or title he didn't know. But even Ralph's childlike sunniness could not warm the darkness in my soul.

I began to wear dowdy, worn-out clothes. After so many nights without sleep, I lost the will to care. My dress became frumpy and low fuss. I'd wear whatever required the least effort to put on, the first item I reached for in the drawer or the first shirt off the hanger in the morning. My mind became a cocktail swamp of warped brain chemicals. The drugs created an odd, altered mental state which had begun to affect my behavior, pushing it to extremes. I then became euphoric on the antidepressants and so became a more aesthetically minded person. Beauty drew me in, captivating me, and I attempted fill my life with as much of it as possible, though it had gone unnoticed before. Silk, soft fabrics, and manicured nails were paramount to me. I actually had the energy to embellish my clothes with appliqués, refurbish my boots, and sew myself skirts made of the most elegant of fabrics as a part of my regular fashion wear. I gave old furniture facelifts and took up crafting. On the pills, I was Martha Stewart on speed. After ingesting them, I was capable of accomplishing the most difficult of achievements—in my sole opinion.

Right before I had to quit my job at the preschool, I kept experiencing moments so euphoric I thought that I lived in a warm bubble that had floated off a glass of champagne. Life was fuzzy, comfortable, very relaxed, copacetic and totally Zen. The two antidepressants I was on at the time ratcheted up the volume on my mood, brought it up too high. Overly optimistic didn't even begin to describe my state of mind. My nerve endings seemed bathed in tranquility. The whole universe seemed to hum with a steady rhythm, like a tuning fork. And I hummed with it, in unison.

And I wanted to create a monument to capture that moment of pure harmony, so I could remember it forever. So that my blissful feelings wouldn't go away. I wasn't sure how to do that, but I tried. I arranged some of my favorite items together in an attempt at creating a tangible collage that captured the essence of ecstasy I felt. It was June. The sunny weather matched my mood. I gathered several unassociated items for my project: one of my favorite CDs; a red rose plucked out of the garden—its petals a velvety lover's valentine, a caress of a flower, fragrant and buttery sweet. Inexplicably, one of the items I collected for my display was a tennis racket with taut strings. It seemed fitting at the time. A crystal wine glass. And lacking any wine to fill it with, I improvised with blue food coloring, filling it up and adding the concoction to my collection. The whole spectacle might have been artsy and expressionistic until the addition of the blue food coloring, when the project began to border on the bizarre. At the time, my collection made perfect sense to me and seemed to provide an equal balance of form and composition. I then photographed the items, sealing the image for memory. I was viewing every waking moment through rose-colored glasses due to my euphoric mental state. Some part of me knew that the moment couldn't last forever, though I tried to preserve it. I wish I could recreate the moment of pure joy I felt that summer, but I've never felt like that before or since. The feeling was exquisite. But it was also over the top and extreme. I'm sure simply observing everyday, ordinary items, like a set of car keys, should not make one's cup overflow with ecstasy. Failing to continue taking psychiatric drugs or any others, I never felt that sense of false euphoria again.

That summer, I would lose everything. My status as a healthy person. My job, my income, and self-worth. Even my freedom and the ability to come and go at will.

After my mom and brother leave to go on the fishing trip, I can't handle being alone with myself. I am drugged, agitated and home alone. The house threatens to swallow me up with its empty, cavernous silence. What is worse, I have only myself for company, and that is the problem.

So I place a call. That one pivotal call for help, without knowing that it would lead to an ambulance and "crisis team" arriving at my door. I call a national counseling hotline but don't expect them to follow through on their vow to get me some help. I entrust the kind voice on the phone with my address. Two police officers arrive, though I haven't committed a crime. I later find that mental health falls under the jurisdiction of law enforcement.

"What seems to be the problem?" they ask.

I mumble something incoherent, stammering about there being an issue with my prescription drugs.

"Well, why don't you stop taking them then?" they say, stupidly, as if the answer is that simple. They are not medical professionals but law enforcement officers, so they don't know that antidepressants can linger in the synapses for weeks. The officers could have benefited from sensitivity training and better preparation. I am sectioned off, their arms as barriers, handcuffed, and taken away. The cold metal cuffs bite into my wrists.

CHAPTER 3

"You Must Accept That You Are Permanently Ill"

The hospitalization was a nightmare. I remember feeling the imposed stigma and the judgment of others, the forced identification as mood-disordered. I remember the invasion of privacy, the inhumane treatment. When my dad brought me my belongings and deodorant, the staff whispered that I was too out of it to care about hygiene, which wasn't true. I did care. I was conscious and listening to every word they said. And I certainly had enough self-awareness to not want to walk around smelly and reeking of sweat, offending others with my odor. I needed deodorant as I always did, even in those circumstances. I could tell the staff thought I hadn't heard their snide comments, but I had.

Upon release from the hospital—a release that is more conditional upon my repeated requests to leave rather than any demonstration of actual improvement—I am advised by doctors to continue on a different drug. One that doesn't really work, either, and instead makes my mind foggy and delusional. My insomnia wasn't resolved during my first short hospitalization and the extent of my issues weren't fully realized. Legally intoxicated, I become euphoric in a simple moment, just from feeling the sun on my face. Such euphoria had been formerly inaccessible while sober. I now have access to a hidden world. It is as if each ray of light dances across my skin, caressing me on a cellular level. I walk to the lakeshore. The sun on my face while I run provides a moment of joy at simply being alive. I run back and forth several times just to test out my newfound glorious capacities.

I run through a field of sunflowers and their bright yellow color is the most beautiful color I have ever seen in my life. Such a rich and buttery yellow! The whole world seems very alive, very vibrant. The planet has a respiration rate. I am viewing the world through rose-colored glasses. It seems grasshoppers hold their breath for me to await my passage. The tiny creatures are my attentive audience. I continue to take my prescribed psychiatric drug as directed.

A pious and chirpy churchgoer of a girl, wholesome and conventional, a brownie-baking piano player, an upright citizen called Debbie makes the mistake of befriending me that summer. There is nothing wrong with Debbie's extension of Christianity. It is simply foolish policy to invite a stoned girl anywhere. Perhaps Debbie is just trying to do as Jesus suggested. Debbie. The short cutesy name was perfect for a girl who's into baking. Her family has always been close. They sit down together at dinner each night, which arrives promptly, night after night, without interruptions or surprises. Then they say a communal prayer and ask each other about their day. But there is something false and unquestioning about Debbie, as if she accepts whatever she is told as gospel. When I press her for explanations, she has none. Debbie wears tame-looking khakis and modest, unrevealing striped shirts that look as if they came from a catalogue filled with smiling, rosy-cheeked, enviable people. Debbie is fresh-faced and girlish with no makeup on. No doubt Debbie's thoughts are always of others, as saintly as she appears. Her angelic demeanor eventually wins me over. I accept Debbie's invitation to go boating with her.

The residents of my home state of Utah know that the Great Salt Lake stinks. Literally. It is acrid with a salt content as high as the Dead Sea's and it could sting or heal your wounds with its purported medicinal properties. But the water is stagnant with few tributaries. Only brine shrimp can exist in such a high saline environment. The water is too salty for fish to call it home. The lake's odor is a major deterrent. The residents know it's a repulsive, noxious body of water. That is why most of the locals nowadays don't get into the water, knowing better than to swim in it and to soil themselves with its rancid offering. I can see a tourist committing that error to test whether they are buoyant in concentrated salt water, but not the locals. They know better.

Debbie's bishop steers the boat like a real yachtsman and for once I am at a loss for words. My mind has gone blank and I can't even manage ordinary small talk. I'm that wasted. I'm incapable of casually conversing with the other passengers on the boat.

I can't even manage a common phrase such as, "Hi, how are you?" I picture people saying, "Cat got your tongue?" I picture them laughing at me. The bishop steers the boat across the bumpy, turquoise waves. Saltwater sprays our faces. Do these boaters know I have recently been released from a hospital? If they did, I would probably be tossed overboard. Debbie babbles on pleasantly. She's talking about her college homework and the church lesson she must prepare. She probably never misses a Sunday's sacrament.

Debbie mingles and socializes with the others as the boat drives on, chirping cheerfully. My mind is blank. A single thought fails to cross it. I can think of nothing to say. Nothing at all. I don't know it, but the antidepressants I am on are increasing my levels of brain dopamine and dopamine can be found in the frontal lobes of the brain, the seat of higher consciousness where our thoughts are formed. I am silent and someone asks if I'm okay and I lie to them and tell them yes, I am. Debbie babbles on about her hobbies. There are many of them. She is multitalented. She is a Sunday school teacher as well as committee organizer, in addition to being the choir director. I hear her, but can't form a single word's reply. My brain feels solidified. I can't muster a response, not for the life of me, nor can I recall what I once said in conjunction with conversations like these, back when I was sane. The boat is speeding through the water and I'm with company, but I am drugged and can't connect with them. The purpose of this ride is for recreation, but I am not enjoying myself. The other passengers are obviously enjoying themselves on this lovely outing on the lake in a boat driven by Debbie's bishop. I'm seated on a ride of terror.

The others, all brunettes in their early twenties, and members of Debbie's church ward, decide to put on swim flippers to dive into the lake. They stumble in their gimpy-footed rubber awkwardness, then splash about. They invite me to join them. I decline. *What would I say to them, anyway? What would I talk to them about, the handfuls of pills I swallow on a daily basis?* I have nothing going for me. My only assets are the orange prescription bottles rattling in my purse, my only tales ones of sharp needles and white coats.

The bishop decides I am his charge now that I'm left alone with him—the others have gone snorkeling. Perhaps he wants to cover up the long pauses and lingering silence. He says something, and I reply with a simple "yes" once again. It seems like the right answer. At least I hope it is. I was just guessing at the proper social protocol. I'm too out of it to be able to tell if it is appropriate. I am a natural-born swimmer, taking to the water like a fish, but I did not get in the water that day. I didn't let a single drop touch me. Looking back, I realize I must have been involuntarily, compliantly stoned that day. Prescriber-ordered, cognitively impaired, on antidepressants that were wrong for me, messed up in all sorts of ways. But people don't want to scratch the surface sometimes, because they don't want to embarrass you or call attention to you, so the bishop never dug deeper concerning my strangeness that day.

An hour of supposed fun in the sun passes. I am unreachable, on my own planet. I am present but not present. A trail of frothy water follows the water-skiers. They laugh at their efforts to remain standing, rather than being dragged behind. Debbie laughs as the bishop mockingly pretends to drive off without them. Giving up the treacherous waterskiing game, they're floating calmly, bobbing on inner tubes now. I wonder why I am associating with Mormons when I am not an identifying Mormon anymore, and I wonder when the ride will end. I'm sure it was my codependent nature seeking to find an identity, seeking to belong somewhere, even with people with widely different philosophies than mine. This is Utah and I was raised a Latter-day Saint, like a good portion of the state's population. I do not count that fact as being among one of my successes, particularly. I was indoctrinated in the faith but after the age of thirteen, I abandoned the church after investigating incidents of scriptural and historical inaccuracy as well as examining its bloodstained history and its involvement in the Mountain Meadows Massacre in the year 1857.

My urge for belonging is as good an explanation as I can find for why I am a passenger on the boat today. The large amounts of pills I am taking might be another explanation. Also, Debbie's invitation seemed sweet and genuine. I was looking for her approval, forsaking my own desire to stay home and vegetate. One of the passengers completes a swan dive, splashing and creating a tidal wave in his wake.

The bishop makes several trips to the beach to deposit swimmers onto the shore. I observe a girl from another church group as she laughingly tries to submerge a piece of driftwood, and I cannot see how she can derive so much pleasure out of her life when I can't from mine. I was too distracted and in my own world to think of the items one needs to pack to go swimming, and I have forgotten my suit and other basics, like a good pair of tennis shoes—vital on an outdoor outing. Packing such items should have been automatic inclusions, and would have been if I still had my powers of concentration. I have forgotten my common sense, the most necessary item to pack.

Fully dressed, I might as well be wearing an itchy wool suit in the hot summer sun. The members of the church group are having a luau on the beach. I should be enjoying myself as well. This is not the case. They laugh and shout, engaging in healthy, athletic pursuits and creating fond memories. They light a fire and dance around it, smiling and talking. I remain silent. The Master of the Bonfire glances at me where I am sitting like a bump on a log, quite literally, and then quickly looks away. Whatever he sees in my face disgusted him, tainted him, and he doesn't want to be a part of it. He knows something is wrong, but he doesn't want to bother to overturn the rock I live under, because he's afraid of what he'll find there. He's young and hasn't seen much in the way of ugliness and horror yet in his short life, so he knows only one way. Fun. He turns away to tease his girlfriend, pulling her hair as she shrieks. His expression is joyous now, having forgotten all about me. He chases the girl across the beach, clumsily spilling his punch in the sand in the process. Time passes at the speed of grass growing. Eventually I realize people are leaving, getting up to go.

The crowd converges on the parking lot. "Come on, get in," Debbie says, hopping up onto the gate of a flatbed truck and offering me a leg up. "We'll go for a ride." Debbie isn't as straitlaced as I thought. If dancing on a flatbed truck to parking lot music could be considered risqué.

I shake my head. "I drove… That's alright. I have to go." I start walking across the lot, with my keys in hand, trying to give her the impression that I'm in a hurry.

"Are you sure?" she asks again.

I cannot speak because my brain won't form the thoughts that I need to communicate my intentions to Debbie, so I shake my head and open my mouth like something's going to come out—but nothing does, much to my despair. I wonder what Debbie thinks of my obvious stutter, my hesitating mind. Without further reply, I get into my car and slam the door. As I turn back to look at her with her sun- kissed hair and cutoff shorts, I see that she's lost her smile. This is not me. I am not me, not myself.

When I'm home, behind closed doors, I shout, "Make it stop!" trying to release my anger. I've never had an angry one-sided conversation before. Now I have.

When shouting doesn't work, I ask for professional help. The nurse practitioner thinks Trazodone will help me sleep this time. But it is like giving heart medicine to someone with knee pain. The wrong issue is targeted. The drug doesn't work for me. At best, the nurse is playing a guessing game, taking a stab in the dark based on the symptoms I described to her. Even with two jobs, one of them for the school district, I don't qualify for health insurance because each job is part-time. I can't afford to see a real doctor, so the nurse practitioner will have to suffice. The drug is supposed to have a soporific effect, but instead it dips me into that level of consciousness so very close to the border of sleep, but not quite there. I am sedated and left hanging precariously alongside sleep, without being able to cross over into the world of blissful dreams. I want the drug to knock me out, but instead I am drowsy, drugged and disoriented, but still not permissibly unconscious. Also, my legs won't stop moving. Later I would find a name for the pins-and-needles feeling in my legs. Restless legs syndrome. I can picture the accompanying drug commercial. I feel an overwhelming need to move, to keep jiggling my legs. Movement, if suppressed, would lead to extreme discomfort.

CHAPTER 4

Failed by the Healthcare System

After weeks of restless legs and little to no sleep, I readmitted myself. I felt it was my only choice. Anyone will break if they go without sleep for long enough. It is only a question of *when*. While interviewing me upon admission for case files and records, the social worker Jeff would write, "Profession: *Track Runner*," though he spent all of five minutes with me, seemed bored, and was ready to move on to the next case right away. He was wrong. Technically I was an out-of-practice journalist. (In practice now, with the publishing of this book.) I have a bachelor's degree in journalism, though I hadn't really used it much, except for a brief stint as a reading teacher for elementary school children, a loosely related field. With my health problems, I was unable to use my journalism degree and instead obtained a series of blue-collar jobs that required little cerebral effort and had flexible schedules. Jobs that allowed my mind to wander and to daydream as my body performed repetitious activities. I am capable of disconnecting the two. Such jobs give me the time and freedom to write.

Catering was one of the mindless jobs I held, for example. In catering, you are wearing white-collar formal wear, but catering is not considered a white-collar job. As a caterer, you are the "event staff," the person scrubbing up the spilled wine at the wedding if you're lucky, and the puke if you're not. The person tugging at the edges of tablecloths and gathering up carafes to place on a Queen Mary overflowing with dirty dishes. The person asking herself, "Where does the salad fork go again?" when she's never eaten at a restaurant fancy enough to have salad forks herself. And, "How many balls of chilled butter?"

Being a caterer means struggling to pronounce the names of fancy French wines and appetizers when you don't speak French. Being a caterer means being one of the people lighting 500 candles a night, then extinguishing them. Catering means folding 1,500 time-consuming napkins into birds of paradise and seashell shapes, like a circus clown making balloon animals. And unfortunately, being a caterer also means cleaning up after those 1,500 people when they go home at night. Catering means you've watched hundreds of weddings, all where the bride wasn't you, though you wish fervently that it was.

I obtained these sorts of jobs as they weren't hard to find or keep, and gave me ample time to pursue creative outlets. As a lot of my coworkers had DUIs and were undergoing custody battles, no one thought twice about my struggles with insomnia and psychiatric drugs, though I never enlightened them much on the issues. That was why I worked in catering and not journalism, because of the amount of tawdry behavior deemed acceptable.

But Jeff the social worker had it all wrong. I simply told him I had done a lot of running that summer. That must have been where he got the track runner title. His error demonstrated a lack of concern for his patients, a lack of caring to get the story right.

My medical records, which would haunt me forever and follow me to a second hospital, were not even correct. To think this messy paperwork would be accompanying me to my next destination... Jeff, Licensed Clinical Social Worker, recorded a few more errors. Lynn, my real father, was listed as my stepfather in my records. My father was baffled by this omission, this mistake, when he received the social worker's report. Jeff was either tired, sarcastic, or he just plain didn't care and hated his job, or was jaded and worn down after witnessing too many people with slit wrists and dull eyes.

Looking back on my hospital records, I see that most of Jeff's notes have been removed from my file, oddly. I suspect incompetency. A mention of him in the notes of one of the doctors lets me know he existed. The doctor wrote in his report: *Jeff worked hard for his [assigned] family*. But there is no further mention of Jeff in my records. And I would have to disagree with that doctor's statement. Nowhere is it explained what "working hard" entailed, nor is his role in my care elaborated. Jeff's own notes have been left out, if he ever bothered to make any.

When I tell Jeff that I don't think the medications I'm on are the right ones for me, he tells me that I will just have to get past my reservations and admit the need to take meds in the first place, for the rest of my life—a prediction that was false.

Elizabeth Richter, author of *Songs of the Captive Unchained: A Collection of Essays from the Heart of the Mental Patient Liberation Movement* provides an example of the sort of incompetency that can occur in medical recordkeeping. Elizabeth writes, "When I asked, the Director of Medical Records at the hospital (McLean in Boston) acknowledged that many people were upset when they read their records because they find them inaccurate." She said that she was only allowed to view her medical records when she was deemed "stable" by her therapist. It seems that medical records for physical conditions are easier to obtain than mental health records. And a therapist's opinion of stable could be just that, a perception. Richter would later find work as an English teacher, a profession that demanded verbal accuracy, casting doubt on her dismal prognosis. She would later petition to have her medical records amended.

According to the Health Information Portability and Accountability Act, or HIPAA, you have the right to request your own medical records or those of a person over whom you have legal guardianship. Records you are *not allowed to request* include psychotherapy notes, information the provider is gathering for lawsuits, and medical information that the provider believes can reasonably endanger the life of yourself or others. Subtracting for the "danger to self or others" factor, why should psychotherapy notes be any different than those detailing, say, a knee replacement?

The answer to this question can be found in HIPAA law, where it states: "Psychotherapy notes are treated differently from other mental health information both because they contain particularly sensitive information and because they are the personal notes of the therapist that typically are not required or useful for treatment, payment, or health care operations purposes, other than by the mental health professional who created the notes. Therefore, with few exceptions, the Privacy Rule requires a covered entity to obtain authorization prior to a disclosure of psychotherapy notes for any reason, including a disclosure for treatment purposes to a health care provider other than the originator of the notes."

I can see how viewing your own psychotherapy notes might be *very* beneficial to your progress and recovery, although the law seems to disagree. Specifically, I could see how viewing these notes might lead you to examine patterns in your past behavior and to adapt and change that behavior if necessary.

Richter wrote about the inaccuracies she found in her records once she was finally allowed to obtain them, and how such inaccuracies can be harmful. "Questions of fact—a person's age or occupation—are very easy to point out and correct. There were some very simple corrections of this kind I needed to make; for example, my mother was an elementary school teacher, not a language teacher. My father, who was actually alive and well and living in New Jersey was listed as 'deceased,' she wrote. I found that Richter's experiences mirrored my experiences with the social worker Jeff.

When Richter finally received all of her medical records, she even found that the pages of another Massachusetts resident's records had been mixed up with her own. She explained that errors in clinical judgment are more harmful. A thin person is described in clinical notes as "anorexic."

In my own case, the nausea that occurred from a migraine I experienced while hospitalized even led to a brief suggestion that I was bulimic, which was completely ridiculous. One can only imagine the errors in treatment that can occur from errors on medical records that are believed to be fact. Such errors in medical recordkeeping can change your whole course of treatment, due to inaccurate labeling.

Through my own experiences with illness, I believe myself to have become a nicer and more compassionate person, due to witnessing the suffering of myself and others. I lost my prejudice along the way and gained more empathy for others' pain. When I was handcuffed and taken to the hospital, it was due to the uninformed, stigmatic notions of others and their fears that I was dangerous. I recall an example of prejudice that occurred in the intensive care unit during my first hospitalization.

"Today he thinks he's God," the orderly said, with a sarcastic smirk. He was talking about one of the patients. Poking fun at this patient's actions seemed not to bother the orderly's conscience much. The rest of the orderlies laughed and rolled their eyes. Then they switched the subject to talk about where they were going for lunch, almost in the same sentence, without skipping a beat. The fact that the orderly made this comment in the first place was not what disturbed me. It was the fact that he said it within earshot of the patient, as if the patient's feelings didn't matter at all, that bothered me.

When I began to be less biased, I realized that human expressions, no matter how illogical they seem, have logical motivations behind them, or serve the purpose of satisfying some need. I'll illustrate what I mean.

For example, you might hear a person who is ill say, "Christmas trees always run away on me," and find it to be total gibberish, complete nonsense, but what he really meant by that is, "I don't like the holidays, my parents divorced on them."

Such statements demonstrate an expression of their feelings in a general, roundabout way because perhaps they don't have the ability to put those feelings into words. Even those who seem to be speaking gibberish or chattering away like a noisy parakeet are probably chattering away like a noisy parakeet to get someone's attention, or they wouldn't be doing it. Or they are doing it to fulfill the basic human need to be heard. In my opinion, there's no real "crazy." And if anyone who has ever felt suicidal is "crazy," then it is more common to have those kinds of thoughts than you would expect. A 2006 survey of Boston college students found that 55 percent of them said they felt suicidal at one point or another in their lives, making suicidal feelings at some point during your life a common experience. (http://www.apa.org/news/press/releases/2008/08/suicidal-thoughts.aspx n.d.)

Psychiatrist Dr. Daniel Dorman gave in his book, *Dante's Cure*, the following illustrative example of how he doesn't believe anyone is crazy, just misunderstood. Here is Dr. Dorman's story of a patient deemed out of control who just needed someone to talk to:

"Dr. Dorman, this is Ruth Sargent on Three West. I think you had better come to the ward."

I (Dr. Dorman) raced over to the ward. A group had gathered in a circle in front of the nurse's station—two sizable fellows, two nurses and three aides, all in white uniforms. In their center stood a young man, about twenty, motionless, his arms stretched out straight in front of him.

Ruth nodded at me, then looked at the young man. "Dr. Dorman, this patient is Roy Ferrar. He was admitted just last night, so we don't have a doctor's order for an injection of Thorazine. He's pretty agitated, as you can see."

I stepped into the circle. Roy was sweating profusely, slowly repeating, "Kill, kill-kill, kill."

"I'd prefer to talk with him," I said to Ruth.

"Well, I don't know," she said. "We should just bring him down with an injection. We have help here who can do that."

Here I was, my first night on call. These nurses were experienced. Ruth Sargent was trying to show me the way.

"I'd still prefer to talk with him."

"If you must, but not alone. I insist on leaving the door open."

I turned to the young man, "Mr. Ferrar, might I talk with you?"

He followed me into a consultation room. I sat down and leaned back slightly in a tilt-back grammar-school-teacher's oak chair.

He slowly approached me, arms still outstretched. "Kill, kill."

The door was open about a foot or two. Faces looked in at us. Roy placed his hands on either side of my neck. I did not resist.

"Where did you get the idea to do this?" I asked. "This is just like a scene from a movie about an insane asylum."

He blinked, removed his hands from my neck, and collapsed in a heap on the floor in front of me. The door opened.

"Perhaps you can just take him to his room," I said.

The orderly, a burly man used to "restraining" patients, looked right at me. "I'll be damned, Doc. You've got—(a way with) well, I'll be damned. Come on, Roy, let's go to bed." Roy allowed himself to be helped up. The members of Dr. Dorman's medical staff declared that he had a talent for deciphering the language of psychotics and for winning their cooperation.

(Dorman n.d.)

Examples like those of Dr. Dorman just go to show what a bit of human compassion can accomplish. Of course, I'm not advocating for the elimination of caution. I just wish that I had known a doctor like Dr. Dorman when I first became ill, and that there were more like him in practice so that others could receive more compassion as well.

My health had reached a crisis point before my final hospitalization. That summer, Debbie was the only friend I spent time with and our boating trip had been a fiasco. Unsure of whether to believe social worker Jeff's predictions or not, my mom invited a neighbor to try to reason with me. She tried to get the neighbor to convince me that lithium was a critical drug and that I should take it for the rest of my life in order to cure my chemical imbalance, which was no different than needing to take insulin for diabetes. But even my mom was skeptical that the pills were accomplishing much and after I demonstrated my sustained period of recovery to her, she would never insist I take the pills again. Instead, she supported the opposite.

My mom raised an eyebrow as I slurred my words and struggled to form sentences after swallowing the lithium.

"I've got gout and I take pills for it. It's no different, taking lithium for what you've got," the neighbor tried to convince me.

Sick as a dog and dehydrated, thanks to the lithium, I decide to flush the pills down the toilet when the neighbor leaves. Cold turkey is a difficult way to get off a psychiatric drug, if you are allowed off of it at all by your doctor, due to a fear of being sued—which eliminates the option of informed consent. Even if a drug is clearly harming you, doctors are reluctant to allow you off them. They feel that you should be maintained on *some* sort of treatment course. *A* treatment is better than *no treatment*, which would look like neglect. If you died, at least they could prove they made an effort to save you. Doctors don't want to be sued for malpractice. They would rather you stay on a drug, even if it is clearly harming you, to cover their bases. But cold turkey is not a good way to stop a drug if you don't want to suffer withdrawal symptoms. A slow taper is preferable to abrupt discontinuation when getting off psychoactive drugs, psychiatric or otherwise. But few doctors are willing to risk their name and put their license on the line by advising you to discontinue medication.

As no one appeared willing to help me get off the drug, I was required to stop by myself, with gung-ho grit and stoicism. Remember that psychiatric drugs are psychoactive drugs, just as street drugs are, and both affect the mind. Rocker Stevie Nicks called her eight-year addiction to psychiatrist-prescribed Klonopin worse than withdrawing from cocaine and heroin and "hellish." And these words come from a rock icon who has seen some hard-core drugs.

In my experience, it can sometimes take a month or longer to return to baseline (your old self) after withdrawing from psychiatric drugs. The longer you've been on the medication, the more severe the withdrawal.

My withdrawal effects were extreme. My brain had become accustomed to having a chemical crutch there to calm down. Without it, my brain wasn't sure how to manage and went haywire. Withdrawing from lithium could spark a manic reaction which may mimic symptoms of illness and resemble withdrawal from other substances. I didn't trust myself enough to realize that the withdrawal process I was going through happened to everyone who stopped taking lithium (a drug that didn't work for me in the first place) and that what I was experiencing wasn't due to some character flaw. I had no reason to self-validate my suspicions. I had been convinced by doctors that I was flawed and told I would need the drug for life. Oh yes, substance abuse, along with sleep disorders, also fall under the realm of psychiatry's jurisdiction. It seems my doctors were treating a problem that they created, and I would have been better off staying away from psychiatric drugs in the first place.

It took time for my body to return to homeostasis after ditching the drug, but I refused to allow myself time to recover and bounce back. Had I been a more experienced pill popper, I would have given myself time, but that was a group I never wanted to belong to. As a first-time crisis sufferer, the demands and expectations I placed on myself were too high. Naïvely, I expected myself to immediately spring back into shape and go back to what was normal for me. When that didn't happen directly after ending the drug, I was terribly disappointed. I disappointed myself by failing to achieve my perfectionistic goals. Knowing nothing about psychiatric drug withdrawal, I assumed the state I was in shortly after quitting was permanent. I was clearly ailing without the drug, but rather than bow out of life, I made attempts to go on as usual and to pass as normal. Or, lacking a definition for normal, to pass for what wouldn't make people emotionally upset, flying under their radar without detection while conducting my usual activities. Despite a defeatist attitude, I tried to pretend I was one of the functioning everyday people on the street going back and forth to jobs, or school, or other meaningful activities. I attempted to mop up the vomit in my bathroom, a leftover from my drug withdrawal, to wash my greasy hair and adopt a positive attitude.

I needed a cause, something to get up for every morning. Because I didn't really have one, I decided to invent one. So even though I had graduated from my alma mater a few years back, I chose to linger in the college's video production lab, making and editing amateur independent films. It was an improvement over the days I rarely got out of bed, zonked on lithium. I didn't have a job anymore. Insomnia and hospitalizations had caused me to miss so much work that I decided to leave before I was fired. Being fired seemed inevitable, so I quit while I was ahead. Instead, I begin to view life through a film strip.

CHAPTER 5

A Distraction

I apparently pass for normal, because I meet someone in the video lab who treats me like I am one of the calm sane-looking people I see on the street. He's ten years older than me, thirty-four to my twenty-four. His name is Brent and he looks like a young Hemingway, all bright-eyed and eager and vigorous. Brent takes to me right away. He's a journalist and like other journalists, he's wordy. This one's double majoring in English. He poetically compares me to literary figures like the Greek goddess Circe. *Please*, I think, *please…* My ego can't handle such ridiculous praise, praise which has no foundation in reality, and his descriptions gross me out. After gazing at the stars by the bay, eating fried skillet dinners at midnight and hanging out at his apartment, he asks me if I will be his girlfriend. I want to conceal the fact that I don't really like him, and that I'm just using him as both a father figure and a nurse during a needy time. I'm dependent on Brent as I regress to an infantile state. It seems that the people who fall for me shouldn't. I don't know how to tell Brent I think he's generic, replaceable, a stand-in; I don't see us making it in the long run, but I do like that he is convenient and available. Convenient and available *right now*, when I need him most. How someone as messed up as me could even think of *dating* seems far-fetched. But I didn't invite him into my life. *He* asked *me* out that day in the video lab, and there were no other takers. I wasn't intending to meet anyone. I was just trying to distract myself from my serious issues. And he was a good distraction.

So now I've got a built-in friend and nurse. Brent thinks it's weird that I sit around making random videos all day and that I don't have a job. But he tells me that it doesn't matter, he's still in love with me and he's sure I'll luck into some position I'm qualified for sooner or later. It's too much too soon, and the message is delivered from an overly sentimental writer, so I do not trust it.

I feel guilty over my lack of interest in him, so I attempt to make him a boiled cabbage and corned beef dinner, Irish style. Only I make a mistake and buy lettuce instead of cabbage, leaving out the most essential ingredient. Brent and I look at the wilted brown lettuce leaves floating in the drain of his kitchen sink. What I've made looks like something let sit too long at a buffet. To top off the awful dinner, Brent cuts his finger opening the can of corned beef. His blood mixed in with the meat makes the dinner look still breathing and bleeding. I gag and retch.

"This is terrible, it's sailor's food," he laughs. "You're a terrible cook," he says, but he pinches my nose playfully and his smile is mild and forgiving.

He made a half-hearted attempt to eat the now blood-soaked meal, then gave up and dumped it in the trash. So much for corned beef and cabbage. I didn't make any other attempts to cook for him after that. I was embarrassed at my lack of skill. Now I am a better cook; then I was young and inexperienced.

I have to keep busy. When I don't, the darkness in my mind threatens to swallow me up. I attend video labs I'm not even registered for on campus, but no one bans me from them. I am gaining use of expensive video equipment for the price of a quick flash of my student ID card, its expiration date unnoticed. It's as if I'm still a student, having gone back in time. I hang out in the video lab, using my editing skills to create cinematic creations. Brent and I collaborate on videos together, combining broadcast journalism techniques. We use industrywide software and string out the b-roll. Making videos is what Brent and I do because I'm not attracted to him, so what else is he good for?

Brent's eyes extend out a bit too far, as if he's got Grave's disease, which ruins his shot at handsome. The rest of his features are decent, even slightly above average. Like a lot of English majors I know, he's somewhat dramatic and intense, veiling ordinary details in a shroud of mystery. He says he wants to run with the bulls in Pamplona, has to before he dies, as it's on his bucket list. Brent says he is attracted to me because there is something waifish and innocent about me. Brent responds to my neediness, to the damsel-in-distress aura that surrounds me. I finally tell him what I'm struggling with. His brother took lithium, he says. Brent calls himself a depressive. No big deal. It seems everyone is on pills. The plumber is on Prozac. The mailman on Milltown. Brent's drug of choice is Wellbutrin. Brent's on psych drugs too. *Ha*, I think. *Guilty as charged.*

Brent is a gentle, mothering man and that is why I like him. I like him, but I don't want to end up with him. Brent is the kind of guy who will make sure that you're safely strapped into your seat before the ride takes off. Brent is the kind of guy who will make you chicken noodle soup when you're sick. He is the kind of guy with drawer after drawer of matching socks. I wasn't capable of caring for myself at that point, so Brent and I were a perfect, if unhealthy and parasitic, couple.

We get into his little Honda. Brent is taking me to The City of Rocks, Idaho, to go climbing. Brent turns on the car's radio and we listen to music down the empty two-lane highway. As far as talents go, Brent sings and plays the guitar. He has the ability to pluck a song from request and turn around play it.

Before this car trip, Brent took me to the park to join a drum circle. Brent's brother was there, too. Scattered across the park's lawn, on towels and blankets and temporary seating, were hippies with henna tattoos stenciled on their limbs.

The air smells of sweat and weed. The park pulsates with sound, vibrating in a multicolored mind warp. And when I see Brent's brother, I know right away that he far surpasses Brent in looks. When the two men stand together, his brother looks like a peacock in comparison with a drab pigeon. His brother's beauty eclipses Brent's. Brent is a few degrees shy of handsome, but his brother hasn't missed the beauty boat and displays those extra degrees on his face. Like Brent, he's got a cleft in his angular jaw, but the similarities end there. Brent's handsome jaw is his only forgiving feature. Brent's brother has the same dimpled jaw, but lacks the bulbous eyes that Brent has. It's not fair to Brent, but I wish that I had met the other brother first. Wishful thinking. Brent's brother has a girlfriend, after all, and she's accompanied him to the park. And at this point I have nothing to offer. At this point I'm a cretin who lives in sweats at the video lab who has no right to stake claims on anyone.

The brothers create a smaller circle of their own on the grass, apart from the hippies. They bounce songs off each other and attempt to make up some of their own. I try to tune in to the music, to feel the grass under my feet. Brent's brother has a pink blossom tucked behind his ear, making him look trendy and non-threatening. I'm a groupie, a hanger-on, a park girl, a drum-circle-joiner and a Millennial, as are the rest of the people in the park that day.

Brent and his brother continue playing guitar together. I fall quiet. It's like the day on the beach with Debbie, when I have nothing to say and my mind is blank.

"How am I doing?" Brent asks. I suspect he wants a critical review of his music.

"Good," I reply, a one-word assessment that I'm sure is inadequate. I fail to say anything else for the rest of the time we spend in the park. I fail to smile and act like I'm enjoying myself. I'm an emotional downer, a real party pooper. I'm not doing this on purpose. I'm frantically searching for something to say, but nothing comes out. My mind is blank. Then again, I'm on myriad prescription drugs. The concoction seems to amplify all that is wrong with my mind.

"You're being weird," Brent scolds when I don't say anything. I try to focus on the music. "Try to act more normal!" he continues.

Brent wasn't always a clean-cut college student, studious and academic. He's older than the traditional student because he dropped out for a few years while struggling with an addiction to heroin, at which point Brent learned some life lessons from the school of hard knocks. He told me he was taking Wellbutrin. Maybe it's to replace all the chemicals he depleted as an addict. I think that his heroin spree was a form of self-medicating for depression. Heroin, it seemed so harsh a drug. The thought of heroin reminded me of holey, disease-ridden people, desperately shooting up their fix. Committing heinous crimes without blinking in order to score their next hit. It was a path I could never take. Why add addiction to my list of numerous problems? Why complicate my life? But he's clean now, has been for a couple years. Brent attributes his success to Wellbutrin and says there would be no way he could get through school without it, couldn't ace the classes he was taking unless he was on it. But he's still a little paranoid about Wellbutrin's long-term effects, saying he's unsure of what it will do to him cumulatively. Having gone through his own struggles with substances, Brent feels protective of me. He does not outright reject me as I advise most people to do. I think mistakenly that Brent has an insider's view of what I'm experiencing, and that he'll understand me. Think that he'd be supportive of me attending a day treatment center. Think that he wouldn't care when I have nothing to report except to tell him about the clay sculpture I made that day, or about the time I squandered in the video lab. So I invite him to volunteer at the day treatment center as a test. He promises to go, but flakes. Just because Brent knows illness firsthand doesn't mean he wants to become bosom buddies with it again. Because going there would cause him to revisit that dark place where he once dwelt. I try to tell him that I'm not strong enough to do this by myself yet, but he doesn't want to hear it.

If my mind goes blank in the car with Brent, at least I can return to the one subject we have in common. Journalism. I graduated two years prior and Brent is in his senior year, though he's old for a college senior. Like me, Brent knows that most people have strong opinions about the press. He knows that our training in media law will prevent us, hopefully, from inventing salacious gossip due to our fear of libel or defamation suits costing hundreds of thousands, or even millions of dollars, to our employer, and with the loss of a job as a consequence. Brent has been trained in the inverted pyramid style of writing and has the *AP Stylebook* memorized. I'm relieved that Brent has deemed me worthy of going on this trip in the first place, given all the odd behavior I've displayed lately.

We pull up to the camp site, step out, and survey the area in the mid-day sun. The sky is as blue as a robin's egg, the clouds like fluffy cotton balls. And before us stretch miles of towering rock. Brent dons a pair of vintage sunglasses from the forties. He introduces me to his friends, who arrived a few hours before us and have already set up camp. Brent's alternative-music-loving, tofu-munching friends from the English department. Brent's friends extol the works of Virginia Woolf. Personally, I prefer F. Scott Fitzgerald and his symbolism—a green light at the end of a dock as a beacon of hope, even if I think it's overdone. It seems to me that Woolf's writing spirals into a black, nonsensical hole without a coherent center, as if she had written while terribly depressed. Brent's friends get into deep thought-provoking discussions on creationism, the way college kids tend to do.

"A level 7.5 climb. Knarly, dude!" says Brent's blond, dreadlocked friend. I privately refer to this guy as Hippie Dude in my head.

I learn new climbing-related vocabulary words such as "crampons" and "belaying." Brent's friends pass me some climbing chalk to dust my hands with. They hand me a pair of climbing shoes. The shoes are small and lightweight like ballet slippers, and have a rough texture on the bottom. The insignificant-looking shoes are actually powerful, useful and effective, and will hold your weight. They're made narrow and moldable so you can jam them into rock crevasses if you find yourself slipping. Brent, in his nurturing way, helps me to hook up my gear. If I was a baby, he'd have dressed me. We have a sick, dependent relationship, but Brent doesn't seem to mind. He attaches the metal hooks, then checks my harness several times to make sure I'm strapped in. He wants me to be safe.

Climbing is a sport that requires muscle, the ability to foist yourself up by the strength of your arms, and agility. I am pleased that lithium has not slowed my twenty-four-year-old athletic abilities. Brent, thirty-four, seems just as capable. At that age, I view Brent as being ancient, but as I get older I realize thirty-four isn't so old at all. But the maturity level between a twenty-four-year-old and a thirty-four-year-old is usually a large distance apart. I would catch up quickly after experiencing extended periods of intense suffering, then reflecting upon them.

After Brent straps me in, he watches me scurry up the rock like a spider. I look back down at where he is on the ground. He looks so small, like an ant. *Twin Sisters rocks, you're no challenge*, I think. I'm unsure precisely which sister, which of the twin rocks, I'm climbing. When I get to the top, I marvel at how blue the sky looks up here, even bluer than it did from the ground. The landscape is picturesque.

"You made it!" says Brent. I can't think of reaching great heights. I can only think of my many failures and the disintegration of my mind.

CHAPTER 6

Reckless

I have climbed to the top of the Twin Sisters peak and I am afraid of falling, but Brent has strapped me in tightly.

"What's it look like up there?" he asks.

"There are a couple of clouds, but you can see for miles," I say.

We pile into the Isuzu with Brent's friends, bound for the restaurant in small-town Idaho. Brent strokes my hair as if I am a small child. Brent is in love with me, and I mistook him for the type of guy who doesn't care if a girl returns his feelings or not. Honestly, is there a guy out there like that? Fine with rejection? Happy to cuddle up to icy coldness? I'm definitely not in love with him and I can't return his feelings. Brent senses that though I'm there and present, I'm not quite within his reach, and he's right; I never will be, not for him. I am remote and removed. I am unreachable and I refuse to be owned. I like having cultivated this independent quality. I am self-reliant, my own island. In this way, I cannot be hurt.

That day, I am reluctantly obedient to him so that we can continue to enjoy a parasitic relationship. I am not his girlfriend, but an imposter. But he's sweet and I don't want to hurt his feelings, so I'll keep pretending for him. Brent keeps referring to me as "Circe" there in the SUV, "Circe," in his overly poetic way. He's comparing me to a Greek sorceress. How mythological. How ridiculous. The name is an overestimation of my looks and personality. I think he should delve a little deeper into character development and gather background data to rewrite the story.

When the Isuzu comes to a halt, hippies and climbing gear spill out. It's all such grungy, sporty fun. The clothes his friends wear are woven and unisex, made for functionality rather than fashion. I sit near Brent in the restaurant and his friends order artisan citrus beer. What else would they drink? I know mixing lithium and beer to be a very risky combination. But I want to appear at ease in front of Brent's friends and the beer might help me achieve that. Good old peer pressure. *They'll notice I'm nervous*, I think, so I take a sip.

To think of turning them down and coming up with a little old excuse like, "No beer tonight, I can't combine it with my psychiatric drugs," is unthinkable at my then immature level.

I am compensating for a lack of personality, and I am trying to prove myself. I do this because I might have to admit the real reason for my abstinence, if probed. Admitting to having a sleep disorder or mental issue is not the same as admitting you have diabetes. The two reactions to your confession would be totally different. One is seen as not your fault, the other probably due to poor morals, bad habits, or a terrible upbringing. Once I am older, I will surely have the strength to say no to the booze and not give a damn about what others think of me.

They explore politics, religion, and science there at the table as they drink their beer. They continue their argument on creationism. I take a few more sips to cover up my nervousness. I've never been much of a drinker. Drinking can be dangerous, much more drinking while taking pills. On this occasion in the bar, mixing alcohol with pills makes me dull and dopey and I start to fall asleep. I can tell by all of their faces that they're expecting me to contribute something to the debate in some way.

"Well?" one says. "What do you have to say about that?"

Suddenly everyone is looking at me and I panic, but I manage to concentrate hard enough to force a few words out in my drugged, impaired state. "Um… So creationism. Um… Creationism, right?" I pause to think. "So… Do you believe in the Big Bang Theory? That must have been how we came to be. Er… In the aftermath of it."

Someone actually responds to my ill-planned response, directing the focus off me without noticing how nervous I am. What a relief. Another even elaborates and goes on talking, using the lead I provided her as a starting point to continue the conversation in a new direction. I think it is the hippie girl with the braided hair in a faded T-shirt who rescues me. I have done my part.

It has taken all my effort, all my energy, everything I have, to eject those words from my mouth. I am silent for half an hour after this exclamation. Exhausted by the pace of the conversation and feeling sedated, I listen to their witty discussion, which moves as quickly as a ping-pong game. Everyone but me is volleying back an answer. The conversation seems to be on fast forward, like the *Seinfield* episode at the hospital, moving either too fast or too slow, but never at a speed at which I can comprehend enough to catch up.

"You're quiet again," Brent says. "Is everything alright?" He hands me another beer, the last thing I need.

I wilt like a flower from both the concoction of substances in my body and my struggle to keep up with his friends' liveliness. I slide back into the booth, slipping under the table. I want to be invisible. I hope that he knows that I tried to be present for him today. Tried, at least. I nap there in the booth as Brent's friends chat away, thinking they can analyze their own existence, figure out life's secrets during one night in a bar. How naïve of them. The hopeful part about them is that they are young enough to think that they can actually solve the world's problems. They believe intense discussions like these will help brainstorm ideas which will move mountains. It's the optimism of youth. I wish I could go back to those days when everything felt so simple. When the world's major problems seemed so fixable. Maybe looking back on these times makes them seem better than they actually were while I was experiencing them, putting a glossy sheen of false idealization over these memories while conveniently leaving out the awkward parts, like the fact that we were all going through an identity crisis.

When we are finished talking, drinking and eating, we grab the check and the hippie girl in the faded T-shirt takes the wheel of the Isuzu. Her boyfriend and partner Hippie Guy, in sandals with a climbing gecko emblazoned on his shirt, rides shotgun. The drive over the winding rural roads seems to take forever as I slip into a state of consciousness that is the after result of a poisonous mixture of faulty brain chemistry, psychiatric drugs, and alcohol.

We drive for what seemed like forever into a black, featureless night. Pitch black due to the lack of street lights and buildings, it is a rural backdrop I find comforting, as if night could sweep away all that was wrong in the daytime. When I try to make out even the faintest of geographical features through the vehicle's window, I see nothing but inky darkness. Once again I feel as if conversation is expected of me, but I have nothing to contribute. I'm just too groggy.

"I've never read that," I respond, when asked about a work of literature, though I have. I just don't want to have to complete my sentences. It requires too much energy and my reserves are running low. And then there is the ever-present blankness of mind, making conversation difficult.

Brent gives me a sharp look that seems to say, *Who are you? I thought you had read that. In fact, I know you have. I know you better than that.* I turn my face to the window, even though there's nothing to look at.

At last the ride comes to a stop, and we arrive back at our campsite. It is dark and there will be stories to be told at the fire, his friends announce. I brighten at the sight of the flames. I imagine myself drifting into them and being engulfed by them. I am not a pyromaniac; at least I can count that diagnosis as *not being among one of mine*, but nevertheless I am mesmerized. I think the others felt that way about the fire, too; they just weren't inclined to talk about it. The primitive fascination with fire dates back ages, to the beginning of human time. What separates the socially acceptable from the pathological is action. I wouldn't actually reach out and *touch* the fire, nor would I express my love for it.

There are shadowed faces in the dark and animated stories and wild gestures. Brent makes them laugh with his story and they say,

"Tell us a joke," so I tell them one I've heard before and memorized, taking the easy way out. At least they haven't heard the joke. Unless they're just trying to be polite.

"Great! That's real funny," they say, quietly, without sincerity.

Then Brent drags me off to bed, to the tent we collaborated on building earlier in the day. Brent did most of the work. I fulfilled his requests to "hand over that" tool or instrument. It was hard to get the poles to bend properly. Through teamwork, we'd managed. Brent kisses me as we snuggle into our respective sleeping bags.

"Is there something wrong?" he asks, when I don't kiss him back. *"Is there something wrong?"* seems to be his platitude lately. Brent thinks that I just need to loosen up a little and warm up to him. But I never will, because I just don't like him *that way*, despite not being entitled to choosiness, being in kind of a bad place in life.

Fortunately, he changes the subject and complements me on the softness of my skin. "Your skin's as soft as a baby's. Or a peach. Can I call you… Peaches?"

I smile at that, but then proceed to ignore him. I don't want to follow up with the Peaches name; it makes me gag to evaluate my own looks. I bury my head in my pillow instead, and fall asleep.

Most likely due to unfinished business from the night before, the next morning Brent and I get into an argument in our tent, which is slightly uphill from the others. I'm sure that sound travels downwind.

"What is wrong with you? You acted like you liked me at first, but you keep pushing me away! You led me on!"

Brent has had it with me. He is disgusted and frustrated by this mad girl who won't even have sex with him to make up for the fact that she's being a real downer, and that he has to drag her along on this trip so that she won't be left alone with her own mind gnawing away at what's left of her sanity. Brent tucks his head back into his sleeping bag to hide, a gesture that states he is figuratively slamming the door on this conversation. He's done with this argument, done with me. Our tent is a testament to sloppiness and depression, and that is exactly what it looks like. Bread crumbs and Cheetos litter sleeping bags. I was a real mess then. My housekeeping skills would improve about the same time I cleared out the chaos in my mind.

Brent tosses off his sleeping bag and looks around. He finds the mess in the tent absurd and points it out. "God, if this is what it would look like if we lived together, count me out!"

As if I ever mentioned wanting to live with Brent. I'd almost rather saw off a limb. He laughs and plucks a dirty sock off his sleeping bag, wads it up, and tosses it in the corner. I burst out laughing because his tossing of the sock doesn't improve upon the mess in any way. But his silly statement ends the argument for good. I know that his points are valid and legitimate, and should be recognized and dealt with. I feel guilty because I know I'm taking advantage of him, horribly so. The mess in the tent is predictive of our future housekeeping styles and a sad metaphor for our non-existent relationship.

I hear his friends approach the tent. The sound of crunching gravel underfoot announces their arrival. "Leave them alone, they need their privacy," someone says.

Far from it. There is no need to conceal anything. I really wish I could be attracted to Brent because he seems like such a great guy. Everyone says so, too. He's now on the honor roll after squandering his youth on heroin. He's really turned his life around and suffers no permanent long-term issues from his stint on drugs. But after his friend's statement, both of us are too embarrassed to leave the tent. We wait until the others depart before emerging.

"Hello, new day!" I say when I emerge, peeling back the tent flap and looking around at the tan cliffs with bits of scattered of vegetation on them. I am greeting the Twin Sisters campsite.

Brent mumbles something inaudible as he dresses for the day, pulling on the same crumpled sweatshirt he went to bed in. Neither of us is exactly a hygiene expert at this point. Brent and I join the others at the fire pit where they are sitting on wooden benches. Kind, *parental* Brent makes me a sandwich on the picnic table. I watch him pull out the slices of bread, the mustard, lettuce, and mayonnaise from the cooler. I reach for the bottles of mayonnaise and mustard and give them a hard squeeze. The condiments are ejected with a loud, satisfying plop. It's a cold ham breakfast sandwich. The thick, cold meat slides around my mouth and isn't to my liking. I disguise my reaction from Brent so he won't be hurt.

Hippie Girl saves the day with her torch-tossing skills by announcing, "Let's grill them." The sandwiches suddenly taste much better. I am glad for the very basic invention of fire once more, and for the cave people who invented it. There is silence as we all munch away, our mouths occupied by food. Hippie Guy pulls out his guitar, to provide background music for our feast.

That this bench isn't our breakfast table, that we have no running water, and that we are grimy and dirt-streaked and living without other modern conveniences sinks in after a few days of wilderness roughing it. Some of us have tree sap in our hair. This enjoyable but hardscrabble trip reminds us of how badly we want to go home. At least I think the others are thinking what I'm thinking, when they speak of the to-do items on their schedules. Suddenly, we come to the conclusion that we must get out of there as fast as possible. We want to go home so we can play our guitars and download music and watch TV. We want to feel carpet under our feet again, a soft mattress supporting our weight. The tents are disassembled, the sand dumped out, the bags zipped, and the Isuzu and Brent's small Honda packed.

But then Brent ominously tells me he isn't *quite* ready to go home yet and that *"We need to talk." Not so fast, sister. You'll not leave Twin Sisters*, he seems to be saying.

"Look—moss," I say, and point. I don't want to get into a serious, lengthy discussion. I'm just trying to enjoy nature and to distract him by emphasizing the beauty of it.

Brent tells me something scientific and noteworthy about moss, a boring fact pulled from an encyclopedia. But not even the beauty of nature can melt my melancholy. I wonder why I don't just tell Brent that we need to part ways then and there. Oh yes, because we had driven up together. I don't want to be stranded and left far from home with only my two legs and my hitchhiking thumb to get me back. I do enjoy Brent's company and friendship, despite our incompatibility, at a time when I greatly need it, but want nothing more. I never desired to be his romantic partner.

Brent, like the journalist he is (he will later find a job as an editor), pulls out his camera and starts photographing me on the moss-covered rock. The mini photographic session works. Distracted, he drops the issue of needing to talk. He tells me I'm a beautiful subject and can I pose "like this" and "like that" for him? Brent adjusts his camera settings, plays with the white balance, and employs the techniques we learned in photojournalism class, for which I received an A-plus.

Stop, I think, under the relentless flashes of light. *No photos allowed! I charge for these, you know*. I am blinded by the glare. Brent smooshes our bodies together and takes a forced picture of us with his arm around me, then smiles falsely. The picture is posed and unnatural and features me in a position I never would have forced myself into normally. This forced cheeriness is too much for me.

When Brent is satisfied that we have taken enough phony pictures, we load our gear into his car and start out for home. I am glad that this emotionally and physically draining weekend is over.

We listen to Brent's music this time. There is something feminine and whiny about the voices of the indie singers he listens to. The songs are too soft and teasing. I don't want musical notes to tickle my ears with a feather as they enter. I want the audio equivalent of a full impact, I want the notes to hit me all at once. I want music that assaults. I want louder sounds, stronger than what Brent's got, something soulful and uniquely American. I prefer bro-country artists with music made by mixing harder rock sounds with hip-hop and country, the way zydeco music blends a jazz and blues sound. Bro-country uses the instruments of traditional country music but with a heavier emphasis on drums and steel guitar, with lighthearted lyrics. Music with pizzazz. I prefer the sounds of Florida Georgia Line, Jason Aldean, Chris Young, Dierks Bentley, and Eric Church. But it's Brent's car, so we listen to Brent's music. Music like mine catapults me out of my sullenness, jolting me out of a rut. Brent's music is mopey and indulgent and I do not want to turn inward and wallow. I am afraid of what I might find there. I don't want to be introspective, because I know I will be overwhelmed by a wave of darkness if I do.

Brent sings along to his music. He taps the steering wheel to the beat as he drives.

"Listen to these lyrics. Strawberries, lost love…" He taps the steering wheel some more. He decides we must stop to do some sightseeing when he sees a field full of bright yellow sunflowers. He wants to take more pictures.

"I *have* to get a picture of those," he says. Reluctantly, I pose among their golden petals.

We stop again when we come upon an old, abandoned train car.

After Brent presses the shutter he says, "Perfect. Perfect!" as if he will treasure these photos forever.

Brent doesn't take me home right away. He isn't concerned about that. His excuse is that he has to drop off the camping equipment. He takes me back to his bachelor pad near the college.

At first I am his quiet companion, part of the background. I explore the apartment, wandering freely, looking inquisitively at his knick-knacks and odds and ends as he goes about his daily activities and chores and dispenses with the camping gear. I am a quiet observer of his routine scene. The apartment offers me a view of what daily life is like for him. The apartment is a slice of Brent, and I'm sure I won't like this flavor at all. He behaves naturally and at home here. I suppose he is comfortable enough with me to allow me access to his private world, to see him as he really is. What's next, letting me see his flaws and vulnerabilities? Allowing me to watch him brush his teeth in fuzzy pajamas? I feel like an intruder but he insists that he doesn't want me to leave yet, when I ask if I am imposing.

"Stay," he insists.

He logs onto his computer and pulls up a homework assignment. He's writing an article for class that will appear in the school newspaper, a right guaranteed to all senior journalism students. If you make it that far, you deserve that guarantee. That seems to be the theory. I hover over Brent's shoulder, offering him suggestions. I try to pretend that I'm not that far removed from the world of student journalism and that I'm still qualified to do this for him. So what if I graduated and later went crazy?

Brent strokes his chin pensively. "Hey, that's good, that's very good," he says, typing away as he adds my revisions.

With my help, he finishes the article quickly, which pleases him. He smiles and says he's done with homework for the night. His voice is low and suggestive, as if his mind is on something else. He slams his textbook and shuts down his computer. His focus is now on me.

"Let's watch a movie," he says.

I don't remember what movie we watched because we didn't really watch much of it. Instead of a couch, he offered me his bed as theater seating. His TV was placed conveniently next to the bed.

"See, your excuse to get me to watch a movie was just a ploy," I accuse.

He laughs. "You're right."

He undresses. And then I see the tattoo. The penis tattoo! I can't sleep with someone who has a *penis* tattoo! Oddly, it's the *only* tattoo he has *anywhere* on his body. What a place to get a tattoo! The tattoo starts just under his belly button and ends in an unmentionable region. Without it he would look neat and ordinary, like the white-collar office worker and senior journalism student that he is. His coworkers in the office would never know it was there, so they'd never have to discount him and write him off as unprofessional. Who would have guessed that practical, studious Brent would have such an adornment? The tattoo makes Brent look rough and hard-core; I know I would feel slimy and regretful if I slept with someone who has a penis tattoo. But the tattoo is a minor issue compared to the bigger picture and doesn't really matter. I wouldn't have liked him with or without the tattoo. I don't like Brent in any sort of romantic way, though the tattoo certainly doesn't help. I just don't feel that special spark which creates romantic chemistry between people, even if I have to borrow from pop psychology to come up with an explanation for why I'm not in love with him. Vainly, I feel that I would have been able to feel that spark had there been more physical attraction between us. But the penis tattoo gives me valid evidence to support the legitimacy of my lack of feelings for him. I doubted the sincerity of my hunches before. Now I have tangible cause.

Suddenly, my mind flashes back to Brent's heroin history. I jump to the conclusion that someone who has tattoos was exposed to a *tattoo needle* at the very least, and probably many more with heroin. His clean-cut college student appearance made me forget to think of the details of his past. I picture him huddled near a graffiti-covered wall, hungrily jabbing a needle into his vein as if getting his fix is more important to him than a lack of shelter. I picture dirty, garbage-strewn alleys, mud puddles collecting water from a rain gutter as he crouches, shoving the needle into his vein, oblivious to his grubby surroundings. The habitat of heroin junkies. I think of catching hepatitis, AIDS, and a litany of other diseases. This is the beginning of the end for Brent. To this day I am still unforgiving and prejudiced when it comes to people who've used heroin or other hard drugs. If I find out you're a former user, even if you used it just once, then I'm very selective. Maybe my stance is too harsh, too strict, but I make no exceptions. To me it seems like the sort of guys who'd be daring enough to do heroin might be daring enough to engage in other really dangerous and unsavory activities. Contrary to the popular belief that women are attracted to "bad boys," they spell out trouble and life complications to me. A girl's got to be safe, after all!

I feel I must exit, so I make up an excuse for why I have to leave his room immediately. "I have to get up early tomorrow," I say. "Real early. Like crack of dawn early, so, you know... Best be going." I point at the door as I speak, and launch my body toward it.

"What happened?" he asks. "What on earth is the matter *now*?"

"Nothing. I just forgot I had to be up early tomorrow, that's all," I say. And I'm gone. I know it's a lame excuse, but I have to leave.

I would never see Brent in person again, though he would be instrumental in saving my life long distance by phone, notifying my mom and the proper authorities when I was in crisis. I don't think that he was being vindictive and seeking revenge by telling my mom of my plans. He was only trying to keep me safe. I'm sure I hurt him more than he ever hurt me. I am lucky someone cared about me at that crucial time in my life, when he certainly didn't have to. He was a kind man. Less patient people certainly would have given up on me long before he did. Perhaps I should have given him more of a chance and preserved the friendship. After all, we could have formed a pact of mutual understanding, each of us having had our share of problems. We could have relied on each other, each drawing strength from the other. At the time, though, the relationship was unbalanced, with me as the recipient of most of the caring as I acted out the roles of sponge and leach. If I'd stayed, perhaps I could have learned some major life lessons from him, lessons he'd learned the hard way. But I have never doubted how I felt in that moment and I have no regrets over fleeing, even though my friends would question my judgment. "Why would you leave someone who has such a good job? A newspaper editor?" they asked.

You see, even before graduation, Brent had already secured an excellent journalism position. His prognosis after graduation would be an upward trajectory. It was hard to get my friends to understand my point of view. I, alone, knew why it was better to walk out and was firm about it. Would Brent have stopped my own downward slide? I doubt it. I think I was headed that way, anyway.

CHAPTER 7

Captured

With Brent now out of my life, I have fewer distractions from myself, and this is the problem.

Brent's friendship had been the equivalent of my water wings. Now that he is gone, without my safety net, I quickly slip down into a dark hole. There is no one to remind me to eat, no one to get up for, to bother to dress for... Endlessly antsy, I feel have to keep moving. If I don't stay in motion I feel like a soda bottle under pressure, on the verge of exploding. So I pace around the block for much of the day because I have to keep moving. Alone, I must face that I was sick all along and Brent was just good at throwing a scarf over my eyes, distracting me from that part of myself and leading me down from the ledge, so to speak.

The pills I am taking are not working for me; they are making me feel, paradoxically, even more depressed. The doctors have not found the right drug that works for my particular brain chemistry. My brain chemicals feel like a messy stew and I wonder if I'll ever return to being the person I was *before* taking them. And that's why I'm depressed. The thought of being permanently stuck in this state is at the core of it. I don't know why I cannot go back to my usual self. I wonder if I ever will. Unaccustomed to taking pills and with less than adequate medical care, I haven't had anyone to tell me that

I will *most certainly* go back to the way I was before beginning a pill-popping regime, once their effects leave my body. The oversimplified advice from church and school, "Drugs are bad, they'll kill you," doesn't serve me well here and is useless. I am too nauseated and depressed to eat. It's been days since I've bathed. I have simply given up. When I do try to eat, my hand shakes so much that I spill food all over my shirt. At this point, I'm completely nonfunctional and in need of a bib.

Days pass with no improvement. I am slipping deeper and deeper into a dark hole. I don't want to slide any further. What would that look like? Complete immobility? I am desperate, so I cry out for help, to anyone, even a guy I don't love, because he babies me and that is what I need right now. A guy whom I refuse to sleep with, even to pacify him. A guy who has assumed a caretaker role and who must be very annoyed with me by now. Seeing him and his garish tattoo in person would be too difficult, so I call him instead. I tell him I need help because I wish was dead. I'm glad I know now that I would never feel that way again. But even then I don't think I truly feel that way; my attempts to reach out are a cry for help. Brent recognizes the urgency of the situation and calls my mom to relay to her what I told him, appealing to her for help. I'm not upset with him for his betrayal of confidentiality, at first. Brent's met my mom before and she likes him. She thinks he's a good influence.

My mom likes him because she knows Brent treats me politely and he works at a news desk and he seems like a nice boy. Boy is overstretching the word. He is thirty-four years old. Okay, so he's a decent man. He pays his bills, helps others, and is no doubt an outstanding citizen in the community with a respectable, responsible job. You'd think his shady past would have turned him bitter. A lot of people are soiled by life's disappointments by the time they're that age. They are headed for a mid-life crisis or in the midst of one. They have been around the block a time or two, they become more weary and jaded. Brent hasn't lost his joy for life despite all the obstacles he's had to overcome. And even though Brent has done heroin, his druggy past was completed in youthful good fun out of innocent curiosity. His drug use, he summarizes, was an attempt to emulate his heroes, Kerouac and Burroughs—nothing more than a period of experimentation, he says. And he is still idealistic and hopeful, knowing he is now on the right path.

After the talk with Brent, there is a quick intervention. In a chain reaction of events, my mom calls Jeff, LCSW, Social Worker and Professional Screwball. Where was he all this time when I needed to reach someone about getting my lithium blood levels tested? Together, they declare the situation critical and develop a plan of action. Part of me is thankful to Brent for alerting the authorities and getting help. But that didn't mean that I wanted help in the form of lockup and forced drugging.

Jeff arrives on foot and I can see the police cars up the street, a block or so behind him. I have familiarized myself with the laws. This time I know what is coming. So I turn and sprint across the lawn of the city block. I sprint as fast as I can. I figure that Jeff, with his considerable paunch, will have trouble catching up to me. I am right. He's a slow, lumbering runner. I can hear him huffing and puffing behind me. I panic. *Where should I hide?* I decide to hide somewhere where I can blend in, with the idea of getting lost in the crowd and becoming part of the background. I dart down the street and dash into a rec center. I flash my gym pass at the startled-looking attendant behind the desk. He accepts it and waves me on through even though I'm red-faced and inexplicably out of breath and shaking. The attendant must have thought I'd physically overexerted myself and was headed back to the treadmills for more punishment. I smell the overpowering smell of chlorine. No use hiding in the fluorescent-lit room with the Olympic-sized pool. I sneak over to the basketball gym, the thought of Jeff in hot pursuit behind me making my pulse quicken with fear. I don't want to go to the institution I'm sure he and the pair of policemen will force me into. I think it's ridiculous that the management of mood and sleep disorders falls under the jurisdiction of law enforcement.

I smell wood varnish and dirty gym socks. Boards creek under my feet with each step. My tennis shoes emit a rubber squeal as they come in contact with the polished floor. It's dark in this gym, a perfect place to hide. I duck under the bleachers and crouch in the dark, waiting, praying that Jeff can't hear me. *Run fatty, run*, I think, knowing my adversary is close behind. I don't want to be locked up. Don't want him to take away the key. For a brief moment, I feel resentful of Brent and the phone call he made which has led me to this situation. I would later forgive him and deem the call necessary.

A person with restless legs isn't the best candidate for success at the game of hide and seek. To be good at concealing oneself, one must possess one very necessary, specific quality, even to the exclusion of all others: the ability to keep quiet. My restlessness is too great to allow me to conceal myself for long. I just have to pace or face an uncomfortable, claustrophobic boxed-in feeling. A feeling as if I can't breathe. I feel so claustrophobic that crouching in my hiding place under the bleachers is impossible. My legs are too restless. A tingly, stabbing, pins-and-needles feeling overtook my extremities when I gave in to exhaustion and let them rest. Basically, I am in sad shape and probably deserve what is coming. But I'm not about to surrender, not without a fight.

Jeff hears me, I can tell. I can hear his footsteps in the gym. *I'm busted!* Try as I might, I can't even *force* myself to hold still, even with the threat of capture hanging over my head. I wonder if the antidepressants I am on have anything to do with my restless akathisia.

Now I am sure that they had a lot to do with it as I have never felt that way again. I have also never taken them since.

Thinking I still have a chance to bolt past Jeff, I crawl out from under the bleachers and race out the gym door. I do not make it off the property. Somehow, I miscalculated his location in the room and walk right into Jeff, LCSW's trap. He's tall, so I walk straight into a solid wall of disapproval. Jeff has a frown on his face. He is panting and out of breath, his black hair shining like a raven, his green Welsh eyes glaring holes into me. His look says it all. *Why did you have to make this so difficult?* I am no match for his heavy six-foot-two frame. He wrestles me to the ground. The officers arrive then, and they put the cold metal cuffs on, as if I'm a criminal rather than someone who doesn't want to go to an institution—and who would, honestly? I peer out at Jeff's face through the window in the back of the cop car. I detect a hint of smugness and triumph in his satisfied smile. He gasps for air and tucks his dress shirt into his pants, straightening his mussed hair. Just another day on the job for him.

"We got her!" is the last thing I hear Jeff, LCSW say, as if I am a prized buck he caught. I see his grin, watch his face fade as the car drives away.

CHAPTER 8

Patient Abuse

I'm gross and disheveled at this point, as I sit here in the back of the cop car. Due to the shakiness the meds produced in me, I wasn't able to properly feed myself and there are bits of encrusted food on my shirt. I am wearing the remnants of my lunch. I'm sweaty from my marathon sprint away from Jeff, grimy because I've been too out of it to bathe or care. I realize I must look like a frantic, cornered wild animal.

I wonder if Jeff ensured that my file will precede me to this institution. If he will assemble a file similar to the first hastily created one in which he got my family details, occupation, and other basics about me wrong. The file with the wrong information in it. This time it is clear that I won't be going to the hospital for a *brief* stay. *Two strikes and you're... where?* I shiver and shift in my seat. My restless legs won't permit me to sit still, though I try. It is extremely hard to squirm in handcuffs.

I am transferred from the police car to a government-issued van, while still cuffed, of course. It's hard to sit in this position while sane, never mind while being locked down and agitated with my wrists tucked behind my back.

And then an ironic, degrading event occurs. Even though I am incapacitated and cannot help myself, I am lumped together with prisoners being carted off to jail. The state must have a limited budget, for I have to share the same van as the inmates. The Department of Social Services must be trying to cut down on transportation costs. It adds insult to injury after having first been picked up by a police car. The van actually slows to a stop and the doors slide open to let in a group of men in jumpsuits. A hefty, orange-clad man climbs into the van. The entire vehicle shakes as he steps up. The van tilts heavily to one unbalanced side as he sits. His knees are the size of canyon boulders, cramming against my side, taking up all that is left of the seat. He's hairy and sweaty. Sitting next to him, I'm too close for comfort. I feel awkward and uncomfortable and imposed upon. Though I don't know the name of the man sitting next to me, I imagine that he would be called something short and choppy. His name would be something like that of a member of a motorcycle gang. I imagine that his moniker is "Butch." He looks like a Butch. Butch's arms are hairy and tattooed in his cuffs. Is riding along with prisoners based on the assumption that immorality and mental illness are often found to exist concurrently? That I am with my own kind, where I belong? Is my present company a reflection on the assumption that those being sent to psychiatric institutions are also likely criminal? I haven't committed any crimes, I'm just indisposed. And now I am being transported with inmates. What did I do to deserve this? I haven't stolen anything, I didn't murder anyone… But let's face it—I'm not exactly in an elite category right now. These men in orange jumpsuits frighten me. Who knows what crimes they have committed? What grizzly deeds they have participated in? The men in the orange jumpsuits and I do not converse. We do not exchange a single word during the entire trip. I don't want to know, don't want to find out. Maybe my opinions of them are as prejudiced as theirs are of me, but I don't want to complicate my life by exchanging stories with them. Whatever they tell me, I'm sure, will be horrifying, sad, shocking, and benefit me in no way. I stare out the window at the barren landscape instead.

The inmates are dropped off. Their departure couldn't have come soon enough for me. I must remain in the van to be driven on to my final destination. I am terrified and crippled by anticipatory anxiety. *At least I have more leg room now*, I think, as I quiver within the bounds of my restraints, counting my blessings. The driver stops next to an ancient, Brick Gothic building with towering turrets. The driver says that I have arrived at the "old part of the hospital." He is trying to minimize the terror of the panorama in front of me and to let me know that there is a newer, more pleasant, remodeled part of the hospital to look forward to as well. His words have no effect. They fall on deaf ears like an attempt to whisper through stone. I shudder when I think about what probably goes on behind those walls.

My mother has been contacted by the hospital and invited to be part of my admissions process. It is as if I am going away to an exclusive private school dressed in the uniform of the infirm.

"Take good care of her," she says to the hospital staff. There is a sad, downturned droop to her eyes. Her loved one is in the care of others now, the situation is out of her hands.

I have to go through the admissions process to be admitted to a place to which I really don't want to be admitted. So I don't try hard to impress. I'd rather be rejected and turned away. I'd rather fail their tests and not meet their criteria. But there is no evaluation process. The decision was made before I even arrived. I answer the administrator's questions as they check my belongings, which consist of the clothes on my back. I'm a mess. On the dehumanizing van ride to the hospital (not helped by the presence of inmates), out of nerves and a fear of the unknown, I have chewed and twisted at my shirt sleeve until it is a clotted ball of damp cotton. My collar is stained with food deposited there after failed attempts to eat with my palsied hands. The nurses take one look at me and express compassion for my defenseless, invalid's demeanor.

"Poor thing."

The administrators seem to take pity on me as well, which is no doubt aided by my forlorn and pitiful appearance. They assign me a kind, female doctor, a Dr. V. Dr. V. is the end-of-the-road doctor for last hope cases, so she has to be competent, innovative and above average. She has to be creative to look for lasting solutions. Dr. V., I would find, is a life-changing, impactful rehabilitator—she'll do anything to get to the bottom of why you're down.

Aesthetically, Dr. V. is unusually tall for a woman. She stands at six feet, a big woman with a hearty, booming laugh and broad shoulders. The doctor behaves as if she experiences supreme mental health herself, as if it is a simple exercise for her to share her joyous, bountiful health with the rest of us in the form of the time and interest she takes in us individuals. The doctor appears calm and laughs easily and often. Her emotions seem genuine, evidenced by the crinkling of her eyes when she smiles. Her booming laugh echoes across the hospital corridors, erasing the gloom.

The nurses say the first order of business for me to attend to is bathing. They have drawn a hot bubble bath for me. They keep a watchful eye on me at all times, afraid of what I might do, but even their wariness is mixed with compassion and is only there for self-preservation. I am like a stray dog the nurses have taken in to clean up. They are not sure if I bite yet.

Rather than feeling like I'm at a gas chamber shower, I am soothed by their soft, gentle ways. "We'll make this quick and painless," they say.

My warm feelings of comfort and nurtured, cozy, envelopment vanish when I arrive on the ward and see its faded green carpet and dingy furniture, realizing it is to be my home. I walk around looking at the dated décor in baggy, donated hospital sweats which the nurses have given me. For furniture to get so worn, it must have taken time. Time to collect dust and wear. And while those chairs were here, other people have been here too. Probably locked in their rooms. I feel trapped, wondering if I will stay here year after year until I sustain the same sort of wear and tear as the furniture. Until I am old and gray. Forever! An eternity! Perhaps I will die here. No one ever instructed me on just exactly how long I would be staying. No one informed me of the checkout policy. They didn't, because they don't know the answer to the question then themselves. People heal at different rates. They don't know when I will, if ever. It is a question that couldn't be answered at the time as it *has no answer*, so they neglected to inform me at all.

I am thinking the answer is forever, though, because when I ask the gaunt, haunted people pacing the halls how long they've been here, they confirm that my suspicions are true. Their stay must have seemed like an eternity of confinement, their days indistinguishable from each other despite whether the actual length of time they've been here is, or isn't. Hospital days are routine and structure-based. And for those who don't get better, each meal must be just another tray put in front of them, each passing second, another to endure.

I need to conduct a quick, informal survey. I walk around asking patients how long they've been here, and some of the patients say "six years." Six *years*! I feel faint then because I think I will be here for six years, too, and that they've taken away my freedom. I am sure I will never see the light of day, or the outside world, ever again. In despair over my incarceration, I see nothing but gloom. With my fatalistic, negative thinking, I am assuming that I am a severe case who will progressively worsen. I think I am a lifer, the bottom of the barrel. I predict I will become a mumbling shuffler, wandering the halls dazed and confused with lank, greasy hair.

In reality, I would be a short stay and was quickly rehabilitated. But it is easy to doubt yourself when people insist that you're mentally ill and will remain permanently so, even if that is not your eventual outcome. It's easy to lose confidence in your actions when you believe your decisions are clouded by a veil of illness. I had no way of knowing what was going to happen at the time, and my depressed outlook convinced me that I would be there forever.

For when you're depressed, all doors are shut, all smiles are frowns, every up a down. All minutes seem to drag on forever and time is unquantifiable. I was depressed because I felt imprisoned.

The walls here are made of concrete and painted cinderblock. I feel them with my hands, fumbling for a crack in the fortress. I know after I scan for escape routes that there are none. It seems futile to try to escape. Our beds are immobile metal frames, bolted to the ground.

CHAPTER 9

The Human Windmill

When I go to my assigned room that closely resembles a cell, I meet my roommate, Alice. We were supposed to be assigned roommates according to like personalities, said one administrator. *Obviously someone has erred*, I think, when I meet Alice.

Alice is a manic-depressive stuck in perpetual mania. She talks too much, *way* too much. She's a constant verbal stream. Her lips move so fast they're a humming blur. Her topics of conversation often have nothing to do with what is occurring in her surroundings, and she does not catch social nuances. Her words are often irrelevant and her interactions socially awkward and inappropriate. Alice laughs at her own jokes. Laughs so hard that her face turns beet red and she has to trundle awkwardly off to the drinking fountain with her lopsided gait, to take a sip and have a breather and calm herself down. She walks with her feet splayed wide, though she appears to have no inherited deformity. Her odd lumbering walk seems more of an affectation and more an expression of deep-felt emotion than an impediment. It is as if Alice is punctuating the ground with her feet as she walks. And why not? The rest of her body is highly expressive, especially her face, so why not her legs as well?

Alice is far from deformed. Actually, she looks like a Norwegian doll. She looks as if she could be made of porcelain. Her skin is like ivory and there is a rosy blush to her cheeks. She flushes easily when excited, which is often. Her hair isn't blonde, it's yellow, and her features are symmetrical, refined and noble-looking. Alice isn't your stereotypical bubbly blonde. She crossed the line into the land of obnoxiousness long ago.

Alice waves her arms like a human windmill, simply because she's alive and she can. It's as if she has been born anew and has just discovered that her body is capable of performing these actions. Her wild motions are a celebration of movement. But no, Alice is more tornado than human windmill, wreaking havoc and obliterating everything in her path. No one can get a word in edgewise, people are often left stunned and confused by her loud displays of emotion, left holding onto their hats as she whirls by, because she often talks right over the top of them. She is incapable of listening. I want Alice to shut up. She is running her own radio show, her own stream of consciousness narrative. She's constantly delivering her very own talk show monologue. I'm pretty sure no one wants to download Alice's channel. She is an outcast, even among the other patients, who are pretty strange themselves. Mention the proper noun "Alice," and expect to hear an abundance of laughter and ridicule. She is, sadly, the butt of many jokes.

After going non-stop, Alice finally slows down and plops down on her bed in a heap of exhaustion. She expels a few last giggles and then, hiccupping, gasps for breath. She behaves as if all that babbling was a fit she had which has now passed. As if the scene she created was something that needed to be ejected and now that it's done, she's content. The storm has been weathered. I begin to realize that there's a person under what appears to be a blonde tornado.

Alice tells me her story. She was captured too, like a wild mustang, she says, mystically. At first she was coaxed into going along with the hoax but when she realized it was a lie, she fought back like a healthy filly, kicking and struggling. She was brought to this institution by her brothers who fed her some line about how they were going to Disneyland and wouldn't that be a nice trip, *dear sister*? I find her story comparable to a child's pet dying and his parents disguising the fact and instead feeding the child a line, saying that the pet has gone to live at a "nice farm in the country." Alice wasn't Disneyland bound, of course. Her brothers drove her here instead. Some vacation. They gave her no say in her fate. They conned her, pulled the wool over her eyes. Alice has been here for five years. Her brothers saw how increasingly destructive her compulsive behavior became. Prior to going to the hospital, she said, her brothers observed that she had been taking multiple daily showers, scrubbing herself so vigorously that her skin peeled off. She had an obsession with being clean.

Alice says that her "cure" comes at a price. She says the meds have given her diabetes, documented by the hospital, and that lithium has wrecked her liver. She says that here, they can force you to take meds whether you want to or not. Here, they can legally rape your brain forever by force-feeding you pills or injecting them into your bloodstream. Here they can turn you into a mindless zombie.

They can do this to you even if you haven't committed any crime. But if you go so far as to mention that you're suicidal, even if you haven't actually harmed yourself, that's a potential crime against yourself and they can lock you up for that. Because then you're a potential self-murderer. Alice isn't in crisis anymore, but Dr. V. has determined that she's too out of step with society, too incompetent to function in the outside everyday world.

So what? Who gets to decide? Would she really be incapable of caring for herself? I try to imagine Alice pushing a shopping cart in a grocery store, doing the errands that ordinary people do. I imagine her bouncing around the aisles in a bunny hop, speaking to each and every customer, telling them jokes with no punchlines while they are left staring, jaws gaping. I picture her being easily misled by a stranger with a convincing story. A stranger with sweet promises for someone naïve. Maybe it's for her own safety, being here, but *really*, who gets to decide what's "normal" and what's not? There are a lot of people with unusual habits and they're not all institutionalized. If Alice is happy being loud and bouncy, who cares? And what if she *was* capable of taking care of herself? Would they ever give her a chance to try?

If Alice is a representative sample, a typical case study, if her future is my future as well, then I can't imagine anything more terrifying. I'll be forced to stay here until I develop diabetes. I'll be disfigured and develop a permanent nervous tick. If this is the place where I am to get better, the statements Alice claims as fact are not exactly conducive to healing. Don't people go to hospitals to heal, not to be tortured?

I am too busy thinking of the worst-case scenario to realize that since there is nothing I can do to change my situation for the time being, I should try to make the best of it. I need to find the silver lining. If I don't, I may never get out. I need to demonstrate improvement to the staff before they will release me. Alice is trying, Dr. V. is attempting to help. Instead I see Alice as a freak of nature and Dr. V. as my captor. Six years with a mechanical wind-up doll for a roommate? How could I ever survive that? Six years of listening to her broken record speeches? You have to really look hard to find the silver lining in moments like these.

Alice is the colorful blur I see out of the corner of my eye in our room. That's her. Always in motion. Our room. The room with the homey, inviting bed which just so happens to be bolted to the floor. *Want to rearrange the furniture today? Nope, sorry, can't.* The cinderblock walls are bare and stark. The interior designer will never be allowed in. Alice has been imprisoned here so long that she's built up quite a collection of possessions, which she's used in an attempt to try to bring a little cheer to the room. I don't care to take a page out of her decorator's book. On the walls are Alice's crumbly, glued-together art projects. Instead of Picassos, she has Crayolas. I see a craft pom-pom dangling precariously off a sheet of construction paper.

This cell is her home. That thought scares me. I don't want to be here long, certainly not long enough to amass possessions. I hope I'm not here long enough to put up a welcome mat or to rent a postal box. This is not my permanent address. From an orderly, I receive a thin, scratchy hospital blanket which smells of sausages, oddly. What is that pervasive, lingering smell? Years of stale breakfasts soaked into the fiber of the linen. I heard that policy dictates that you can make a phone call home to request a personal blanket, but I feel too doomed and depressed to feel like calling anyone. I wouldn't want to explain where I was and how I ended up here.

As a new admit who has not yet been seen, I'm in bad shape. I sit shaking on the immobile bed, waiting for my chance to see the doctor. My condition upon arrival could be why Alice, in particular, was assigned my roommate. It has been days since I've slept. I have a frantic, exhausted, nail-biting, on edge feeling. I'm a frayed wire. My eyes are bloodshot, my palms sweaty. I can't sleep, nor even hold still without being overwhelmed by my restless legs. Essentially, I'm in the same boat as Alice at this point. The difference between us is that through intuition, I seem to recognize when I'm making others uncomfortable, and Alice does not.

Lying in a bed feels confining, suppressive and smothering. I can't stand it! I *have* to get up and move or face the painful stab of a thousand pins and needles in my legs. This is more than sheer restlessness. If I can't move, I feel as if I will burst. How did I get this way? I was on two antidepressants at once, and this is the result.

That night I don't sleep at all. Not for the entire night. I know, because I watch the clock tick by, hour by hour. The members of the night staff are stricter than the day staff. The night staff see patients only while we sleep, so they assume the worst about us, not knowing what we are like when we are awake. There is no chance for the night staff to get to know who we really are and what our personalities are like. All they see of us is a dark, sleeping form; they let their imaginations fill in the rest. When a patient pokes his head out of his room, they assume we're either sleepwalking or breaking quiet hour rules. Either way, their reaction to our nightly awakenings is not good.

The response is always, "Go back to bed." Of course I am breaking the rules. But I can't help it. My restless movements keep Alice awake, but try as I might, I just can't force myself to hold still.

Somehow, I survive the night and make it to the day that follows, having spent the night tossing and turning. Raggedly, mechanically, barely, but alive. Alice's sleep must have been disturbed as well. She must dislike having me as a roommate as much as I dislike having her as one. Later, once the effects of the antidepressants wear off, I stop having restless legs. I *knew* that the drug was the culprit. My suspicions were founded. There is no reason for someone so young to experience such anguish without artificial interference.

CHAPTER 10

An Eternity

It's daylight on the ward. An orderly who looks like a Hawaiian surfer dude with long, wavy black hair falling over one eye, chuckles at me, but in a nice, teasing sort of way.

"Look, you can't keep this up forever. You'll wear out," he says.

Ryan is one of the kinder members of staff. Patients have our rating systems, our naughty and nice lists. We have to keep safe, to advise each other to avoid abuses of power. Ryan is a college student gaining clinical experience here—he is studying behavioral science and psychology. He is here to study our brains. To observe the case studies in progress we are.

I try hard to follow Ryan's advice to rest, but it doesn't work. I can manage to lie down for as long as my legs will allow, which is all of five seconds. It takes every bit of my concentration to force myself to hold still and even then I can't manage. I've developed blisters on my feet again from my consistent pacing.

The orderlies tell me I will get to see the doctor soon, to be evaluated. Dr. V. is not laughing her big, hearty laugh this time. She seems suspicious of this new intruder on the ward. This is her flock of sheep, these people on the ward, and she wants to protect them from this newcomer, me. She only behaves this way until she gets to know me, until she knows I can be trusted. Doctors are human too, who experience human emotions and are prone to errors of judgment.

At first, these patients are better off than me, if only because they've had more time to recover. I would later become better off than ninety percent of them, however and would be considered a "high functioning patient," but it would take time.

"Geodon, that should slow you down," says Dr. V. She doesn't know me yet, doesn't know that I get akathisia from all antipsychotics due to their dopamine-blocking, movement-suppressing effects. Stubbornly, I tell her I will not consume an agent known to harm me in the past.

"I won't do this willingly. I'll put up a fight," I say, trying to put up a tough façade.

Because she doesn't know me yet, she says, "This is part of your treatment. Try the Geodon."

Ryan and the stern-looking nurse force me to go to the Quiet Room so that Alice can get some sleep. I also suspect I'm being detained until I willingly agree to take their awful pills. Pills that I know don't work for me. They make me sleep in a vault-like chamber of a room with padded walls and a bed that is bolted to the floor, a common sight in this place. It looks like the inside of a very restrictive space ship. Windows line every wall in the room. It is, after all, an observation tank. I can see the nurse's station on the other side of the window. I must undergo twenty-four-hour observation. My dignity and privacy are gone. Fortunately, I haven't much dignity left at this point.

The Geodon is a form of pure chemical torture. It worsens my restless legs, and I am out of my mind with agitation. The agitation is jaw-locking extreme this time. My bones have turned to jelly and I quiver uncontrollably. Psychotropic medications, for the most part, just don't agree with me. They all produce a foggy, altered state of consciousness that gives me the awareness that I've just consumed a mind-bending substance, be it prescribed or otherwise. I've tried dozens of them and they *all* make me feel stoned.

My restlessness makes it impossible to sit still, so to cope I rock back and forth on the foam pad. The agitation is so extreme that I pray I will fall into unconsciousness rather than bear it another second. Finally, my body can take it no more and I fall into a deep, blessed sleep for which I am extremely grateful.

I wish that psychiatrists administered actual measurable tests prior to beginning treatment. I wish that there were legitimate, tangible neurotransmitter tests to diagnose such illnesses as depression, anxiety disorder, manic depression and schizophrenia, as there are for many physical diseases. I wish that brains could be scanned, in a noninvasive way, to pinpoint evidence of specific diseases leading to accurate psychiatric diagnoses. But at the time of this writing, there aren't any. Psychiatrists make diagnoses based on observations, their best guesses, and by following criteria laid out in the *DSM* (Diagnostic and Statistical Manual of Mental Disorders), their guidebook which tends to generalize and diminish you as an individual.

Then you will be put through a trial and error period as they attempt to find a drug that will work for you, as you act as guinea pig. It is an inexact science. But the initial trial could mean taking the wrong drug as they struggle to find one that will work with your brain chemistry. Some of the drugs can potentially make you even worse. Psychiatric drugs, don't forget, are mind-altering drugs. We all have a unique brain chemistry so treatment should be individualized. The human brain is a complicated place, containing over 86 billion neurons and over 300 brain chemicals, only some as yet identified. Ghrelin is a neurotransmitter discovered *as recently as 1996* that was found to govern wakefulness and appetite. I wish that the current psychiatric treatment process was less akin to a walk in the dark. Perhaps the future will bring such advancements. I hope that there will definitive diagnostic tests in the future. The instatement of neurotransmitter tests would be a precise and excellent addition to the psychiatric setting.

CHAPTER 11

Guinea Pig Test Subject

Dr. V. comes to the ward to check on me. She wants to see if I have improved while on Geodon.

"The Geodon, it should be working," she says, and turns to go. "We'll try it for one more week," she adds, before retreating down the patient residence hall to her office.

A week later, Dr. V. still doesn't know how to proceed. The drug is clearly not working as evidenced to anyone with eyes. My condition has worsened. Her staff holds a meeting to discuss my situation. Nurse Stern and Ryan are included.

I do not have any hospital privileges yet. Privileges are what you get once you've proved yourself. Rules are, you have to start from square one and then work your way up. To do this you must be on your best behavior, attend groups, and demonstrate your compliance to staff. Obtaining a hall or grounds pass is a privilege. I do not have a hall pass yet with which to stroll the rolling green, pine-dotted campus. I cannot come and go at will. Although the place was remodeled, I suspect it was a once a Gothic institution. The rumor is that lobotomies were once performed here. The thought makes me shiver. I need to get outside, to breathe fresh air. Freedom beckons through the streaky windows in which I can catch glimpses of the lawn beyond it. As a new admit with zero privileges, I can't even make a phone call, nor wear my own clothes yet. I cannot even leave the Quiet Room. The rewards system enforcement seems childish, like giving a child a gold sticker for completing a task. But without rewards, few would be motivated to improve.

CHAPTER 12

Kyle, Orderly Mentor

As I daydream about my release date, I am convinced that staying here won't be so bad when I lay eyes on Kyle, an orderly. But *what an orderly*! Calling him a mere "orderly" does not do him justice. Kyle is twenty-seven years old, he tells us, because he's friendly and open to questions and comments from his patients. His hair, jet black, curls around his head in a flattering, face framing helmet. It wouldn't be accurate to call his eyes simply "blue." His eyes are, at times, icy pools to get lost in; other times they're aqua, the same color as the warm water surrounding the Bahamas. Kyle's eyes are hypnotic and resemble actor Bradley Cooper's. Depending on the occasion, Kyle's eyes look like wolves' eyes or the eyes of a madman, depending on the light—only Kyle is on the *other* side of the desk. His intense eyes sometimes have a far-off gaze, as if Kyle is looking at something pleasant that exists in another galaxy known only to him. There is a mysterious birthmark, a possible port wine stain or scar under Kyle's right eye that adds to his allure. Where this mark came from is never explained.

We later find out that he *was* once on *our* side of the desk, on the receiving end. He is a manic-depressive in remission who wants to share his knowledge with others. He is a peer counselor now, on a mission to mentor us. Kyle is an orderly who eschews hospital scrubs and instead wears only designer brands such as Calvin Klein and American Eagle and affects a cool, casual, indifferent air. He prefers pop-country artists like Jack Johnson and other artists who frequent the beach. And Kyle works at displaying his mellow, placid temperament. He is positively nonchalant at all times. His voice is soft and calm, so this job is perfect for him. Getting too upset would be "uncool." In a post-feminist era, Kyle is Mr. Nice, Mr. Sensitive. Kyle has a laissez-faire style of governing the ward. He behaves more like a security guard sitting in a watch tower, while reading a novel and paying us little attention. Leave him to his computer games at the nurses' station, don't make any waves, and he'll let you spend your days the way you want.

Nearly all of the female patients have crushes on Kyle. The depressed girls became less depressed looking at him, the manic girls more manic; the delusional, caught up in fantasies that he could be theirs. Kyle is our keeper. The one holding the keys. He watches the camera afternoons and nights, and I catch him peering at me through the glass. If you are hurt and vulnerable and trapped and are required to have a face observing you at all times, it might as well be a handsome one.

There is something slightly off about Kyle's mannerisms. He doesn't advertise his issues, but if you struggle, he will share bits of wisdom. In a quiet voice, he confides to me that he is a manic-depressive on lithium maintenance treatments who is currently in remission. Kyle knows the tricks of the trade when it comes to dealing with mood disorders. His emerged when he was seventeen, so he has dealt with it a long time.

Make my bones stop aching, I silently plead with him, with my eyes, though I know this is magical thinking. I am still experiencing restless legs. But only Dr. V. can institute any changes. Kyle is my daily caretaker, my source of entertainment, my advisor, a friend. A watcher and shepherd. He is not my prescriber, nor my savior.

Kyle is armed with a large supply of practical tips on how to survive within the hospital walls. Having survived and thrived himself (fifteen percent of those with his disease will be lost to suicide), Kyle has advice on various topics, such as how to brush your teeth while your hands are trembling from lithium toxicity, and how to hold a brush steady. He imparts a few survival tips to me. Kyle tells me to chew gum when my mouth is dry from the pills because it helps prevent gingivitis. He has tips on how to become more like him because look, *he's* the one behind the desk now. Maybe they hired him so he could relate to us. Smart, this mentoring technique, very progressive and innovative. Kyle has made it through hell and back and is alive and well.

As Kyle guards the door to the Quiet Room, I sneak glances at him, trying not to be too obvious about it. Kyle's chameleon eyes change colors. Today they are snow caps in winter. I want to drink his eyes—they make me thirsty. The port wine stain on his cheek makes me think some creator has put a stamp on him, singling him out and marking him as "special." Either that, or a fairy kissed him under his eye.

Unfortunately, Kyle is also one of those guys who *knows* how good-looking he is. He's probably received a lifetime's worth of compliments on his appearance. Kyle is kind, but he *does* realize the effect his hypnotic eyes have on people. He realizes the effect produced when he smooths his black, wavy hair across his forehead. Not that he'd have to try hard to impress in a place like this. It's not as if he wants to.

While I huddle on the mattress in my cell, Kyle spends hours grooming himself at the nurse's station. He's very meticulous when it comes to grooming. He pulls out a comb and styles away multiple times a day. I watch him file his nails. He scrutinizes them closely, buffing them, then blowing away the debris. Perhaps Kyle is bored and is just looking for something to occupy his time aside from his observation duties. I think it would be boring watching camera footage of patient activities eight hours a day. Eight hours of watching someone sleep. How fascinating. There isn't a TV in my room and I don't have a book to read, so Kyle becomes my only form of entertainment. Kyle gets up from his computer and adjusts his designer sweat jacket. I see him turn around and I admire his denim-clad bottom, using the glass from my observation tank as a mirror. Kyle won't let me out until I come up with a phony "I'm all better" statement, or prove it to him. And it will probably be phony because Geodon is an awful drug and under its influence I cannot possibly get better. Kyle parks a chair next to the door of the Quiet Room where he reads a book, taking time to glance up at me every few minutes. They are trusting a manic-depressive with my care.

Like a lot of manic-depressives I know, even one in remission as he claims to be, Kyle has a flair for the dramatic. In addition to carrying a comb in his back pocket, he is also prone to wearing ascot scarves casually tossed to one side, like a film noire star, over the designer labels he wore. He favors red and white knit caps with little white pom-poms on them, even indoors. Kyle and I have a master vs. student relationship. I resolve to learn everything I can from Kyle about survival. Kyle shoves a tray of food my way. It contains grilled chicken, mashed potatoes, steamed vegetables, and a dry bread roll, each divided into their respective plastic compartments. It comes with a plastic fork as well. The Quiet Room doesn't come equipped with a kitchen, as kitchen utensils and appliances are considered "sharps." So I must improvise. Is one supposed to earn a badge of honor for having spent time in this room? I should have received a medal for having survived its gritty minimalism. My dining options are either to place the tray on the bed, or to sit cross-legged and eat my food on the floor. I feel like a neglected shelter dog who has been brought my kibble. The Quiet Room isn't meant to be long term quarters, so I won't have to eat off the floor for long. We talk sometimes, Kyle and I, short conversations so as to abide by the rules. Officially, my head should be in my room, not poking out into the hall, but Kyle lets me stick it out sometimes to chat.

I must have endured the Quiet Room for three days before Dr. V. decides to change her treatment strategy. She sends the social worker to ask me what's worked for me in the past and asks how they can help me in the future. The information the doctor gets from the social worker will give her an idea of what will work for me. She finally wants my input in my care, I suppose. I don't know why that wasn't the first question she asked me upon admission. It's another example of their lack of respect for patients, of their lack of confidence in "crazies." They viewed me as too "out of it" to be able to include me in my own treatment. Had I been there for a knee replacement, I'm sure I would have been asked to collaborate from the start. Matters of the mind aren't afforded the same respect as physical ones, though they should be.

"Lamictal has *kind of* worked in the past," I tell her, though it hasn't really. Nothing really has. But I know Lamictal produces fewer side effects than Geodon does. "No drug" isn't an option. So I choose the lesser of two evils.

Dr. V. immediately stops the orders for Geodon. At last I am off that skull-seizing, mind-numbing med. It was hard to even squeeze out a single thought on Geodon. I was a zombie. Lamictal is milder than most other anticonvulsants and doesn't require blood monitoring. We've reached compromise, the doctor and I.

With the removal of one detrimental drug and the instatement of another and all major crises at bay, I begin to absorb my surroundings. I can even start to find humor in this dark, disturbing environment. My jaw doesn't feel wired shut anymore, as it did on Geodon. I discover I can make people laugh again without making a spectacle of myself. The nurses, Kyle...

We can never let the orderlies witness our unruliness. After all, they write up daily reports about us and keep them in our charts. But in private, Alice and I jump on the rigid beds and sing. Two lively females, we can only escape the staff in our shared cinderblock room. We jump on the beds and sing and laugh like two girls at a slumber party, rather than where we are and who we are. I have to do this to let off steam from being under 24-hour observation. Mostly though, I try to avoid hanging out with Alice because I want to get out of here and I want to appear normal and rubbing shoulders with her doesn't look good. Alice is, well... unaware, to put it mildly. I dislike the drugs as much as Alice does, but I'd never mention this to staff. To do so would appear as if I wasn't compliant with my treatment plan and I do so want to get out of here. Out of the hospital, I will become more stable as time passes, freeing myself of the drug's influence and gaining the freedom to choose what I ingest.

"Here are your pills," says the nurse. She glances at the clock and seems bored.

Meanwhile, I realize that maybe my outlook isn't so bad, maybe if I just swallow these pills like I'm supposed to, I can get out of here. Dr. V. isn't so hard to get along with, after we get over our initial misunderstandings. The difference in my demeanor, the *improvement* is noted and orders are written to allow my release from the Quiet Room. The Quiet Room form of punishment reminds me of a torture chamber and seems extreme, but how were they to know what I was capable of? I have since tried to forgive.

Kyle starts a movie on the DVD player in the commons room and as the other patients rush to take their seats, I think that this is nothing at all like the stereotypes of what a hospital should be like. This is not like *One Flew Over the Cuckoo's Nest*, where they pass out cigarettes and try to reason with each other's neuroses. I realize that life in here isn't much different than outside life. There are people who are kind and people who are not so kind and some who are in between, just like anywhere else. Of course I'd rather *not be here at all* if I had a choice, but I don't, so I might as well make the best of it. Others have not come to the same conclusion that I have and have sort of let themselves go, forgoing showers and any attempts at civility.

The movies Kyle shows us are all by Disney and are purposely upbeat and motivational. They're meant to cheer us up. They're picked because they will not enrage the patients and there is no violence in them, only happy endings. That day Kyle has a characteristic breakthrough manic quality about him, despite being on his lithium. After he presses 'play,' he does not return to the nurse's station, nor bother to sit down. Instead, he stands, arms folded across his chest, tapping the remote control and pointing it at the screen, or fidgeting nervously while jiggling his leg. Kyle has *improved*; he's not perfect. I can tell he still harbors a good deal of restlessness. Or maybe he is the same as anyone else, only now that I know he was a former sufferer of illness, I am now watching him more closely. My opinion of him could be biased. I shrug and turn back to the movie.

It is later determined that I am healthier than Alice, and we are no longer suitable roommates because she talks too much and this disturbs *my* sleep. The tides have turned. This time it is Alice who is the disruption. So I am assigned a new roommate. Her name is Kate. Or Karl. I'm not quite sure. At least *I think* Kate is female. She is overweight with a short, choppy haircut, and at first I mistake her for a man. But then I think, *they wouldn't have me room with a man*. I realize that Kate's short hair is a survival mechanism. She wants people to mistake her for a boy so they don't hurt her, I wager. She's a tough kid who says she has grown up on the streets. Kate's short hair isn't indicative of inherent lesbianism. She just wants to appear capable and the people in her street crowd, she calls them "gigolos," all had short hair. Upon arriving on the ward, Kate immediately develops a crush on Kyle, like all the other girls do once they first see him, even the mannish-looking ones. Heck, even some of the *guys* have crushes on Kyle. Behind closed cinderblock, we discuss our daily interactions with him, saying, "He *smiled* at me today!" And, "Did you get a look at those eyes?" or "Kyle said he'd give me a pill if I did what he told me to,"—a phrase *I* never found myself uttering, personally.

CHAPTER 13

The Others

As far as other patients on the ward go, there is Jack... Jack has a toothless laugh that bubbles out uncontrollably, turning into a hyena's giggle which interrupts the movies we watch.

Heads are torn from the screen. "Shut up, Jack!" they say. "We're trying to watch a movie!"

Jack thinks everything is funny, even if it's not funny to anyone but himself. He finds humor even in the blandest of situations. Jack thinks "noses" are funny and he finds "tables" equally funny. He thinks rose bushes are as hilarious as paying taxes. Jack says that is why he's here, due to his uncontrollable laughter. He can't stop laughing and no one has been able to stop his giggles either, not even Dr. V. Jack has been laughing since 1967, at his own private jokes. Jack is not a success story. He is not someone you see on the cover of the hospital pamphlet, with a happy beaming smile, advertising its amenities as well as the virtues of its rehabilitation programs. Not that you have to advertise boarding here like you would at a prep school. No one wants to come here willingly.

Like most patients, Jack has a story to tell me, his journey from sane to here. He bounces up to me, childlike and brimming with joy. His eyes crinkle up at the corners, and he reveals a thousand-watt grin. I wish I had Jack's illness, the blight of too much happiness. It seems like something you'd want to catch. Wait, I take that back. Perpetual laughter would be as bad as a permanent case of hiccups. No, probably worse. You could choke. Jack's eyes are very expressive, oozing happiness. They are happy, too happy—bright and shiny with an odd gleam in them. As always, Jack's presence is announced by his loud, obnoxious laugh.

"Ha, ha, ha, hee, hee, hee, ha, ha, ha! You know how I got this way? It was all thanks to a little blue pill I bought from a Mexican on the street corner!" he giggles. "A little blue pill. It made me see things, that pill. A little blue pill or maybe it was a powder. Never buy stuff on street corners if you don't know what it is!" he advises. Excellent advice to follow.

Jack laughs so hard at himself that Beth, the resident Queen Bee and borderline personality disorder sufferer, pleads with him to stop. Beth looks after the hard luck cases like Jack, but is less kind to the ones who are well off like me—I believe she thinks we don't need protection and can fend for ourselves. She even seems a bit envious of our wellness. She takes the really mental ones under her wing. *Don't do drugs like Jack*, I make a note to myself. And buy nothing suspicious off street corners, maybe nothing at all off street corners, unless you're a broke, desperate tourist, and maybe not even then.

"Jack…" Beth says mildly, chiding with him to stop. I think the reason Beth is mothering is because it appeals to her own need to be loved. She's hardly had any love in her short, empty life. She was a foster kid, unwanted. An extra mouth to feed. If someone weak and helpless drops their books in Illness Management Class (a required class for all patients), she stoops to pick them up, returning the books to the owner with a smile. Secretive, concealed patient relations are a no-no here, but sometimes she'll save an extra juice box for Jack. But she is only nice to those who can't help themselves. Beth loathes me.

I could never hope to meet such interesting and extreme people in my life elsewhere. The people I met in that hospital were so *unusual*, I knew I could never meet anyone so interesting on the street. They'd have to be locked up and preserved like rare butterflies. Their idiosyncrasies, their various oddities would have to be examined and studied as if they were rare specimens in a zoological collection.

Then there were patients from whom I didn't learn much, but who were interesting nonetheless. "M" had a rare genetic disorder that was causing his brain to shrink. Only staff knew his real name, but they never called him by it. The last thing he was able to write was the letter 'M' so everyone just called him M. M was losing gray matter volume at a rapid rate. Soon, doctors predicted he would lose all capacity to function and become a vegetable due to his illness. It was written in his chromosomes and was his destiny. He spoke in one-word, nonsensical sentences. The doctors couldn't figure out how to help him. He was one of the most unusual cases they had ever seen. He was slowly dying. The hospital functioned as a hospice for him. It would be his final resting place. What I gained from M was gratitude. I compared my situation to his and was glad mine wasn't worse.

"Tree," said M, randomly. He often peed his pants and had to be told to go change but he couldn't remember to do that, so he often smelled awful. There was nothing interesting about that. M was twenty-three years old and dying. It wasn't fair. Life isn't fair. I was forced to accept this concept a young age: It could always be worse.

CHAPTER 14

Hope Mentoring

K yle imparts more bits of wisdom. He should teach a class called Side Effects 101. When I mention the tremors in my hands, Kyle tells me that he brushes his teeth with his left hand now because the tremors seem to affect his right hand more, for some reason.

"There's ways of getting around issues like these. There's usually a way to deal, to counteract the bad. Take the good with the bad. You gotta take the good with the bad in life. It's a sweet life," Kyle says, with a wistful, satisfied half-smile, as if he is glad to have shared his deepest secrets with me. He seems so wise, like a Buddhist monk. Kyle reaffirms the flaws of our shared human condition and makes me think, *Life, you know how it is. It's wonderful and it's horrible all at once.* He doesn't sound regretful that he now has the physical capacities of an eighty-year-old, despite being only twenty-seven. Kyle copes—it's what you do when you're short on options and it's the best plan you've got. Your last resort. I am suddenly grateful that I was assigned to Kyle's ward. Studies show that when cancer patients are exposed to music, they report lower pain levels and heal at faster rates. Kyle is a similar motivating factor for me, like sun to a plant. Talking to him brightens my mood. Actually, because he's so young and handsome, his very presence brightens my mood. I am sure that Kyle is a positive factor.

Beth may be one of the most intelligent people I have ever met. She is hyperverbal. Every word in the English language seems a close friend of hers. She has a sharp wit in her criticisms of others— her comments are biting and accurate. When Beth constructs a sentence, it often dazzles with its complexity. Beth sounds just like a college professor delivering a lecture, even in casual conversation. Often her well-placed comments hit their mark, destroying the egos of her intended prey. Beth is someone you don't want for an enemy. She could humiliate you—and she's not afraid to do it in front of an audience. She could pick you apart truth by truth, insult by insult.

Jack is sprawled out on the couch, his belly button showing through his too short, faded, hand-me-down hospital-issued shirt. Jack lost the will to care about his appearance about the same time he lost his mind. He laughs during every scene of the Disney movie, whether the scriptwriter intended the lines to be funny or not. Jack's corny-sounding laugh disrupts the harmonious pact of pre-agreed-upon silence that we have created by group consensus.

Everyone turns their heads to glare at him and hiss, "Shh!" Even the ever-patient Kyle lightly reprimands, "Jack… C'mon..."

Beth is seated as far away from me as possible. Beth sees me as a rival because I am not helpless, nor severely ill. Jack is Beth's pet because he is helpless. He is, to her, an invalid who needs her protection. I have a theory that because I am the only other young, thin female on the ward, she sees me as prime competition. The rest are chunky or old or too sick to function. Beth acts as if my every action is an imposition. She is sarcastic and mocking. She behaves as if I intend to slight her, as if I'm going out of my way to purposely do so. I never expected to find a repeat of high school cliques in this hospital. Beth, Queen Bee.

At lunch Beth points to me, rolls her eyes, and whispers a comment to her chubby roommate Lila. With heads bent together conspiratorially, they laugh at their private joke. When I try to sit at their table, Beth moves away as if she's saying, *we're better than you, don't sit here!* Denying people makes Beth feel important, I can tell, by the satisfied gleam in her eyes after she rejects me. Not that I'm really looking to make lifelong friendships in here. Still, Beth's behavior stings, as we currently share the same space. I try to forgive her, knowing that she was a foster kid and came from an environment that probably damaged her.

Beth's roommate Lila is a severely depressed mother of six who, after becoming terribly frazzled under the hectic demands of motherhood, just sort of lost it one day. I don't blame her. Imagine caring for all those kids. One day Lila tripped over one of her kids' toys and sprained her ankle. The inconsiderately placed toy was the last straw for a neurotic mind already pushed to the brink. I'm not sure which part of Lila's mind encouraged her to get hold of a dangerous weapon, but that's the next thing that occurred to her to do. Fortunately, she drove herself to the hospital before using the weapon. Of course, a lot of housewives find motherhood stressful and they don't *all* reach for knives. It is clear that something went wrong. Lila has a tough, persistent case of psychotic depression. She has tried nine different antidepressants with little success. Lila's even experienced "Prozac Poopout." Prozac lost its effect on her after years of use and can no longer make a dent in depression that deep.

I begin to feel like a survivor. Our circumstances feel much like incarceration. At least I have entertainment.

Kyle occasionally displays behavior that is slightly off and I wonder if he is slipping up. Regressing. Then it hits me that he's *one of us* and he probably likes working in a hospital because everyone's weird and he can feel free to be himself. Once I catch Kyle brushing his teeth at work at the sink near the nurses' station.

"Um, Kyle, are you sure you want to do that?" None of the other staff members are around. We are left alone that afternoon with Kyle in charge. Kyle, Orderly. He's supposed to be *on the other side* of the desk.

Kyle gives me a big, foamy grin and bites down on the plastic handle, scrubbing furiously. He turns his back on me, spits the white foam into the nurses' sink and laughs. He looks at me and smiles. "Didn't get the chance to brush at home," he says.

Kyle is wearing a designer sweater with a tiny green alligator emblem on the breast. Other days I catch Kyle tossing a football back and forth from hand to hand at his computer desk. He explains that he needs exercise and needs to keep active. Technically he's performing his job duties; he keeps an eye on everyone at the same time. He is charting as he clutches the ball, so his supervisors do not chastise.

Dr. V. is less cruel and impersonal than I originally thought, after we establish mutual trust. Privately, in her office, she admits that she believes in God and she hopes that I do as well, so that I can find my way.

"Faith. It helps," she insists.

I'm not sure if I do or not, but it's nice to know that I'm under the care of a doctor who believes in *something*. Especially someone so omnipotent, so benign and loving.

I thought the hospital would be grim and unbearable all the time, but it only is some of the time. The days of ice packs and lobotomies are gone and being here is supposed be therapeutic. It is a mind-rehab center like a rehab center for any other type of disorder, and most of the staff members seem like they're here to see us get well, despite a few ignoramuses who treat us badly. They are usually the ones who are prejudiced toward "crazy" people. They have stigmatic preconceptions regarding the mood-and-bodily-rhythm- disordered, whom they view as needy, irrational, and attention-seeking drama queens.

There's Nurse Grim, as I call her in private—she doesn't allow laughter because we need to "behave." She registers contempt and disgust for us on her face. Nurse Grim, who thinks we're "dirty" and makes comments like, "You can't trust these patients, they're really too out of it to know what's going on and they lie to you all the time. Make sure to wash. Scrub between your toes." She speaks condescendingly, as if we are little children. But for the most part, the rest of the staff acts like they're here to help.

We have Crafts Class and Art Therapy and music and woodshop classes as well as Illness Management. Ann is so crafty that the shop instructor asks her if she'd like to sign up for the advanced class.

"Can I do that, too?" I ask.

I dangle my woodshop project in front of the instructor's face, hoping he'll take it into consideration and allow me to enroll. My project is simply my name scratched into a board with an X-Acto knife (the razor is available for use in that class *only,* for obvious reasons). I'm neither very creative, nor particularly handy with wood. I'm more of a verbal athlete. My simple project isn't good enough for the advanced class, and despite my requests to join, it is Ann's enrollment he solicits. The fact that I am feeling competitive about a silly hospital woodshop class shows that I care about something, even if it is only something trivial.

Kyle is a huge sports fan. He often forces us to watch football in the commons room whether we like it or not. And he keeps a football under his desk at the nurses' station in case the urge to play strikes him at any time. Jack, Ann, and I sit on the couch in the common room as we stare with glazed eyes at a team of men doing what appears to be running back and forth on a green field, occasionally smashing into each other. At least that's what it looks like to me. It's one of Kyle's football games. Alice wanders around babbling, as usual. Her chatter is so annoying. She sleeps up to fourteen hours a day. A massive dose of lithium and Seroquel always knocks her out. She's surprisingly hyper for someone so heavily sedated.

Sports are Kyle's field of specialty. He sets up a game of horseshoes for us.

"C'mon, this is about to get wild!" Kyle says excitedly. "Alice, can I trust you with this?" he asks, handing her a horseshoe-shaped beanbag. Real, metal horseshoes would be too dangerous and considered weapons. Instead we get boomerang beanbags.

Alice babbles on in her usual motor-mouthed way, so much so that everyone stopped responding to her long ago. She usually goes unnoticed, so she is eager to talk to Kyle. "Oh, thank you! Give me that!" she says overenthusiastically, as she rips the beanbag from Kyle's hand. Alice's sweet, angelic Grace Kelly look belies a hyperactive, loud, and generally unfeminine person. She grabs the beanbag from Kyle and launches it with a forceful arm. It hits its target.

"Score! Score! Score!" she shouts, then jumps around, pumping her fists in the air in a victory dance.

"Look at that arm. Maybe I shouldn't have trusted you with that." Kyle launches a couple of long range shots of his own. The nurses all stand around to watch our game. Apparently games like these aren't common, so they are curious, whispering to each other.

I launch some beanbag horseshoes as Dr. V. walks in. "This looks like fun," she says approvingly, with a crinkly-eyed smile. We are red faced and happier than usual from the physical exertion and the change from the usual dull hospital routine.

CHAPTER 15

Safe from Whom?

Nights later, a horrifying event happens. Afterwards, my parents try to threaten the hospital and hold them liable for the resulting physical damage, as it hadn't been *their* idea to send me here in the first place—it was the social worker Jeff's. My dad will threaten to sue. I will wonder why dangerous incidents don't happen more often in a hospital like this, considering some of the people housed in it.

It all starts with a patient called Dan. Rumor has it that he tried to murder his mother. Dan has pale blue eyes like Kyle's, but unlike Kyle's very alive eyes, Dan's eyes are dead and devoid of all emotion. I always think of Dan as an empty, harmless shell, a person too vacant to cause much trouble. He usually sleeps quietly in the corner or infrequently mumbles something incoherent. I am wrong to underestimate him. No one can truly know what dark thoughts dwell inside the mind of another.

I am in the exercise room, minding my own business, pedaling the bike and watching TV when out of the blue, Dan lunges for me. I feel sharp, talon-like nails dig into my throat. I feel a spurt of blood rising from my veins. When I look into Dan's eyes, I see that Dan is not home. Perhaps he has not been home since he murdered his mother, like they say he did. The attack on my throat is startling, shocking, bloody and painful. I'll never know why Dan chose me as his victim. How do rapists choose their victims? Dan digs his long, claw-like fingernails into my throat so forcefully that he lifts my feet off the ground, holding me afloat under my chin in his viselike grip. I scream as loud as I can, as I assume it is the proper etiquette when being throttled. This is prison violence, this shouldn't be happening in a *medical facility*. I don't panic, though. When it comes to fight or flight, I fight. It is the quick thinking back to classroom self-defense lessons that saves me. I scream at the top of my lungs, and then I scream and kick some more.

Kyle is on duty that day. He immediately rushes to my aid.

"Dan! Stop that now! Put her down!" Kyle ordered.

Kyle knows instinctively how to tame the especially dangerous, the weakest of the weak. He has a way even with the lowest functioning patients on the ward, such as the organic brain disease patient M, who can only speak one word now: "fence." Kyle mesmerizes the severely ill with his hypnotic eyes, sending them into a trance. Dan stops being angry and immediately calms down when Kyle gazes at him. Kyle leads him away by the arm, like a lamb on a leash.

Amazingly, Dan obeys and slinks off meekly. The bright red gash on my neck causes a stir on the ward, mostly amongst the medical staff because they feel guilty as if there should have been some preventative measures in place. My dad makes a fuss and the hospital doesn't want to be sued. So the staff fawns over me and files an official assault report. A hospital administrator photographs my wounds with an instant camera, waves the photo back and forth, and then files it away. They sterilize my wounds and apologize over and over. A nurse is sent to change my bandages daily.

The general practitioner who works separately from Dr. V. knocks on the door of the room I share with my recovering meth addict roommate, Christy. I have no experience with street drugs myself. Kate is gone, she has been discharged. The general practitioner examines my neck wounds. He winces, but tells me that it is healing nicely. The administrators send me a teddy bear and flowers and a "Get Well Soon" card.

Their offering doesn't take away the trauma of the situation, nor the fact that it happened in the first place. Nor does it dissolve the irony of my predicament. I was put here by doctors to keep me safe from myself, but I've now been attacked by someone who may have strangled his mother. It is absurd how this supposedly healing environment sometimes—isn't.

My dad, upon hearing of the incident, decides to visit the hospital to check up on me. He remarks that the hospital looks like a private children's school, perhaps one for bright children with a tailored curriculum. My dad is being optimistic. He's trying to cheer me up. He says the hospital is nothing like he imagined—like a cement dungeon with chained-up people drinking from bowls.

Brent, the journalist with whom I rock climbed over the summer, never visits. Brent fell into a depression over my condition and his own part in my confinement, I later learn. I read somewhere than ninety percent of the relationships of people with mood and sleep disorders will fail. The odds were stacked against us. Not that I really wanted to be more than friends with him in the first place, which further complicated the situation and justified its disintegration. Brent's own problems were a barrier to the continuation of our friendship. What is the failure rate for relationships involving not one, but two people with these sorts of problems? Nearly one hundred percent?

Brent's depression contributes to nebulous thinking. I can tell from his occasional calls that the pictures he paints in his mind's eye of this place are of a dark dungeon, a far cry from reality. Brent is too afraid to visit. He wants the girl he went rock climbing with back. I must admit, I do harbor a bit of resentment against him for having called Jeff the day I was admitted. I try to keep in mind that he had my best interests at heart.

When my dad visits the hospital after the incident with Dan, it is acting as a father whose daughter who has been injured. He wants to fight back against the system. He talks to the social worker and he tries to speak to Dr. V., but she shies away from conflict and directs him to the administrative staff. Perhaps she is simply afraid of retaliation or wants to avoid a lawsuit.

I am traumatized. I fear Dan will escape from his room at night and attack me again. Sometimes I think fear is a gift. If I fail to be vigilant with Dan, if I fail to watch out for him, then he could get me again. Fear is an automatic response, there to warn you of impending doom. Fear is present when a man offers to help you with your groceries, but you detect something odd about him and have a hunch you shouldn't let him. Fear has served you when you later find out the man is a serial rapist and you're overcome with relief that you didn't let him help you with your bags.

Fortunately, Kyle is also concerned for me. He puts Dan on a 24-7 watch and doesn't allow him to leave his room.

CHAPTER 16

Creepy Lord Cade

As if the incident with Dan wasn't frightening enough, I would soon endure another scary incident. That it occurred is not surprising, given my surroundings. The people I had to associate with, the patients, some could become a bit... obsessive. I became the victim of a stalker. Statistics show that one in six American women will become the victim of a stalker. Given where I was, the chances seemed even more likely. The difference between me and other victims of stalking was that I could not escape my attackers by relocating. I lived with them, involuntarily.

A former patient was released, one who had paid too much attention to me while he was at the hospital, and he began to call the ward, leaving cryptic messages which described what I was wearing that day. As in, "I saw her walking to the canteen wearing jeans and a blue sweater." After asking to speak to me and having his request fiercely denied, he would hang up.

Then the creepy former patient, whose name is Cade, says he remembers my room's floor plan exactly, detail by detail. He says he has drawings and maps and he knows how to break in. The hospital administrators do not want to play around with this guy. They don't know what he's capable of, so they take his creepy threats seriously. Besides, it's just good policy and it covers their bases. The administrators hand me the proper forms and tell me to fill out a restraining order. I thought I was in this institution to save myself from myself. But now I'm again facing danger from another's impositions instead.

Cade refers to himself as "The Lord" in the letters he mails to the hospital and when he speaks to Kyle on the phone. I'm not sure why they deemed someone who calls himself "The Lord," who doesn't actually happen to be a wealthy British property owner, fit for release. I'm not sure which competent psychiatrist determined that someone who calls himself *The Lord* and who creeps around peering into women's windows at night, making harassing phone calls and describing their clothing, as stable. Cade is clearly grandiose and an egomaniac. I wonder if he is homicidal.

"Today she was wearing a blue sweatshirt, a white baseball cap, and jeans," Cade, "The Lord" says. "I've got a present for her. Let me in and I can give it to her."

"Go away!" says Kyle, slamming down the phone.

The restraining order finally stops "The Lord" from completing his creepy plans, however deviant. Well, at least the restraining order stops him from calling. But the order doesn't stop him from sending letters. Cade somehow found out my parents' addresses, probably due to the invention of modern technology like the internet. He wrote long, rambling letters to them professing his love for me and his desire to make me a duchess to go along with His Lordship. At least Creepy Lord Cade was good for something. He made my family laugh. They really cracked up when they opened his letters and found out that he claimed to be a genuine *lord*.

CHAPTER 17

Fainting Spells

One day a particularly handsome patient was admitted. A new patient was big news on the ward, as our daily life involved a monotonous routine of Crafts Class followed by lunch, followed by dinner, followed by Snack Time. In our spare time we stared at the walls, shuffled about, or watched sappy Disney movies imposed on us by Kyle. The new patient resembled a young Charlie Sheen.

It was 2010 and Charlie Sheen was in the news for his bipolar antics, for his erratic *Entertainment Tonight* interview in which he confessed that he had "tiger's blood" and was "bi-winning." This was back when Sheen thought he could sleep with anyone and be immune to all disease because he was superhuman. He was above consequences. This was before Sheen was diagnosed with AIDS and his former "Goddess" Bree Olsen denounced him to the media for concealing his contagious disease. While denying that he was manic-depressive, it was clear to everyone watching that he probably was. I hope that Charlie Sheen brought the issue of mood disorders and drug addiction to national attention, and that politicians watching him thought about signing new bills related to the expansion of mental health services as they saw the need and urgency for these enactments. Especially after his *ET* interview. I hope that children tuning in changed their minds about wanting to try drugs. I hope that something came of the Sheen interview rather than the public's expressions of disgust over the plight of a wild man, and the media circus that ensued. But in the end, I think he just became another tabloid sensation, fodder, smut and gossip. In the infamous interview, Sheen's hair was a mess, there were bags under his eyes, he talked about smoking crack and having special powers, and he looked strung out. Charlie Sheen lost his major TV contract with the producers at CBS because he had some kind of episode that made him think he was special and that he didn't need to be respectful of his bosses like everyone else. That he didn't need a job like the common people, even one that paid millions. *That he was above consequences*. So the buzz was all on Charlie Sheen that year and, consequently, viewers were probably thinking *bipolar,* not *bi-winning*. Because Sheen's name was splashed about in the media so much then, he was on my mind when I noticed that the new admit, James, looked just like him.

When James introduced himself to me, he seemed beyond exhausted, unsteady and ready to faint. He seemed on the verge of collapse from a case of "manic exhaustion" or a "fainting spell" of antiquity that called for smelling salts. His palms were sweaty when I shook his hand, so my own hands slid right out of his feeble grip. I wasn't beneath shaking hands, even here in the hospital. I treated all people equally at first, unless they proved undeserving. My own cheerfulness, I thought, might improve others' outlook and well-being and thus improve overall ward safety and cooperation. I made friends because I preferred to dwell in harmony, not conflict.

James' breathing was labored and each breath he took looked to be a struggle. When one doesn't sleep, one's heart never gets the chance to rest, but must work overtime. I should know. Periodically, James' eyelids would drift closed as if he just couldn't bear to keep them open anymore, yet he was still unable to get tired enough for sleep. Every breath he took seemed painfully drawn.

Yet James appeared not to have lost his enthusiasm for life. Despite his ghostly pallor and his frayed exhaustion, he was able to show me his poetry books and share with me some of his favorite poems. Being confined to the hospital was particularly difficult for him. He was accustomed to being very active otherwise. He told me he felt cooped up and penned in. James shared with me the inspirational message he had written on his forearm in ink as a reminder, in case he lost his faculties. He knew he was hanging on by a thread and might need to look there someday. It read: *Just. Keep. Going.*

I empathized with James. Before Dr. V. took away the Geodon, I was just like him. My mom used to spend her hospital visits massaging my feet because I walked on them so much it felt as if my bones were wearing through my skin. I hoped that Dr. V. would be able to help James with the medical science available to those of us living in 2010, and that he wouldn't need a coroner. I hoped that he would not succumb to "manic exhaustion," a legitimate cause of death in the 1800s for people with conditions like his, pre-technology. James seemed on the verge of collapse. I could see his pulse pounding frantically in his neck.

Mania may be caused by physical conditions such as epilepsy, thyroid disorder and more, in the absence of a history of primary bipolar disorder. It may be a good idea to have a physical exam to ensure the correct diagnosis when obtaining mental health services. Here are some physical causes of mental conditions that may even be the primary cause of the symptoms you experience.

- Genetic disorders
- Chemical imbalances
- Thyroid imbalances
- Blood sugar dysregulations
- Hormone imbalances
- Inflammation
- Adrenal fatigue
- Inability to convert folate to folic acid due to a gene mutation. A deficiency could affect levels of neurotransmitters
- Gut flora imbalances (leaky gut)
- Hydrochloric acid deficiency which does not allow pepsin conversion in stomach, involved in protein metabolism
- Food allergies/brain allergies
- Pathogens (yeast and parasites)
- Specific nutrient deficiencies: usually vitamin D, zinc, B6, B12 and essential fatty acids
- Toxic metal buildup (mercury, lead, etc.)
- Being under the influence of stimulant drugs, psychiatric, street, and herbal. Stimulant

psychiatric drugs: Adderall, Celexa, Prozac, Ritalin, etc. Stimulant street drugs: Cocaine, methamphetamine, etc. Stimulant herbs: St. John's Wort, etc.

I was not subjected to any tests at all prior to immediately being placed on drugs and given a diagnosis. But what if I wasn't crazy at all, but instead suffering a delirium from the effects of poisoning? What if I had been bitten by a tropical snake and was undergoing a hallucinatory fever? None of the admitting doctors bothered to ask questions before bombarding me with pills and injections. Then again, there are no tangible tests for mental disorders. But other conditions *can* be ruled out and excluded. I don't know if testing would have changed my outcome or not. But it would have made my care more comprehensive, more thorough and complete. The brain is an organ, just as the liver is. My mania did not come about naturally but chemically, after I had been placed on two antidepressants. I think that it's easier for doctors to prescribe rather than question. Easiest to extend the least effort. There are no blood tests for depression.

Psychotropic drugs didn't work for me and made me feel worse than when I began. I'm much more stable now that I'm off of them. In fact, I don't think it would have been possible for me to write this book under their mind-clouding effects.

CHAPTER 18

Poetry

B reathing heavily, eyelids drooping from the effort to keep them open, James jiggled his knee and read aloud from his book of poems. "Can I write you a note?" he asked. Of course I said yes. I was curious to see what he had to say. What did someone as tired as he have left to express? Did he plan to write a desperate "rescue me" S.O.S. note?

James handed me a slip of paper with a poem written on it in the stereotypical chicken-scratch handwriting that people refer to as "dude writing." Whereas I've noticed that a lot of women tend to employ cutesy bubble writing, dotting-the-i's-and-crossing-the-t's with circular dots, James' writing was more jagged.

I unfolded the piece of paper and read it. It was another motivational message about finding the will to carry on.

"Well, thank you, James," I said, pocketing it.

I stored James' poems in a folder on the desk in my room. We were allowed desks, even if they *were* bolted to the floor. I had to find ways to amuse myself in what amounted to, what seemed at times, to be a prison-like hospital environment. Reading poetry was one method of passing the time.

I had also developed a sense of gallows-ready acceptance as a way of coping with the daily gloom that surrounded me. My new roommate, Christy, the recovering methamphetamine addict, explained her methods of coping both inside the walls and in life in general. Like Kyle, she had developed ways of her own for dealing with what at first may seem disadvantageous. She made her setbacks workable. If they weren't workable, what choice did we have? To give up would have meant becoming a chronic patient with "why bother" hygiene, on whom the staff had given up hope. The alternative would have meant staying here and staying stagnant, and that was never an option for me.

"I had to teach myssself how to talk again. I was in a drug induced coma. Or maybe it happened after I slipped and hit my head on the ice. It took me two yearsss to learn how to talk again," Christy said. "I sat on the couch for *two whole yearsss...* All I did wasss watch TV and try to sssound out the words. And then, you know what I did? I picked up the newspaper and ssstarted pronouncing wordsss again, word by word, sssyllable by sssyllable. I ssslowly rehabilitated myssself. I taught myssself to talk again," she lisped. Christy had such a great attitude. I really admired someone who had lost one of the body's most basic functions, a function so central and necessary to the human experience that it is used to define our humanity—and then found it again.

Imagine going two years without being able to speak! The only remnant of her tragic past and miraculous recovery was a slight, yet ever-present lisp and the lizard-like motions of her darting tongue when she formed words. But compared to where she had been before, what an improvement! *Don't do drugs*, I made a mental note to myself, once again, especially after noting the experiences of Jack and Christy. I felt there was no further need to scramble my already funky brain chemistry. Christy was a saintly example of a roommate, with her positive attitude and her refusal to give up. As saintly as someone who had once regularly polluted her brain with crystal meth could be. The point was, she had learned from her experiences and those experiences had not managed to destroy her fighter's spirit. Christy was self-deprecating and, recognizing that there was something exaggerated about her lisp, used it to emphasize her points for their dramatic effect. Christy was a caricature of herself with a healthy sense of humor, and she made the best of things.

CHAPTER 19

Informed Consent

A rare few, like Alice, struggled with mood disorders not tempered even by large doses of drugs. Alice was an exception to the usual rule of the expected projection of gradual improvement. Alice's joy, her perfect simple joy for life, was endearing in a way. Bubbly, blonde, and looking the picture of robust health, you would think she was just like any other twenty-eight-year-old. Until the jokes got too loud, the laughter a little too explosive. She laughed so hard at her own jokes that her face went beet red several times a day, and she had to gasp for breath and run to the drinking fountain.

Alice's dilemma reminds me of an ethical question, one that was posed to me as well. It's the matter of consulting with patients on their treatment without dismissing them as either too "crazy" or "out of it" to know about their condition, or too ill to know whether the problem they are presenting is real. The matter of inclusion in treatment decisions and informed consent. In the mental health system, physical complaints are often dismissed as being "all in one's head" or "part of your illness." But maybe Alice's stomach *really did* hurt, though you couldn't get a doctor to legitimize her complaints. Is it really possible that people suffering from mood disorders experience no physical health issues at all, because all somatic complaints are in the patients' heads? That mental patients are immune to physical problems?

Psychiatrist Esther Oh, who wrote on psychiatry vs. internal medicine, said, "Patients with mental health issues can present with real acute medical problems. Yes, they are notorious for being demanding, difficult to work with, unpredictably violent, poor historians, or acting strange, which can make the evaluation process frustratingly time-consuming and challenging. It's easy for physicians to dismiss patients' physical complaints or label them 'crazy' or individuals who don't have 'real illnesses.' This leads to incomplete care and treatment of the patients."

Alice was just "out of it" to the doctors and her complaints were not seen as legitimate and were therefore not to be taken seriously. They left her groaning in the corner with an "imaginary stomach ache." A patient could have a foot rotting from gangrene, but due to clinicians' fear of getting close to the patient or dismissal of his complaints, the patient is never heard. Most patients will find a drug, *that one effective drug*, or a combination of two or three or more, that will eventually work for them. Alice never did, and considered herself a victim of the system. Alice had been cheated out of a normal life. Five years of her twenties, that critical time period for growth and development, had been swallowed up by the hospital. Maybe it was the best place for her. I doubted she could function in the outside world. She was too socially inappropriate and probably would have found herself in legal trouble. But those were only my perceptions and estimates. They could have been as false as the doctor's predictions for her. People can surprise you.

CHAPTER 20

Goals

When the medication I was forced to take caused me to over-salivate and drool on myself, Christy was there to hand me a stick of gum she had purchased at the canteen with the money her parents sent her. She seemed a true friend, a friend for all seasons. Christy had been unable to speak for two years; a little extra saliva should leave me with nothing to complain about. Christy taught me to be proactive in my approach to problems. It was best to do something about them rather than to ruminate over them. Rumination was completely unproductive. Christy toughened me up, much like a basketball coach would, or a drill sergeant, just as Kyle did. If you removed our surroundings, the bleak, beige cinderblock, the bolted down cots, and stripped us down to what we were, then we were really just two roommates who had become friends.

Kyle was a favorite topic of ours, but only when the door was closed and we were safely in our rooms and when he was behind the desk and out of earshot, so that we could not be penalized for insubordination. Beautiful Kyle, with the keys that jangled in his pocket and his strange habit of bouncing athletic equipment off the walls when he was supposed to be charting. Kyle, who brushed his teeth at the nurse's sink because he was obsessive about his breath and probably performed regular sniff checks. Christy and I spoke endlessly of our admiration for Kyle's hypnotic, aquamarine eyes, and of petty ward gossip. There was plenty to talk about, with people behaving so strangely around us.

Life went on in the ward as usual, as life has a habit of doing elsewhere. It was as if we lived in a sort of Gothic finishing school. Groups and classes were held, on schedule, to distract us from our minds and to teach us life lessons. Stress reduction techniques were taught. James was often truant, attending class only rarely, when he wasn't busy pacing the halls. Alice attended a single class, choir, because when frenetic, singing is an activity one can participate in. Her loud, cheerful, belting voice dominated the choir room, overpowering it and drowning out everyone else.

I tried not to let the behavior of others affect my personal journey toward my goal of discharge. I thought more about my plans for the future and what to do after I left the hospital. I was given weekend passes and allowed to go home more frequently. Dr. V. said she saw progress being made.

As time went on, James' raspy breathing regulated itself. He seemed to have improved immensely. He still paced the halls to work off nervous energy, but now he could keep his eyelids open for stretches at a time and he didn't seem to be resting on death's doorstep anymore. He paced so much that his flimsy sandals started to fall apart. I found one of my meds stimulating, which made it hard to sit still, but it wasn't exactly in my four-year-plan to spend my life in a hospital, so I figured I'd get better in a hurry. As in yesterday, so I hid this annoyance from staff.

At this point, I learned the art of ingratiation. Psychiatrists are human, too, and so can be swayed by their emotions just like anybody else. I learned ward politics so I could speed up my release. And as there are no blood tests for mental conditions like these, there is no way for psychiatrists to know whether you're bluffing when you say you are fine, or if you are just telling them that to further your own agenda. So when asked, I told Dr. V. I was "fine." It isn't common to submit patients to a lie detector test to prove it.

According to my observations, those who said they were "fine" were often released from the hospital much sooner than those who said they were not. And there was no way of really gauging if you were, other than to take your word for it. The doctors couldn't go inside your head and read your mind, they weren't clairvoyant. "The Lord" Creepy Craig, who had secretly harbored predatory thoughts, had been released after managing to put on a convincing act. And no one had been the wiser. I wasn't like him at all, but I put up my own façade to speed up my release.

Of course I was ready to leave. I had been ready to leave since day one. I missed the little things about life on "the outside," everyday occurrences which had been denied to me, simple experiences that I had taken for granted before. Fresh air, freedom, a watermelon picnic. Walking barefoot on freshly cut grass. The taste of chocolate. What it felt like to kiss a handsome man and his firm, stubbly mouth. Memories. Precious memories. So to the standard questions, "Are you suicidal?" I always responded "no," and stated that I was "fine."

Mostly, though, saying I was fine *really did* make me believe that I was fine. Thus is the influential power of positive thinking.

In accordance with my ingratiation campaign, I attempted to befriend the nurses and other members of staff. Even the stern ones with the chilly attitudes. I pictured the end in mind, the finish line, the day I would leave this place and never lost sight of my goal. As charting was completed by staff members every fifteen minutes, including periodic safety checks, I made sure to never let them catch me acting "weird" or to let them see me slip up. It's hard to say what defines "normal," but I did my best to act polite and civil at all times. It could only help my case for release if they wrote down that I was polite and cooperative.

Some were easy to befriend, like Nurse Megan, who insisted we refer to her as just "Megan." Young, pretty, sweet and bubbly, she practically sang her way onto the ward each day. She looked like a Disney princess with her high cheekbones, oversized eyes, long lashes and perfect figure. She was young, only twenty-seven, like Kyle. Megan demonstrated a great deal of compassion for her patients. She actually *listened* to us and responded to our needs instead of dismissing us as crazy. She nurtured us the way a nurse should. You'd think that listening to patients would be common sense, but so many of the other nurses invalidated us and brushed us off.

The gauge on the unit's happiness meter usually went up a little when Megan was on the unit. It was as if, upon her arrival, she had slipped a pair of rose-colored glasses over everyone's eyes and made us happier. Her shiny, fawn-colored ponytail bounced as she waltzed down the halls in her neatly fitting uniform. She was kind and understanding and she spoke to us as if we were real people who mattered.

CHAPTER 21

Skull Seized

When the worst experience of my life thus far occurred (even worse than being attacked by Dan), it was Nurse Megan who saved me. After being injected with the drug Geodon by Nurse Nasty one night, which was completely unwarranted, I developed a case of akathisia. Nurse Megan told me that she would quickly obtain an order for something to counteract the effects, because she saw that I could endure the effects of this chemical torture no longer. I had run into the hall and screamed a pained, mournful howl, begging for help. I must have sounded like a cat whose tail had been set on fire, and Megan responded. I was in a complete panic due to what I later figured out was restricted blood flow in my brain, due to the suppression of the essential movement-controlling neurotransmitter dopamine—to get technical. At the time, I panicked. In some, the body comes up with an automatic response to counteract the effects of dopamine suppression from antipsychotic drugs, and your body will attempt to increase its movement by producing more dopamine. The body deals with foreign invaders by attempting to return to homeostasis. My body kicked back too hard. *Way* too hard. I thought about these things when I wasn't trying to forget the incident, which is the worst thing that had ever happened to me, and truthfully, still is. The sensation I felt then still gives me nightmares, so indescribably horrific it was. My legs were so restless that I could not hold still even for a few seconds and my muscles attempted to force me in several different directions at once. The large dose gave me akathisia worse than I'd ever experienced before. I felt so painfully agitated that jumping out a window seemed a legitimate outlet, and I would have, had the option been available to me and if the akathisia had lasted much longer. The impact on the pavement I would have created seemed a less painful end than facing the hideous agitation. I felt like a marionette whose strings were constantly being pulled upward. My jaw felt wired shut. There was an icy feeling in my spine, my brain itself felt numb, and the feeling penetrated beyond my head, into my nervous system. No wonder these drugs were called neuroleptics and, once invented, had been used in veterinary medicine on cattle. I felt like a dentist had crammed a cold, metal drill into my brain and begun his work. The akathisia from the drug and its resulting agitation seemed to have soaked into the marrow of my bones and hijacked my skull. Every cell in my body seemed to want to reject the powerful drug coursing through my veins. I ran around screaming for help. It seemed the only thing to do. My brain had been seized. The sensation was far more painful than a bee sting, even several hornets at once; worse than the car accident I had been in. I had been injected with liquid horror.

Nurse Megan acted quickly. She knew the desperate state I was in, and stuck me in the bum with a needle full of Ativan. I had never felt such sweet relief. I passed into a blissful sleep. Nurse Megan had seen akathisia before and knew how desperately I needed it to stop, and she thought fast and saved me. Nurse Nasty saw my screaming as bad behavior. But I was in pain and desperately needed help, and Nurse Megan had listened.

Nurse Megan would be my advocate in other instances. "Oh, my gosh, they gave you *that*? But that's such a harsh, old-fashioned drug," she sympathized, blinking her large round eyes, which were reflective pools of sympathy. "I'm sorry. I hope things get better for you. Come see me at the med window later, let's talk," she said.

I knew she'd not only be ready to lend a listening ear, but that she would stand up for me in her talks with the doctor, relaying my comments and concerns. I felt confident that Megan and I could solve any issue together. In fact, when I had first arrived at the hospital, Nurse Megan's first item of business was to conspire with the surfer-dude orderly Ryan to buy me a meal from Burger King, which they secretly transported into the kitchen—a special treat. I must have looked thin and starving when I first arrived. In any case, Megan and Ryan went above and beyond in their professions, while others simply fulfilled the minimum requirements in order to keep their jobs, or worse, demeaned their patients. It wasn't necessary for them to be as kind as they were. They told me that though they didn't bend the rules for everyone, they were making an exception for me by buying me that delicious, crunchy sustenance.

Dr. V., Kyle, Ryan, and Nurse Megan made up a caring, pro-patient team. They went the extra mile for me and I wondered why I, in particular, had been singled out and deemed deserving of such kindness. I lingered over my crunchy fries and delicious burger, savoring every bit. Far from being just another ordinary meal, the food comforted me and quenched a need at a vulnerable time. I hadn't had a burger and fries in such a long time.

CHAPTER 22

The Tongue Depressor

To help pass the time, I observed the interesting behavior of the other patients. Ann, in her mid-forties, is kind and sweet in a cheery, if delusional way. Her view of the world is so optimistic, it's massively inaccurate and that's probably why she's here. In her fantasies, she's won the lottery and rubs shoulders with movie stars. Ann is sugary, syrupy sweet and if you ask her what her mood is, she will most likely say it's "wonderful" and inquire about yours in a selfless way. She's a goody-goody and has a pristine innocence about her. Have a smoke? Ann would never defile her perfect lips in such a way. I can tell Ann probably came from a home where she was loved and that most of her life thus far has been comfortable and easy. Because people have been kind to Ann thus far, she is kind to others. Talk of crime and sex would be more shocking to Ann than it would be to most people. She has never heard of those things. Ann is deeply religious and attends the hospital chapel every week. I can see her baking a casserole for a sick neighbor. She probably tries to make the world a better place, and I admire this, while at the same time disbelieving the reality she has constructed for herself. Ann can often be found dressed in a modest-looking forest green coat buttoned up to her neck, a prayer book in hand with a little silver cross dangling from her throat. She looks like a Christian missionary. She is delicate, angelic, and somehow fragile looking. Her blonde hair is shoulder-length and frames her face like an angel's halo. Ann is an excellent pianist, a real asset to someone so churchy, and she sings in the hospital's chapel choir.

Ann's delusions tend to be grandiose in scale. For one, she thinks she's Yanni's wife. Yanni, as in the famous pianist. To try to verify Ann's story, on a trip to the hospital library, I look up Yanni's spouse. I see no mention of someone named Ann. Not that I really believed Ann's far-out tale in the first place. Ann is persistent in her delusion that she was Yanni's wife, and said she had to get out so she could accompany him on the piano. Ann is such a brilliant pianist that her weird tale is almost believable. She entertains us on the hospital piano, dazzling us with her long symphonies. She says she has to practice to keep her skills from getting rusty, ostensibly so that she can return to play with Yanni. I tried to imagine what it would be like to wake up one day after a head injury like the one Ann had had, not remembering any facts pertaining to myself except for one major erroneous detail, that of being Yanni's wife. That would be insane, of course. Unless one really were Yanni's wife, which of course she was not.

I watch Ann steal a tongue depressor from the cup on the nurse's counter. She uses the tongue depressor, meant for involuntary force feeding, to pick at the wallpaper which resembles papier-mâché. Ann has found a new toy.

The staff won't bother to stop her. Kyle, who has his own issues to battle, believes in individuality and creative expression. Besides, the tongue depressor is made of thin balsa wood. Kyle *does* raise an eyebrow from behind his desk at the nurse's station, but on his lithium Kyle is passive, a guard dog with NyQuil in his bowl. He turns his attention back to his computer. Ann's behavior doesn't set off any immediate alarm bells in his head. Kyle is a very easygoing peer counselor. It's easy to get away with stuff on his shift.

Ann says, "The wallpaper is uneven." She uses the tongue depressor as a leveler and aligns it with the wall. She seems to have an obsession with perfection in architecture. I predict that she'd be great at sewing sweaters with bunnies on them; she'd have to get the button eyes just so. No wonder Crafts Class is Ann's favorite.

Ann doesn't like swallowing her pills. Who can blame her? Sometimes they don't give you the right ones, or they give you ones that make the problem worse until they *might or might not* find one that works. In the meantime, the pills could make you nauseous, make you shake, and distort your personality. Some of the pills are the size of horse pills and they make you gag. I hear the nurse pleading with Ann to please take her pills.

Ann shakes her head, babyishly, and sticks out her tongue, which she is able to do without a tongue depressor.

"I hate this stuff," she says. Perhaps that is why Ann took the tongue depressor, as a sort of regurgitation tool that she's saving for later. I don't blame her. The pills are gross and they make you feel pretty spacey and weird sometimes.

I see that she uses the tongue depressor to scrape at the ceiling, examining the crumbling detritus with a perfectionist's eye before brushing off the resulting powder.

The wild antics of others distracted me from myself and I slowly began to heal. *What wound did ever heal but by degrees*, wrote Shakespeare. In my case, I demonstrated this by sleeping a stable six hours a night, a record for me on Lamictal. When I stopped taking Lamictal after my release, I slept a more refreshing seven to eight, as if the drug had made me slightly hyperactive.

In that hospital, I got to glimpse a section of humanity at its best and worst and everything on the spectrum in between. I had seen unusual behavior tempered, I witnessed triumph over adversity. I had seen some abuse their power over the weak. I had seen some choose kindness, despite the fact that they would receive few rewards for their good deeds. Yet somehow I'd been lucky as far as my care went. Either lucky, or smart and capable. I tried to make myself likeable to my captors, to establish rapport with them in the hope of achieving better treatment and an earlier release. And it worked. As I was young and healthy looking, personable and cooperative, I was told I would have a better prognosis. The older, the lame, the less attractive ones, were sometimes treated like children, sadly.

I read a lot of books to pass the time. Fortunately, the hospital had a library where Kyle and Ryan took us on weekly field trips. If we had earned our privileges, we were even allowed to check out books. An imagination is a hard thing to eliminate. A body is easy to chain, but the imagination is more elusive to capture. The moments between dinner and med time were free moments I spent reading, dreaming and picturing myself in a new life beyond the hospital walls.

Ryan always had a joke up his sleeve. Ryan particularly delighted in telling us jokes in the med line, so that he could get people to laugh at an opportune moment, just as they tried to swallow their pills, which led them to spit up. This would often result in spills and choking, as we struggled to swallow the meds and choke back laughter. But he never took the jokes too far. I'm sure he'd have given us the Heimlich maneuver if necessary. Or given us a tongue depressor to unclog our throats with, had Ann not confiscated them all. Ryan saw us as overly serious and haunted and wanted to put a smile on our faces. He would usually just make a slight comment here and there about something ironic that he'd observed, and it was enough to set us off. In a hospital for "crazies," there were plenty of anecdotes. He wasn't being cruel, he was only commenting on the irony of what he'd observed.

To keep our minds active while being locked up, Kyle led us in Current Events Group, where we'd watch the national news and then discuss what we'd learned. I'm sure this class was required so that when we left the hospital we did not become hermits living in abandoned shacks in the woods who were completely out of touch with the outside world. Kyle, the instructor, had a beautiful backside. He loved both fashion and sports—he kept a compact mirror in his pocket as well as a football under the desk. He was a macho-man dichotomy. He was in touch with his feminine side. Christy and I would nudge each other every time Kyle turned to change the channel in Current Events Group because we'd get to look at his backside when he did. Hello, nurse!

Giancarlo was a patient of Italian ancestry. He was also legally blind and manic-depressive. *It could be worse*, I thought, until I observed that Giancarlo seemed to be handling our confinement even better than me. Despite his limited vision, Giancarlo always managed to look trendy, stylish and presentable, just like a well-sighted boy who was capable of dressing himself. Giancarlo was a real fashion plate, looking as if he'd stepped off the pages of a magazine. He looked as if he employed a personal stylist. He was very handsome with a head of thick, black, wavy hair and creamy, pale skin. I thought that in order to look so fashionable, Giancarlo must have held his clothing very close to his barely sighted eyes in order to dress himself. Whatever his method, it worked, because he always looked great. He had more than adapted; he should have been heading a clothing line. Giancarlo may have been blind and manic-depressive, but he was far from a burden to others in his social stratosphere. Instead, despite his disabilities, Giancarlo inspired and even became the envy of the other guys on the ward. They said stuff like, "He could probably get all the chicks he wanted." Perhaps because it took him such effort and concentration, Giancarlo dressed better than most of the well-sighted guys I had met.

Though he had limited eyesight, Giancarlo could still see tiny objects up close under a microscope and it delighted him to use one, as magnified objects were the only objects he *could* see. That was why Giancarlo said that high school biology class was one of the highlights of his life. Not because it was the class where you learned about sex, as was the explanation given by a lot of red-blooded guys, but for what he could see when he couldn't otherwise.

One night the hospital held a game and movie night, and Giancarlo chose me as his partner. I was thrilled. He chose me because he liked the sound of my voice, I suppose. He didn't *look* blind. He was wearing expensive-looking leather pants and a rock T-shirt and his black, spiky hair was casually, yet purposely, tousled. Patients who had earned their privileges were allowed to wear street clothes. I didn't pity Giancarlo at all, I liked how calm he seemed and I was curious to learn more about him and to hear what he had to say. I mean, how many guys get excited over a high school biology class and call it the highlight of their lives? Naturally one wishes for good looks, for excellent health, for riches, for eternal youth. But if that's not possible, then we deal with the cards dealt us. Giancarlo wasn't a saint, of course, but what twenty-two-year-old man is? He threw Helen-Keller-sized tantrums sometimes, out of frustration with his limited capacities and the strictures placed on him, out of his longing for normalcy. Then after having calmed down, he promptly forgot about them and went back to being his usual, calm self.

CHAPTER 23

An Evolutionary Advantage

O bserving hyperverbal and intelligent people like Giancarlo, James, and Beth, it seemed to me that manic depression was both a blessing and a curse. In the process of evolution, there must have been an advantage to being able to think faster than others, to figure out your next move ahead of time and to withdraw into depression, into a state where one could conserve energy when one needed to lie low to escape predators. If not, these abilities would not have survived and been passed down from generation to generation. There must have been an advantage to predicting what would happen before danger struck. In the process, some might have developed thoughts that moved *too fast* as evolutionary features sought streamlining. Blessed with creative abilities and a quick mind, one feels emotions more deeply and can paint with a broader palette of life's colors. From that well of pain, one can draw upon their experiences for a source of creativity. Feelings of intensity drive art. It is not bland acceptance of the status quo that inspires.

As a side note, Ludwig van Beethoven, Edgar Allan Poe, and Winston Churchill are all thought to have suffered from manic depression. "I do believe God gave me a spark of genius, but He quenched it in misery," said Poe.

Not that every manic-depressive is some great genius. There are drawbacks to feeling so deeply. "Complicating matters further, certain life-styles provide cover for deviant and bizarre behavior. The arts have long given latitude to extremes in behavior and mood...," wrote Dr. Kay Redfield Jamison, an American clinical psychologist whose bestselling work has centered on manic depression, in *Touched with Fire: Manic Depressive Illness and the Artistic Temperament*. (Jamison n.d.)

Dr. Jamison studied psychopathology and suicide in British poets born between the years 1705 and 1805. To perform her study, she obtained the medical records, available letters, books and journals of the poets. Jamison studied the lives of poets Samuel Johnson, Thomas Gray, William Collins, Christopher Smart, Joseph Wharton, Oliver Goldsmith, William Cowper, James Macpherson, Robert Fergusson, Thomas Chatterton, John Bampfylde, George Crabbe, William Blake, Robert Burns, Joanna Baillie, William Wordsworth, Sir Walter Scott, Percy Bysshe Shelley, John Keats, and more. Out of the thirty-six poets she studied, only the records of *four* poets showed that they had never suffered from a mood disorder as evidenced by recorded periods of melancholia, institutionalization, suicide attempts, insomnia, and recorded periods of "nervous fever."

A posthumous study by Dr. Colin Martindale, who examined the lives of twenty-one eminent English poets born between 1670 and 1809, found that more than half had a history of breakdowns, suicide attempts, alcoholism and other "psychopathologies." One in seven of the poets had been institutionalized in an asylum. Indeed, the artistic temperament and neurotic illness seem to go hand in hand.

Speaking of disorders that go hand in hand, migraine is comorbid in bipolar II disorder, and both disorders often afflict the creative. A study performed by the *Psychiatric Times* which interviewed people with mood disorders found that migraine was a common condition in those with bipolar I and II, occurring in a whopping 82 percent of those with bipolar II, and in 27 percent of those with bipolar I. The researchers found an especially high occurrence of migraine in those with panic disorder and insomnia and also found that migraines occurred in 51 percent of patients with unipolar depression. (Oedegaard 2001)

Both migraines and manic depression involve imbalances in the dopaminergic and serotogenic systems of the brain, which cause a cortical spreading depression in migraine, and may lead to mania in manic-depressive disorder.

I had plenty of time to philosophize in the hospital, plenty of time to think and to study neurobiology in the monastic hospital library, as my life resembled that of one who is enrolled in a Gothic boarding school. I was confined, given a regimented schedule and there was a lot of routine in my life. Like a scholar, I was forced to attend classes such as Illness Management and Crafts. I was also required to participate in Group.

CHAPTER 24

Cupid's Arrow

Donna was a patient who seemed to have bought too many self-help books on the psychology of men, as if she were in perpetual man-hunting mode. Donna was an unlikely victim of a misguided Cupid's arrow. She was a romantic, in love with the idea of love, even if she had to resort to dreaming and scheming to get it. Men were Donna's whole world and her raison d'être. She was a follower of pop psychology, and read articles with titles like "10 Ways to Tell if He's Into You or Not." Donna eagerly recited her self-help tips in the hopes of betterment.

"Work on your waist line. Let him do the calling. Act helpless to flatter his ego. I'm going to marry a rich, *rich* man," she would say, a shiny glint in her gray eyes which gave her a remote, faraway gaze.

Her eyes were like the marble ones of stuffed animals. The fact that Donna wasn't exactly a typical man magnet with her size thirteen feet, round, manly shoulders and wispy blond mustache, did not seem to faze her. Donna was a heavy woman who no doubt needed a makeover, a new wardrobe, to learn some social skills, and to adopt a bit of feminine mystique, so that she could enchant the man of her dreams and drive away in that red Ferrari with him. I figured she'd need to present a very good façade and would probably need pure magic to trick someone into wanting her. Meeting men, specifically a rich one, was all she talked about. If Donna had a mental issue, it was her disillusioned obsession with love. Donna would pull out one of her dog-eared, well-used self-help books, which she was allowed to keep in her room, and read aloud within earshot of everyone on the ward: "To meet rich men, you have to know where to find them. On the polo field and at horse races are good places to start." No one was interested in her self-improvement program.

Another simple, but vitally necessary, important fact—the fact that Donna wasn't exactly free to socialize beyond the walls of the hospital—did not distract her from her efforts to meet Prince Charming. Donna was certain that, upon her release, she would find and marry herself the man of her dreams. That is, if she followed the proper guidelines and advice written in her self-help books.

Speaking of tragic, foolish, unrequited love, secret institutional romances did occur. They were always taboo, and I always tried to avoid being drawn into one, but I was willing to make an exception for James because he looked like a movie star. I found the idea of institutional romance absurd, as such liaisons distracted from the focus of our stay, mainly the health issues we were there to resolve in the first place. Even so, I was willing to bear a measure of risk for James. Our minor flirtations ended up leading nowhere and consisted of innocent hugs. James was cute, and I felt imprisoned and bored. I was also a twenty-four-year-old young lady—girl, really, given to the flighty behavior of my peers. Occasionally, James would sneak me a hug just out of sight of the nurse's station.

Our clandestine romance involved coded signals to avoid detection. The forbidden romance had to occur in total secrecy, due to rules and restrictions imposed upon us by staff. Our special signal was a spritz of well-timed perfume which I had secreted in under the staff's nose. Much like the sender of a jailhouse note, I would dare to brave punishment to tap out my Morse code. I enjoyed thumbing my nose at authority figures, but only in private. I didn't believe their dictatorial power over my life was deservedly theirs to be had. So I would spray a bottle of floral-smelling perfume in the hallway, which I had concealed under my clothes, for James. When James walked down the hall he would sniff the signature scent, recognize it as mine, and sneak me a hug. Wrapped in a cloud of perfume, he would find me and we'd quickly embrace, but nothing more. The thrill of the anticipation of handsome male company was enough to alleviate my boredom. When we met briefly, privately, in the hall, he would share his motivational poetry with me. His sayings were written all over the backs of his hands in his cramped script. James would read the poems he'd written in a lyrical, expressive voice.

Eventually a nurse caught a whiff of eau de floral and they put an end to our forbidden meetings, which consisted only of innocuous, pathetic attempts to meet and read poetry together. Nurse Nasty put both James and me on "Area Restriction," a foreboding-sounding punishment, meaning we could not come within a certain distance of each other's *area*s, which had the limits of the maintenance of fifteen feet or greater at all times. Our hall passes were revoked and James and I were instructed to ignore each other, even while in the same room, and to avert eye contact.

Where outside of an institutional setting would an authority figure swoop down upon two adults and take away the freedom to choose with whom to associate? Where outside of such a setting would someone take away your hall pass if they didn't like whom you were talking to in public? Who got to decide to whom you could and could not talk? I pictured a gym teacher figure tracking down a *Sex and the City* character, an independent, cosmopolitan sophisticate, at a French restaurant; then blowing a whistle at her as she gazes across the candle flame at her date. I pictured the gym teacher saying, "No, you can't go out with that man! It's not allowed!" and dragging her out of the restaurant by the sleeve of her expensive gown. The imagined scenario made me smile. The Area Restriction Rule was another way that life in the hospital didn't resemble the order of the outside world. If the training administered in the hospital was meant to be realistic and to help develop life skills, then the preparation wasn't adequate. Outside the hospital walls, you are free to suffer the consequences of your actions. To sink or swim, to fail or succeed, to learn from your decisions. This process *must* involve failure or you cannot learn from your mistakes. The rules were not mine, however, and I had no choice but to comply. Due to our imposed restrictions, James eventually fell for a Nordic-looking blonde housed on a different ward. Because she was on another ward and managed by other staff, there was no Area Restriction rule for her. Not that I was jealous. My friendship with James had simply been a way to pass the time. He had been a toy and an interesting diversion for me.

Speaking of institutional romances, Victor seemed to have

developed a pretty heavy crush on me. I did not return his feelings. Victor was a young, blond college student who had spent his summers as an oil field worker prior to his admission. Victor looked like an All-American quarterback. He was one of those guys I imagined other girls would find attractive; for good reason, I did not. I was drawn to alternative types with a sullen air of mystery about them. Besides, I had learned my lesson. The whole Area Restriction Rule was a major barrier. Victor wore his emotions on his sleeve. While other patients seemed dead, zombie-like and overmedicated, there was something very alive in Victor's green eyes and the way they flashed.

Victor's crush on me was obvious. "Hiii…" he'd say in a long, flirtatious, drawn out way, making goo-goo eyes at me as he rushed to greet me as soon as I appeared in the hospital cafeteria. I'd look over my shoulder at the table where he sat and he would give me a big, goofy, finger-fluttering wave and invite me over. But most times I just wanted to sit by myself in the cafeteria as I felt my pills made me too dull and stupid to have an intelligent conversation. I didn't have a hearty constitution made for taking pills without consequence. Even small amounts of medication made me feel doped.

"You fascinate me!" Victor breathed, not at all subtly, as he parked his tray next to mine in the cafeteria.

He hadn't gotten the message, hadn't interpreted my avoidant, dismissive body language as a sign I didn't want to speak to him. He had taken my hunched shoulders and the aversion of my eyes as signs he should plunge ahead anyway. Yet his complimentary statement raised my self-esteem, even if it was coming from an undesired source.

The hospital's privilege and rewards system, complete with its hall passes and Area Restriction Rules, did help one prepare for the outside world, *in a way*. Its series of colored hall passes carried with them certain allowances. If you got a white pass, you could join the other hundreds of patients in the cafeteria, an orange one and you could go on temporary leave from the hospital, and would be able to see your family. The staff met actions with equal, reinforcing reactions. But perhaps they succeeded too much. The system gave birth to what seemed, at times, to be a harsh militaristic environment. But such a strict environment prompted one to change one's behavior in order to avoid punishment, and to reap a reward that eventually provided for greater freedom of movement. The privilege system prompted the formerly unruly to conform, to bend to the standards of civilized company and to behave. Unfortunately, some were too sick to ever hold any level of responsibility, and those people would never get to hold a real metal knife and fork in their hands, only plastic ones.

When I earned enough privileges to work at an on-grounds Supported Employment job (a job assistance and employment maintenance program for people with medical issues), Victor also applied. He could have applied for a number of hospital jobs in various locations, but he chose to apply at the canteen, as I did. I was upset that he applied as well because I wanted to be alone, a silly assumption in a customer service job. I felt he only applied for the job because of his crush on me. Still, any other coworker would have been preferable to one who was far too attached to me. His crush was obvious, annoying, and an impediment to my recovery. Most of all, Victor's actions distracted me from my work. I struggled to keep a conversation going with him, feeling doped as I dodged hot fry batter and swept the floor. The drugs made me dull and quiet, so I preferred to be the hand behind the drive-through window which dispenses the food, not the beaming Employee of the Month. It seemed whenever Victor turned around and tried to start a conversation, I couldn't, due to my foggy, muddled mind. So I stared at the crackling fry grease and chicken poppers instead. But it was no use trying to hide from him. I had no luck there—we were stuck together half a day, every day. And our work release hours were strictly monitored. When the doctors came into the canteen during their lunch breaks, I was sure to load their plates up extra high to suck up to them because I thought perhaps they'd discharge me sooner that way.

CHAPTER 25

Mindfulness

W hen one is under 24-hour observation, a prospective discharge must learn not to let oneself laugh just a little *too* hard at jokes because it could be a sign you are flipping out. Any display of extreme emotion had to be controlled. I felt myself stiffly monitoring my behavior and trying to conform. In Crafts Class, I acted like gluing pom-poms on Santa hats was my favorite and that I enjoyed performing other mindless activities. This expression of contentment with routine wasn't that difficult to accomplish. I was glad just to be doing something with my hands to take my mind off the whole grim situation. Mindfulness Class was my favorite because we were required to do little more than to be aware of our surroundings, to soak them up and to feel the sand under our feet, figuratively and literally speaking. We were asked to hold objects and to simply be aware of the sensations in our fingers, to hold and mold Play-Doh. The instructor handed us squares of fabric and carpet and asked us to pet them and then make observations about them and to write them down. I found these sorts of exercises calming and therapeutic. To James, everything was a chore; he sighed deeply and looked glum as he was asked to feel objects.

"When are we getting out of here?" he kept saying. I wanted to get out too, of course, but I thought, maturely, that there is a time for everything and that we would leave when we were ready.

My parents would comment on the striking difference between my level of performance before becoming ill and my current level of productive output. They said that making Santa hats appeared childish, unstimulating, and seemed way below what I was capable of. But wounds don't heal overnight, and in the meantime, I needed a break. Making greeting cards is perfectly acceptable at times like these. Such activities will reduce stress and are a great distraction from one's problems. Therapists even have a name for distracting activities that focus on awareness of the details of everyday life. It's called Mindfulness. If not for my rock-climbing friend Brent and for his intervention, maybe I wouldn't have been able to make greeting cards at all. Making greeting cards is yards above the motionless invalid.

Hospital life was not complete without the occasional visit to Dr. V.'s office for a tune up. Her office was filled with New Age, stress-reducing knick-knacks such as an aromatic bubbling desktop fountain and Asian artifacts. Dr. V. was good at finding irony in life, and then gathering up and storing such amusing incidents in her mind to chew over later—fortunate for someone in her surroundings. She had this in common with Ryan, the orderly. Sometimes the visits had no purpose, except to serve as regular check-ins. We'd discuss some hilarious occurrence on the ward and she would ask if my accommodations were alright. She asked me if I believed in God and though I wasn't sure that I did, knowing her faith was at the helm of my care led me to put my confidence in her hands. I figured she couldn't be that bad if she believed in a force for good and tried to follow His example. Even if He did not exist, it was a nice thought anyway, to imagine that someone who was caring for me believed that He did.

CHAPTER 26

The Stoner Mix

"Here, come and get it, come get your stoner mix!" Kyle said, dipping a spoon into the viscous brown goo and slapping it down on the paper plates. Every night at 8 P.M. we'd have snack time, usually administered by Kyle. The brown goo was Kyle's special recipe. He joked that he was creating a "stoner mix" made of graham crackers, caramel spread, marshmallows and other unidentified ingredients, for prescription pill junkies like us and himself. His joke was kind of funny in a twisted way. He was trying to lighten the mood on the ward. Kyle referred to himself as a "necessary stoner." So were we, by default. Pills were mandatory and served to us nightly with a paper cup to wash them down with. We gobbled up Kyle's strange Stoner Mix. At times like these, our nightly caretakers consisted of Kyle and another staff member, often reading a book behind the nurse's station.

CHAPTER 27

Captive Christmas

I walked into the hospital gym festooned with red and green balloons and hanging streamers. Crimson tapestries and poinsettias covered the tables. Fake snow, tinsel, trees, and glittering lights adorned the room. The scene was set for the annual hospital Christmas party.

Ann insisted that the décor was put up for her husband Yanni's award show, an obvious delusion that she still carried. I half expected Ann to walk onstage to try to wrestle the awards out of the hands of doctors and nurses, to claim them for Yanni. M was not allowed to go as he was sadly nonfunctional and bedbound. Though Alice was allowed to attend, she babbled on so loudly on the topic of Mormons and politics that no one could hear the old-man fiddle band onstage. I tried not to laugh as the geriatric entertainment struggled through their motions on stage. But I couldn't help it when I caught Christy's eye and saw her laughing out of the side of her crooked, methamphetamine-damaged mouth at the failed talent show. Christy and I were seated at a table with Alice. Christy had a very measured, deliberate way of speaking. She even had a very purposeful way of laughing, almost as if she had to force her laughter out slowly in halting spasms. I giggled and snorted as I struggled to gulp down my holiday red fruit punch.

Then I stood and followed the Santa figure across the hospital gym, my cup of fruit punch in one hand, ready to mingle with the esoteric company. My favorite nurse was dressed as Mrs. Claus, in a red and white faux-fur-trimmed dress and a red felt hat. She was a petite blond with a Southern accent, the instructor of our Medication Management class. I trusted this nurse because she always gave me honest answers. I knew I could pose a scientific question to her without receiving some phony, glossed over reply only tossed out to try to make me feel better. She would give me the straight goods. The ill, especially, with a great deal of intuition and sensitivity, can detect whether they are being lied to or not. She was one of the few nurses who didn't insist that everything I was experiencing was "all in my head." I politely pulled her aside to make sure we were in a private area and that our conversation was confidential.

Then I asked her in a whisper, "Do these medications cause permanent brain changes?" It wasn't your typical festive party conversation but I felt I had the right to know as I was being administered these drugs myself.

And the nurse answered point blank, "They do cause changes. We're working with brain chemicals here. But whether they cause permanent changes or not is unknown. At this point in time, we haven't discovered that much about how the brain works."

That was her frank answer. *Great*, now I felt like a guinea pig test subject. I swallowed my punch with a lump in my throat. I was grateful that the nurse didn't beat around the bush, though. She didn't shrug me off or try to pawn my question off on someone else or try to mask reality. I pocketed her answer and filed this information away in my brain, taking it for what it was worth.

"Thanks for the honest answer," I told her.

I was sure that this nurse, with her years of experience, would know. She smiled and walked away, a small woman in a red Santa suit. Sometimes answers come from surprising places. Even from the North Pole.

Giancarlo was also at the Christmas party. He walked up to greet me. It was as if he had some sort of bat radar for navigating his way across a room. Despite being blind, he always managed to find who he was looking for.

Ryan, the orderly, saw me talking to Giancarlo and laughed. "I always know where to find *you*, my dear. I can always find you talking to the cutest guy in the room."

I was not sure that Ryan even knew that Giancarlo was blind, as Giancarlo was housed on a different ward than ours. To Ryan, he probably looked like any other handsome young man as there is nothing revealing about Giancarlo's eyes, no structural defects or cloudy look. Giancarlo looks stunning in tailored Italian pants and a black cashmere sweater. I'm impressed. Frankly, if I was blind, I'd settle for the easy way out and wear a muumuu and sweatpants every day, or grab whatever I could reach that first came out of the drawer.

"Stop it, Ryan..." I say.

"Back with Alice and Christy and the others," Ryan says, smiling and motioning in the direction of the other girls.

CHAPTER 28

The Pot Skit

D r. V. is disappointed with Bobby. Bobby is a young, athletic-looking patient who went out on a home pass and abused his privileges by smoking marijuana while out on pass. Despite the heat of the hospital, Bobby wears a North Face ski jacket every day, bizarrely, as if he was just about to go out on the slopes when he got carted off to a psychiatric hospital. Dr. V. tells Bobby he'll have to do something to make up for it and that he must admit his mistake to all of us, as punishment, during Group. Bobby can't ski his way out of this one. Dr. V. is waiting for an explanation. Inspiration strikes! I decide to help save Bobby from embarrassment. I have a plan to make his confession less awkward.

This was before the day of the approval of marijuana in the form of cannabidiol for medicinal purposes. Later, I'd come to know patients who had been prescribed cannabidiol by their psychiatrists for their mental conditions. But those laws were too progressive for Dr. V. Drugs were bad, and Bobby had to pay.

Having regained my cheer at this point, I felt a desire to help others. I tell Bobby that his punishment doesn't have to be so terrible. We can make it fun! Bobby is at a loss for what sort of speech to make to everyone during Group. He doesn't know what to say. Dr. V. has indicated that it better be good enough to make up for his serious transgression.

So I tell Bobby my plan. I ask the nurse at her computer station if she'll print off a play script for us. I must have a certain charm, because she agrees. This play will allow Bobby to be forgiven and accepted back in the circle, this production will be huge. I will be the director. Bobby will play a role. It's too bad Kyle is not allowed to participate—he has real star quality—but he's too busy grooming himself and typing up notes in our charts. Dutifully, the nurse prints out the five pages of the script for me. They're for Bobby's "Pot Skit" as Kyle later dubs it, looking back humorously upon the whole debacle. Because the nurse has printed the materials, I have the supplies I need to produce and direct a homemade version of the singing show *American Idol*, somehow tied into the theme of saying no to weed. I'm sure the whole thing will please Dr. V. and that it will be enough to allow Bobby back into the circle. It will be performed for the ward, so we'll have a built-in audience. It's not as if they'll be released anytime soon.

I glance at Bobby's North Face ski jacket with its many pockets. The myriad pockets are probably for storing his weed. No wonder he wears it in the heat. Bobby is sort of a Negative Nancy with a perpetually gloomy outlook. His face is always stormy and his brows furrowed. I never see him smile. Bobby, like James, Beth, Ann, Jack, Lonny, Giancarlo, Alice, Donna, Kate, Victor, Lila, Christy, and everyone else, also finds our whole situation stifling and confining (Bobby would rather be in the woods smoking pot). But Bobby seems to complain a lot more than the others, who've adapted to our unfortunate circumstances and have become accustomed to them. Bobby's refrain is, "Why do I have to be stuck here?" and he repeats it often. He complains even more than James does. I'm sure we're all tired of hearing him say that over and over again.

I attempt to pitch my script to the others, like an aspiring screenwriter. I'm also the casting agent. First, I ask James if he'll play a role. He says no. It's the whole Area Restriction rule. But nearly everyone else I ask says yes. Most people have been stung by Beth's sharp barbs, including Ann. She has since switched her loyalties over to me, so she agrees to participate. I direct people to their costumes and props—the only available materials at the time: a leftover Christmas orange, and a pencil someone has been trusted with, probably to fill out a crossword puzzle. I stab the fruit with the pencil and juice leaks down my arm, but despite that minor inconvenience, we've now got a microphone, a homemade prop. I choose a quiet, mysterious patient named Lonny as my co-host, because I can tell he's got the mind of a fantasist. I've seen him sketching cartoons when he's not pacing about the halls.

His large imagination is apparent when I hear Lonny make statements like, "I wish I could find my happy bubble. Happiness is like a chakra. It's gotta be right here," as he gestures to his heart region. In Lonny I detect a flare for the dramatic, hidden under his quiet, contemplative exterior. He daydreams a lot, lost in his own world. I'm correct, and Lonny agrees to become the show's host.

I wasn't sure where Lonny's chakras are located, but he made an agreeable co-host. Lonny would flatter the camera if there was one. Lonny loves the idea of having everyone's eyes on him. I can tell he is somewhat egotistical. Lonny grasps the microphone tenaciously, like he's not about to let it go. He wants to bask in the spotlight. Sure, his hands tremble from his meds when he holds it, but that doesn't matter. In knowing we're all a little weird, we at once accept each other's idiosyncrasies as we collaborate on this artistic endeavor. The play is, of course, on the subject of marijuana. The hastily pulled together script and the casting will make it a riot, I'm sure.

Dr. V. is in the audience opening night. The play took about two hours to organize and half an hour to perform. Our production costs were zero. Kyle is also in the audience for the premiere. He has to be, as he's scheduled to be on duty that night, as opposed to Ryan. He sits behind the nurse's station and looks on attentively. I can hear him laughing at the funny parts. Kyle is a captive member of the audience. Preppy, handsome Kyle. His bizarre habits and beauty are incongruous. At least he didn't bring a football to work today and he isn't brushing his teeth at the med sink. Kyle's behavior can be a bit unusual sometimes. He blames it on his manic depression while tossing out motivational messages to us, suggesting we modulate our actions and adjust to social norms. He seems to take his own advice most of the time, but sometimes he forgets. Prima Donna Beth is in the audience too. She always tucks her feet under her when you've got her attention, and she has them under her this time in her perch on the couch, I observe from the "stage"—which is really just a clear space in the common room. I can picture her mocking the play, tearing down our achievements. But tonight she is all ears. Beth is sitting with Lila, the housewife on the fritz with too many kids, the homebody who pooped out on Prozac. Lila will go home shortly. The humorous play seems to thaw the last remnants of her depression. Maybe she realizes her children are better behaved than the residents here.

Lonny I attempt to make small talk as host and co-host while following the script's instructions: 'Make small talk.' Lonny loves to be the center of attention. I was a little concerned about his literacy level, but the slow deliverance of his lines and clever ad-libbing only makes the audience laugh harder. I'm delighted that they are enjoying themselves and enjoying the play, performed in the oddest of settings. I can tell by the laughter and applause that the audience loves it. The theme of the play is hilarious—an anti-marijuana campaign based off the singing show *American Idol* with patients as contestants belting out their anti-pot slogans.

Ann is a contestant on *Weed Idol*. She confessed her delusion to me during casting, that she had lots of vocal experience gathered during her years touring with Yanni. Ann says she learned from the master. Skeptical, I gave her the benefit of the doubt, took a chance, and cast her. I was short on qualified applicants.

"Don't lose hope, don't smoke dope…" Ann sings in a high clear voice.

Jack plays the show's judge. He's usually incoherent, so I have supplied him with easy one liners. He forgets his line and has to be prompted to remember it. "Oh yeah… Five stars! Thumbs up!" he says in response to Ann's performance. The laughter is uproarious.

I hear Dr. V.'s husky laugh. James is laughing, too. Kyle's thousand-watt sideways smile and dimples are all I can see beyond the glare of the spotlight.

Bobby has a line at the end, "Just say no!"

I hear another final burst of applause and we receive a standing ovation. Lonny and I start to bow, but Dr. V. is thinking like a psychiatrist and says everyone should stop because our adolescent egos cannot take such praise, that we'll be spoiled by it, turning arrogant from admiration, even while admitting that she loved the play.

The play is such a success that Kyle attributes queen bee Beth to having directed it because she's the unofficial queen of the ward, bossy and brilliant. When he finds out it's me, he says, "Kids, you kids. You little punks. You held a play on smoking pot!" and laughs.

Kyle is my mentor, and I'm glad I've won his approval of my creative effort. A fellow who carries a football and a toothbrush is a fine enough mentor sometimes. Kyle was permissive and lenient enough to allow us to express ourselves creatively. He's a stickler about following other rules, but he's not like Nurse Nasty. He realizes that fun and laughter can do no harm and will likely only further our progress.

CHAPTER 29

Freedom is Near

At my provisional job at the hospital chicken kitchen, I see the handsome Giancarlo come in with his friend—a young depressed man who watches sports when he's not depressed, and also when he is. I am wearing an apron and I am smeared with grease. Giancarlo's friend favors athletic wear and seldom smiles. The friend is sighted. Sometimes he helps guide Giancarlo. But not often. Giancarlo seems very capable. The two young men sit down together at a table. The friend rests his head on the table, buries his face in the sleeve of his sports sweatshirt, then pulls the hood over his head and cinches it, a figurative hangman's noose that is probably indicative of his usually glum mood.

"Hi, Giancarlo," I say.

I don't acknowledge the friend because he seems to not want to be spoken to. His sports hoodie is a protective barrier against the world. He looks comfortable in his cotton cave. Giancarlo actually recognizes me, and calls me by name. I am pleased that he was able to identify me based on my voice alone. I wonder if it is true that blind people develop an advanced sense of hearing to compensate for their lack of sight. Giancarlo catches me at a good time during my hospital stay. I would soon be released, and have already been notified of my impending freedom. I was delighted. Knowing I'm going home soon puts me in a good mood. So I smile at the two boys when I serve them their chicken. And even if only one of them can see my face, I'm sure that Giancarlo can hear the smile in my voice.

The aftermath of the play performance must have demonstrated to the doctor that if I was capable of organizing that many people, I must have an orderly mind. Dr. V. has spoken to the social worker, the therapist, the nurses, and viewed the daily notes from Kyle and Ryan. Nurse Megan has favorable opinions of me and my progress. I am not sure what Nurse Nasty wrote. But eventually all agree that I am doing well, sleeping enough, and that I am likely to do well in the Outside World. I have only to endure a few more days at the hospital. And once I have learned enough life lessons—or pretend that I have (it's really hard to tell from a verbal tally), Dr. V. allows me to go. I spend a lot of time counting down the final days left until my discharge. I am released in April.

CHAPTER 30

New Beginnings

April, spring, a time for earth's new beginnings. Upon my release, I must renew myself. I immediately go about rebuilding a life. I must restructure what was missing before which led to me ending up where I was, so that I never go back to that dark place again. I must rebuild what I lost during the time spent away and make new connections to replace the ones I lost. I will have to learn to live as other adults living in society do. A society where choices aren't made for you, and help isn't dispensed freely and easily by mentors.

I will later get my own apartment and become self-sufficient, but for now I have to pay my dues. As a transition from the hospital, I must first live in a group home. Doctor's orders, after a discussion on where I should go after my departure. I am assigned a roommate at the group home. Her name is Patty. Patty is a streetwise former circus dancer with a daughter she never sees. She says her daughter was an unwanted accident. The daughter is being raised by her parents. Patty has been with abusive man after abusive man, but she wasn't exactly their hostage—she chose them. She's been an addict, she's been homeless. Patty has tried nearly every mind-altering substance known to man and has used them for the entire ten years since she left home. I don't have the authority to judge her, nor her past. Because if I did, she might judge mine. Out of necessity, I must accept whoever has been assigned to me.

As roommates, Patty and I now must work together to scrub the floors for Inspections, a weekly ritual performed by staff. Our shared room must undergo a white glove check. After all, the government owns this property, not us. Patty works hard, getting down on her hands and knees, scrubbing every corner. She is meticulous, a perfectionist even. We have to be, in order to pass the cleanliness test. Patty even dusts the blinds. Wielding a mop, she polishes the floor until you can see your reflection in it. Patty and I even push the heavy beds to one side so we can attack the fluffy dust bunnies hiding underneath them, sucking up and eliminating them. There is something sickeningly satisfying about the plopping sound which signifies that those feathery bits of dust have been swallowed up by the vacuum, and are no more. Patty doesn't want to fail Inspections, so she leaves nothing to chance. She puts on the white glove and runs her hands over the entire room. If it isn't clean, we get kicked out: those are the rules.

But our lives aren't all work and no play. To escape the strictures of the group home, Patty and I hang out with another resident, a Navajo guy named Tim. A huge fan of the *Freddy Kreuger* horror series, Tim's really into slasher films. He walks around in Kreuger claws, slashing the air in front of him and acting as if he's ready to pounce. I imagine the Kreuger claws slicing up my skin, gashing me and turning me into strips of bacon. Tim was the medicine man on the Rez, but medical personnel with European ancestry tell him he's crazy. They say the portents of the future he sees simply mean he's hallucinating, and that they are not predictive dreams. His beliefs denounced, facing large degrees of incomprehensible cultural dissonance, Tim grows depressed, fat and gray—he's lost his original tan complexion and now looks sickly. Tim's not even up to watching *Freddy Kreuger* movies anymore, even though they're his favorites. He spends all day staring at his hands, waiting for them to sprout Kreuger claws, I suppose. He turns them over to examine the backs of them. He has let his fingernails grow unusually long, and now he files them into points. He would make a fearsome opponent.

After asking for permission, the three of us are allowed to leave the group home together to go on brief outings in the city. We make the most of them, packing as much fun into the short amounts of time as we can. Patty, Tim and I buy cheap junk food because it's all we can afford on our disability checks.

My dream is to become a writer. I have a college degree. I can see myself discarding the invalid label soon. So what if I had a few trials and setbacks? I hope that they haven't ruined my chances at the success I hope to achieve.

Patty, Tim and I buy Diet Cokes with lime, bags of chips, and candy. It takes us an hour to walk five blocks in the heat of the unusually warm spring day, because we keep stopping to pop in stores to browse. We are thrilled with the chance to spend a few hours away from the group home. Simple pleasures mean a lot to us because we are usually confined indoors. Tim insists we visit his favorite video shop and he searches for old, obscure black and white vampire movies. Since the movies are rare and dated, we never find them. Patty and I buy plastic keychains which we will promptly lose in the disorder of our discount purses, never to be found when needed.

After a few weeks, we are all able to leave the group home. Patty doesn't see herself wearing the invalid label long, either. She's ambitious and she has plans. She decides to enroll in beauty school. She jokes about being a celebrity stylist. Patty finds an apartment in the same city where the group home is located. I want to distance myself, and so I find an apartment in the state capital instead. I've always wanted to live there, anyway. Starting over presents me with a perfect opportunity to do that. I hope people are less small-minded there. Even though we live a good distance apart, Patty and I remain friends—on weekends, I drive up to visit her.

After Patty starts beauty school, she takes a class where hair models are needed. She tells me I have a fantastic head of hair, so why don't I become her model, her living mannequin? I see her course as an opportunity to get my hair styled for free. I feel Patty's icy fingers scrunching my hair. The cold permanent waves and tedious 1920s style crimping of the mermaid wave she's trying make me glad the curling iron was invented. The instructor is called over to take a look at my hair, and Patty passes the skill.

But Patty's shadows keep haunting her. They follow her wherever she goes. She starts regressing and going back to her old ways. It's almost as if she can't bear having her life go swimmingly, and now needs to go back to her old habits to "live a little." Patty's using meth again. Like she did for the ten years she lived on the streets and worked on and off for the circus. She doesn't *look* like a meth user. She looks like a dancer and still has all her teeth. But she told me she was back to using, a coping mechanism for her. Was it an escape from the trauma of having to stand next to the sword swallower or the bearded lady, while working for Ringling Bros.?

Patty finds a new boyfriend, Ben. He fits right along in her string of abusive men. He's shady and hoody. I sense he's up to no good. I can't figure him out. He's lying to her and telling her he's sober, but she knows he's using because she saw his stash. There's a change in Patty's optimistic, responsible nature. Now Patty says strange, nonsensical, crack-up things when she does talk, if at all. It's rare when she does speak, responding monosyllabically or agreeing with whatever Ben or I say. The doctors say she's brain damaged from her many years of drugging. This latest relapse can't be helping her gray matter recuperate. She's an agreeable Yes Girl with no mind of her own. But when she does say something on her own, it's usually profound, as if to make up for all those times she was quiet.

One such significant time, Patty comes up with her theory on the purpose of life. "Nothing matters. We're all going to hell anyway. We're all black anyway, even though we ain't black. You know why? Because we're going to turn black like blackest, blackest night, like burnt toast." The druggy's statement doesn't make sense, and sounds defeatist besides.

I am at Patty's. After sharing her unsettling theory, Patty's eyes lose their light and she eases her five-foot-nine frame back onto her ruffled, pink, very feminine bed and giggles. She laughs maniacally with her blonde head thrown back. Her sleek, bouncy, beauty-school-perfect hair is still unsoiled by episodes of drug use. Ben tries to get Patty to stop laughing and I can't tell if he's just glad she finally said something after being silent for days, or if he just wants her to stop laughing at her own twisted statement. He asks if he can speak to her privately in the other room. I hear them raising their voices at each other, but can't make out the words. I'm sure this is a dangerous place for me to be, caught in the crossfire between two drug users. I care about Patty, though, and I want to make sure she's okay. Ben storms out, letting the screen door slam behind him. Her boyfriend's petulance does not affect her. Patty and I watch chick flicks starring Jennifer Anniston on her bed until we fall asleep. Patty sits very close to the edge of the bed staring at the screen, blankly.

I tell her I'm not tired and ask her if I can borrow a sleeping pill, one of her prescriptions. This is a mistake common to newbies and to those recently released from group homes. It's obviously a good rule of thumb never to share, trade, or borrow prescription pills! To do so is to make a grievous error. Death could even result. And I learn that night to never try this again. Patty's pill knocks me out of the ballpark. Into blackest, blackest night. One like the one she described in her disjointed, drugged-out statements. So this is the dark place she had been babbling on about.

Help me! I'm trapped! I feel dead inside. The way I feel must be due to Patty's pill and the suppressing effect it has on my lungs and psyche. I don't know what day it is. I've lost track of time. I'm screaming inside because though I'm usually capable of feeling emotions, any, either good or bad, now I feel none at all and their absence leaves me longing for their return. I am emotionally flattened as if I'm lying in a coffin underground with no way to contact others. I feel submerged, thanks to Patty's pill. Mood-altering drugs seldom have good effects on me. They will prove this to me time and time again. This isn't the sharpest decision I've ever made. It is one that Jack from the hospital would have made. I'm a million miles from earth, orbiting Pluto's icy atmosphere. Mentally, I have to literally order myself to move, to avoid paralysis. I actually have to will the thoughts, 'move your arm now' and 'lift your hand' to my brain before my body will obey the commands! The pill eventually wears off, many hours later. Because of this occurrence, I avoid Patty for a while, even though she's my best friend at the time. My mind links her to the bad experience and forms negative associations. I had a bad trip at her house and will not to forget it. I've learned a lesson, learned what not to do again.

Patty's next roommate is named Marylee, and she's a big, dramatic woman who looks as if she'd make a great opera singer. Marylee is fond of frumpy thrift store clothing in bright floral prints. She rarely leaves her couch and she's also a perpetual motor mouth, blabbing right over the top of commercials for products like the Wonder Mop and Crisco. Marylee's arms are butcher's wife fleshy, her cellulite dangling and jiggling like Jell-O. She spends her days watching forensic crime shows and trying to solve the mystery before the 48 edited-for-TV hours are up.

Charlena is Marylee's friend, couch companion, and fellow crime-solver. Together they're taking a bite outta crime and bringing justice to the world. Charlena is a young black woman who favors an all-purple wardrobe, like the late singer Prince. She's got a loud, raucous sense of humor. Charlena visits so often you'd think she lived there permanently and that she was also one of Patty's roommates—but she isn't. Patty's other *real* roommate is Marylee's dog, Bitsy.

The tiny Pomeranian is sent to the groomer to get regular shampoos and trims, to have her nails painted bright pink and her fur adorned with tiny pink bows. Bitsy is a pampered, spoiled little dog. Her owner seems to spend more money on Bitsy than she does on herself. Though they're poor, Marylee says Bitsy is worth the financial sacrifice. Worth every penny for all her adorableness. The dog is an attention-loving ham, walking on two legs and performing tricks for treats. Marylee and Charlena both smoke indoors, as if they exist in a time before the passing of the Clean Air Act. I wonder why, if Bitsy is Marylee's little pageant queen, they don't seem to care about exposing the little dog to secondhand smoke. I wonder this especially when the poor creature develops a hacking cough. The remnants of Marylee and Charlena's cigarettes end up in an ashtray which they leave resting on one arm of their couch. The ashes frequently tip over, peppering the couch with gritty debris. The couch cracks are stuffed with old candy wrappers and potato chip bags that never make their way to the garbage. Patty is neat and organized, a legacy of her days at the group home, but Marylee and Charlena are more than a little grungy. With those two, it's hard to find a clear space anywhere. The coffee table is also covered in ashes and the carpet severely dirt-tracked, stained by paw prints and Bitsy's urine. I think the carpet was originally white, but now it is a sediment-covered dingy, yellowish brown.

"Oh, no, girlfriend, that is not true! *I know* who did the stabbing!" Charlena will say, and then she will laugh along with Marylee, clapping her hands together and jabbing the air, creating stabbing motions along to the latest *48 Hours* mystery.

There's something macabre about their crime scene analysis sessions. They're like two witches, clapping their hands with glee at others' misfortunes. Charlena is the sharpest detective, always solving the mystery first, figuring out who the killer is before anyone else. Marylee comes in a close second at guessing "whodunit."

Patty and Marylee don't have a car, so I become their designated driver. Maybe I've acquired transportation because I had a healthy period of development in my early youth and came from more stable beginnings than others who came from the group home, with a head start on my savings. Somehow I am always the more put-together one, the one with the most cash on hand. Somehow, despite my history of hospitalization, I was always the one with the assets most valued by society. I have a job, a car, an apartment to myself, even the occasional boyfriend, if he would stick around. My role as chauffeur in their lives becomes an automatic delegation as a trade-off for the free dinners I eat over there, courtesy of Marylee. I drive them to the local Family Dollar for a grocery run. Marylee can cook with most everything found at the Family Dollar, a store whose food I consider junk and processed, but which she somehow manages to make taste delicious. Despite the unhygienic environment from which her food spawns, Marylee is a gourmet cook when it comes to classic American cuisine. Her fries are crunchy, her burgers rich and greasy tasting. Her macaroni and cheese doesn't taste like it came out of a box. The heat of the grill kills germs anyway, sanitizing her meals. Marylee is a whiz at pulling together side ingredients and leftovers into one whole, cohesive meal.

When we return from our jaunt to the store, the place looks untidy as usual, so I try to clear off a space on the kitchen counter. It's a futile effort. The trash I slug bounces back at me, spreading itself across the counter as if to mock me and let me know it is insurmountable. I make only a small dent in the mountain of trash on the counter, but at least it is enough to set a plate on. I help dice onions as Marylee takes the helm at the stove. I like that Marylee shuns rare meat, roasting hers black. I prefer my burgers so well done that they resemble charcoal. I can't bear to think of meat that bleeds. Marylee's burgers are burnt black as tar, "as black as blackest night," as Patty would say in one of her meth-fueled ramblings. I think that Marylee has been a good influence on Patty because she hasn't used at all lately. Maybe all Patty needed was company and somebody to understand her. Someone to force-feed her. Marylee's burgers are perfect. There are fresh, juicy, purple onions in them. The mustard is hot and acidic and drips down our throats when we bite. I'm in ecstasy.

Ben arrives. Great, Patty's dirtbag boyfriend is here. "Hey, you guys got food!" I'm not happy to see this scavenger looking for his next meal, one that he hasn't helped procure nor prepare.

We've all gone back to the living room to watch murder

mysteries when Ben walks in. Marylee and Charlena are chain smoking on the couch with one hand and eating burgers with their free ones. Bitsy is tucked into the enormous, worn leather couch somewhere, her tail curled around her. She's a mini ball of fluff. I am sitting on the floor in front of the TV chowing down on my burger. Patty is in the kitchen fixing herself some toppings.

"Hi," Ben says, clearing his throat. "Patty home?"

I don't like his look, his sly malcontent look, but I tell him, "She's in the kitchen." It's too bad we let him in. But I figure Patty is an adult and can handle herself. I hear shouting in the kitchen. They argue and Ben stalks off, slamming the flimsy door behind him.

CHAPTER 31

Another Nest

I had to get out of there. I have to be able to control my own environment and what happens in it. I find a one-bedroom apartment in the city and living alone suits me. I find a job and I go to work. I am relieved to leave the group home behind, though I would say it did serve its transitional purpose.

And then I meet someone. After leaving the hospital, I am just grasping for someone to cling to so that I can prove that my new persona, the one I created, is valid in their eyes. I need that confirmation desperately, as I seem to have no identity. I have had to, after all, reconstruct my life and start anew.

"God... You've got your own little bachelorette world. This apartment is so you... Yours..." the young blond guy who resembles actor Matthew McConaughey breathes.

His pupils dilate with wonder when he speaks as he looks around. He is Scottish-American with a peaches-and-cream complexion and symmetrical features. Growing up with five brothers, he knows no other way but the masculine way and confesses that he doesn't understand women. He's a whiz at working on cars, at fixing things. He's clueless when it comes to matters of the heart.

His name is Ian McLellan. He doesn't take life seriously; he does the minimum to get by so the rest of his time can be spent in pursuit of fun. He performs excellent parodies and impersonations of others. Spot-on impressions of accents and mannerisms. Ian is anxious and shy but he uses humor to cover this up. He's proud of his accomplishments, however small. He has a souped-up sports car that looks like the Batmobile with its shiny black paint, chrome, and fins. A backyard mechanic, Ian spends his time buying and installing parts for his car, fixing it up in his garage. His car is his baby; he treats it like a family member. Ian keeps his feet covered at all times, capped in their little white socks. An odd mannerism. He must feel comfortable that way.

When I first lay eyes on him, I think someone must have created Ian with me in mind. He is the perfect height to make us a matched pair. He's just the few inches taller needed for me to fit perfectly in a coveted little spot on his shoulder.

Ian's best stand-up impressions are of his aging former hippie, father, who treats Ian more like a friend and equal than a son. No rules or discipline, so your kids will feel like you're a peer. They were friends rather than having a father-son relationship.

"Well, son, whatever you think is best," was Big Ian Mac's advice for his son whenever he would ask. His father is sixty-two but acts nineteen, having separated from Ian's mother to find a much younger girlfriend and become a father again at a later stage in life. A midlife crisis, for sure. All this, despite the fact that his father still professes to be in love with Ian's mom. Ian's parents are still legally married even though they don't live together under the same roof anymore—despite Ian's dad having a new girlfriend and

Ian's mom a new boyfriend. Ian's dad is a romantic and his mother is dry-eyed and practical, I learn. It's his dad who wants to keep the marriage intact while his mom rolls her eyes at her husband's new girlfriend and baby. I find this all very romantic. An undying love, unchanged despite different living situations that had lasted twenty-plus years. I don't how having his parents still married with all this going on under various roofs affects Ian. Likely, it probably confuses him. At least they are still married.

Ian sets the scene for his impressions like a stage actor does. He waits until everyone has his attention, until he's got the floor, and then begins. "Everyone" is usually just Ian's friends and me. We are his audience. And then Ian *becomes* his father, stepping into the personality seamlessly. He adopts his dad's gravelly, smoky-sounding voice. Puts on his father's limp.

"I said, boy, get your ass over here! I'm a gonna tell you the story of your creation. I'm a gonna tell you about the night your momma and I spent at that motel in Vegas, didn't take long. The night you was made."

Ian chuckles at his own vulgar impression, then decides to switch tasks and make an improvised marijuana pipe out of a hollowed-out soda can. He's lacking in social graces, devoid of most knowledge of etiquette. Growing up with five brothers was more conducive to learning the art of burping than to learning table manners. But we're at a small house party with his friends with no need for formality.

Ian picks up the Mountain Dew can, pokes some holes in it with a nail, drills out the tin, and shoves some marijuana leaves inside the empty soda can before continuing on with his impression. It seems nearly everyone my age, then twenty-four, smokes marijuana but me. I tried it once and it didn't do much for me. "Your mama thought I was better than the postman or that delivery guy," Ian says, blowing gray-green smoke out of the side of his mouth, speaking slowly.

His *real* dad calls five minutes later, as if he knew we were talking about him somehow, and Ian's impression sounds exactly like him on the phone. When Ian hangs up, we watch country music videos on YouTube. One reason Ian and I get along so well is that we both share similar tastes in music. We bounce songs off each other, each of us asking the other if we've heard this one or that one, caught up in the music and the onscreen images.

Our song, our official couple's one, is Gary Allan's "Smoke Rings in the Dark." There is a haunting, longing quality in Gary's voice that appeals to both of us. The song is prophetic as well, because so many of my dates with Ian end up with him blowing smoke rings in my face. I'll only allow certain people to do that to me, and they had better be cute. Annoying people and smoke rings don't mix. Our kisses were donut-shaped, smoke ring kisses. Ian even fancied himself a car just like Gary Allan's in the video, so he went out and bought a little black Miata sports car, complete with a retractable top, and turned it into what became The Batmobile. Ian laughs as he watches Josh Turner grace the YouTube screen with his guitar and he sings along to the music video.

"God, that's an attractive man," Ian says. "Listen to that deep voice." I am taken aback. *What did the comment mean?*

Thomas, Ian's brother, is gay and has stated so himself, with pride. Thomas displays no outward signs of femininity. He's a roughneck oil field worker who also happens to prefer men. He prefers tossing back beers after a long day in the field and playing footsie in work boots. Thomas' boyfriend is equally masculine and equally handsome—a big and burly construction worker. Without doing some serious research, you'd be hard-pressed to discover that Thomas was a homosexual.

After the comment, Ian's cousin Darren tells me that I had better watch out for Ian, as homosexuality runs in the McLellan clan, and that Thomas is gayer than a fruitcake and a New York fashion consultant put together. I am only mildly disturbed because I want Ian to prefer *me* and not some guy. Were there any other indications of his orientation? Ian does behave indifferently toward me at times. I watch him carefully, looking for signs that he isn't who he said he was. Other than the Josh Turner comment, there are none. I chalk the comment up to a joke because I don't want to ruin anything between us. *It's not possible, he can't be gay and want to spend so much time with me*, I think.

After so many hours spent watching YouTube, I am tired and want to go home. Ian turns testy and abusive. "God damnit, you bitch, all you ever try to do is ruin my fun and tell me what to do! If I want to sit here and smoke with my friends, I should damn well be able to!" Ian says.

But the truth is, I *don't* try to prevent him from hanging out with his friends. It's just that we've been here for hours and it's a normal reaction to want to go home by now. I'm stung by his words, but also trapped without a ride home. Ian was my ride. I came here as his girl.

Seeing the look of shock on my face, Ian seems to sense that he's gone too far and changes the subject. "I guess I'm tired too. Let's go out to the lake."

We get into The Batmobile, his polished pride and joy. Lonely desert, pale dirt, dry sage highway is the sequence of the scene that blurs past, empty and flat. Ian stares straight ahead at the road. I feel comforted looking at the scenic, open expanse. It's as if the world has a spacious outlet door for filler space and this is it. Ian and I arrive at the lake.

The water is so clear you can see twenty feet down, all the way to the pebbled bottom. The lake is a scuba diver's paradise. But on that day, there are no divers present. The strands of bluegrass growing around the lakeshore look as if they are out of a movie scene set in heaven, so gently are they caressed by the wind, swaying back and forth. The sun beams down on the lake through grey cloud auras in light-filled shafts.

Ian takes out his fishing pole and bait and casts his line. "Let's go sit on the dock," he says.

His attention is focused on the water although I whisper-read a book to him on the dock to entertain him while he fishes, but I keep the volume low so as not to scare the fish away. I bite his ear and kiss the side of his face and he smiles while keeping his line in the water. I'm worried that Ian is upset, that I was too demanding back there with his friends. I believe that I am somehow responsible for his mood, for the way he feels.

I call him "Little Boy" because he has little feet for a guy, capped in those white socks that he refuses to take off, socks that he leaves on even in bed. Our relationship has a teasing, playful quality. I poke him mischievously and force him to read a line in the book aloud as we sit on the dock. He grasps the book and laughs and reads: "There was a patch of a pot leaf stitched onto the knee."

"Is this about the whole smoking thing?"

The sun starts to set. There is a lapse of silence between us. Ian is easily bored, frequently anxious and uncomfortable with silence, while I am fine with it and take advantage of it. Silence gives me time to think and reflect. Ian's eyes dart back and forth, his look nervously expectant. He reels his line in, looking disappointed that nothing was biting. Having run out of patience, Ian sighs and then starts packing his fishing gear.

Rising to his feet, he says, "Let's go." The setting sun announces that this moment must eventually draw to a close, but Ian wants it to happen immediately.

On the drive back to our motel, Ian tells me a long and complicated story. Something about his parents and how they're currently married but living in separate households, each with a new significant other and how it's working out. Their story would make a good country song. Semis whip past us on the two-lane highway, their headlights blindingly bright in the darkness.

We arrive back at our motel in the western gambling town which features an in-house casino even though it's second-rate and shabby. Ian parks the little black Miata in the motel's parking garage on the roof.

"Oh, look, they pulled out the high-roller carpet for us," I tease, and he laughs.

Ian has many addictions, I find out. Gambling is one of them. As a general assumption, I find that the odds of the house are usually stacked against you, at which point gambling becomes pointless to me.

In the motel's casino we are surrounded by bleeping machines, bright lights, and gaudy décor. Occasionally the machines let out cheerful, encouraging slogans in their mechanical cartoon voices. Ian sits for hours, burning through dollar after dollar. I quickly run out of the little money I brought with me, but Ian seems hell-bent on staying until he wins. He's worse than a gambling grandma with buckets of quarters and a shaded dealer visor.

"Ian, let's go," I plead.

"Sweetheart…" he says and grabs my hand. When he calls me "sweetheart" or "hon" I wonder if he affixes a generic label to me because he can't remember my name and if there's some other girl—or even *guy*—in his life. He calls me "sweetheart" only when he's trying to be convincing or get his way. Exhausted, I amuse myself by watching his handsome profile lit up neon in the light of the blinking machines. It's the face of greed, but let it be my sin.

A cocktail waitress with her breasts popping out of the top of her glittering uniform walks by, balancing a tray of frothy beers on her shoulder. Ian's eyes don't leave the screen, not for her, not for anyone. He observes the waitress from the corner of his eye, without turning his head. He asks me if I'll be his little errand girl and to please go fetch him a beer. I do as I'm told, wanting to win his favor. I'm suddenly Anonymous Beer Girl, his girl Friday. His right-hand woman.

"And tip that chick, those people work hard for their money," he says, handing me a crumpled wad of cash.

"Thank you, sweetheart," he says in a distracted, offhand way when I return with the frosty beverage.

Hours later, Ian and I move on to yet another part of the casino. He's fall-down drunk by then, and ready to pick a fight like a Scotsman shorted a few sheep. A security guard nearly has to wrestle Ian to the floor as I try to get him to calm down and go back to our room. Ian's public behavior is mortifyingly embarrassing.

"But hon... I'm not done yet," he whines, stumbling and veering to one side.

I put my hand on his chest and pat, attempting to calm him down. The security guard asks for some identification. I'm insulted. We're young, but not *that* young. But part of me accepts that the man's just trying to keep us safe. Ian produces his driver's license and I glance at the photo, which I haven't seen before. Ian's driver's license photo looks like a Hollywood glamour shot. His hair looks especially wavy and he is pulling off a pouty, brooding look. His skin looks clear and his eyes bright. Ian even manages to look better in the driver's license photo than he does in real life, which is the exact opposite for most people—the poor-quality driver's license photo is notorious.

"Yep, you're real. You're twenty-two, you ain't lyin," says the security guard. "But I think you're done for the night, son," he suggests.

"We sure are, sir," I say. "We're leaving *right now*. C'mon, Ian."

I drag Ian to the elevator and shove him in. He tries to kiss me, but he's sloppy drunk and falls all over me.

"Listen here, you don't have to be afraid of me…" Ian slurs, his words making no sense. "Look into my eyes. Find the truth." I do, but he's wasted and his eyes are bloodshot. I don't have the slightest clue what he is talking about.

I, myself, would never have created such a public scene like the one Ian threw downstairs. I find myself longing to take a refreshing shower to wash the smoke out of my hair and to lie down on a soft mattress. Ian moans pitifully and places a hand to his forehead. He says his head hurts. I place a cool, damp washcloth on his head. I don't want him to be sick in the morning. I tuck him into bed still wearing his clothes. He is clumsy and indisposed.

In the morning I hear him retching loudly into the toilet. I find him hugging the porcelain bowl. I ask, with concern in my voice, "Are you okay?"

He looks up from the sparkling throne, where he is clad only in his boxer shorts and says, "I love you. Look at you, asking if I'm alright like that, looking after me…"

I am pleased that he notices I care. A brief tender moment passes between us as he gazes at me lovingly. He is probably just hungover and grateful for a babysitter. Not that I enjoy getting barfed on. He wipes his face on a towel. I try to make him some black coffee to sober him up, but the cord to the pot is tangled up in the cords to our phone chargers, where we left them on the counter the night before. It's a hopeless rat's nest and Ian gives up. He tells me he'd rather have a drink of orange soda instead.

Ian heads for the vending machine, whistling cheerfully, his pocket jingling with change. He quickly downs two bottles of soda.

"Someone's been drinking an awful lot of orange pop on this trip," I say.

He smiles and settles down on the patchy motel room comforter with his prized soda, sipping as he reminisces about the past. He tells me about the pretty Pakistani woman he convinced to sleep with his cousin Darren—they met her in the casino parking lot, this very one, last year.

"But it's fine to tell you about this now because it's over and done. And Darren needs help finding his girls because he's not as cute as me." He changes the subject. "We're going back to bed now, because we didn't spend much time in it last night," he announces.

Ian never asks, he simply orders. And if his stories aren't the kind I would like to hear, I listen anyway.

We look out the motel's window after hearing a savage wind whipping against the building. It's a blizzard, with huge white sheets of ice falling from the sky. We're snowed in. It will be too dangerous to drive in this frozen treachery. Ian and I remain in the hotel, holding court from bed, as if participating in a John and Yoko Bed-In. We pause to make trips to the hotel vending machine for more orange soda. He looks out the window to check the weather again. Still snowing. So we know what to do. Ian crawls back into bed. I can feel his pulse somewhere deep, his throbbing warmth. His strawberry shampoo tickles my nose.

Ian doesn't want to go home yet. There's been a change of plans due to the weather. We'll find local entertainment; there are some friends he wants me to meet.

We arrive at the run-down trailer park. His friends would probably be considered trashy by most definitions—they live in mobile homes and have bad table manners, grammar, and multiple legal problems, but I'm not one to judge. Certainly I'd never use the word "trashy" in reference to them. At least not to their faces. Instead, I try to seek their approval so that Ian will keep me in his life because, after all, they're his friends. His friends have plenty of children, all from different fathers or mothers. I don't like children very much in general, much less children spawned in unhygienic environments. Having been a preschool teacher makes me realize how messy they are. Even the ones that come from clean, stable homes I find messy and unpredictable. I prefer babies because they can't talk yet.

Ian's friend is wearing a tank top and cutoffs and has bare feet. Her hair looks to have been bleached with peroxide, an inch of dark roots visible. She hands me a pudgy, adorable little guy with dimpled hands and large, questioning brown eyes. I cradle him close and rock him back and forth.

Ian gives her older kids—they are six and seven—quarters for candy. They pedal their bicycles away, shrieking with delight at their good fortune.

"Someone's been busy. New baby every time I come here," Ian says, laughing at his friend.

Ian is an excellent friend. He's generous and giving and he

doesn't forget people from his past. He has known this lady for years and has kept in contact with her and her children. I hand the baby back to his mother.

Ian says there are other friends to visit. A housebound grandfather who was kind to him when he was a boy, something that Ian has always remembered, is next on the list. The people Ian has for friends have been his friends for a long time. Ian and I knock on the door of their trailer.

"Oh, looky here, it's Ian!" says the old woman at the kitchen sink. She wipes her hands on her apron and grabs Ian's face and kisses him. She's so obviously glad to see him.

I flash back to the early nineties. I try to imagine this old woman handing a blond boy a slice of warm, homemade bread. Ian is one to return a favor. Which is why he is still in touch with these people.

"This is my girlfriend, Marilyn," he says when he introduces me. Girlfriend? He never calls me that. So this is one of those rare times when he's proud to show me off. I am pleased with the label. I don't understand why Ian is so ambiguous about my title, what he's ashamed of, or why he feels the need to conceal my status. It makes me suspicious, makes me wonder.

Ian and I remain standing in the trailer's kitchen. The trailer is small and there isn't much standing room in the first place, but that isn't why we can't sit down. His morbidly obese elderly friend is occupying the whole couch. The old man is no more mobile than a concrete wall, and he is breathing through an oxygen tube. It touches me that Ian still keeps in touch with the helpless fellow, when he doesn't have to. We stand in the doorway and chat with the old man's wife while the old man dozes.

"He's been awfully sick lately," she says, glancing worriedly at her husband. When he awakens, Ian helps the old man locate his reading glasses and helps prop him up on the couch. Ian also completes a quick wellness check on the old fellow with the efficiency of a doctor, and decides to leave only when he is certain his health is not in peril.

On our way out, Ian decides to give me a tour of his old neighborhood. He points out his old trailer home. I glance at the slumping, weathered structure with its peeling paint.

"Nice," I comment because there's nothing else to say about it. It's not really "nice," it's crumbling and decrepit, but it's who lived in it that matters, and the memories that were created there, not how it looks—in this case, particularly. Ian is introducing me to the places and people he loves, which is the bottom line. I take this to mean he must like me and wants to introduce me to his world both past and present.

Ian was kind to his friends, but the material he was made of didn't translate into making him a thoughtful boyfriend. Some might have even called him abusive. Ian will be one of many in the string of abusive men I seem to attract like a magnet. Ambivalent about my title, he would rather let me linger in uncertainty than introduce me as his.

In the car, Ian interprets my expressionless face in the passenger seat as disdain. "Look, I don't understand you! I try to set this up, make this fun for you, take you to complete a little charity work and this is how you're reacting?" Truthfully, I wasn't thinking of *anything* at the time. I had been staring out the window looking at the scenery, certainly not counting my regrets over the visit with his friends. I didn't view visiting his friends as a chore at all. It had been interesting to discover whom Ian associated with.

When Ian raises his voice, I start crying and can't stop. I'm a leaky faucet. I'm not sure why my feelings are so intense. Such comments don't usually produce such devastation on my emotional horizons. I have crawled out of much greater wreckage in the past and survived, stoically. The truth is I'm not crying because I had to do charity work for invalids and trailer park residents, I'm crying because I'm unsure of what I mean to him, if anything. Ian occasionally refers to me as his girlfriend in public, but in private he tells me that I'm meaningless and that we're just killing time together. And now he's yelling at me after I tried my best to make a good impression.

When Ian sees the flood of tears, they move him to apologize. "I'm sorry, hon...Things will be alright. Let me get you some food. Maybe that will help, to have some food in your stomach." He swings The Batmobile around to a taco stand. Ian brings me the food as if he is now waiting on me hand and foot, indulging me, trying to calm my outburst.

"Thanks for the taco." He seems to think the simple gift he bestowed upon me will undo any of the damage he's caused. Then he changes the subject. "Sweetheart, would you like to learn to drive my car?"

I only have experience driving cars with automatic

transmissions, and zero experience driving manual cars with stick shifts. I don't want to drive his car, but I sense how important it is to him that I learn how to drive it—in case of emergency. Yet I am sure that this moment will go down in history books as the one where everyone in town had to evacuate the road at once, like they had to during the Great Flash Flood of '97 or something. When everyone had to clear the highway to prevent injury and death.

Though I am fearful for our safety and for the safety of others, I say, "Sure," because I know this is what Ian wants, and we trade places and I get behind the wheel.

He gives me few instructions beforehand. My only guidelines involve a lot of hand waving and cursing. All I can say for my efforts was that I managed to get the car to the gas station in one piece.

"I'll show you which type of gas to get. Not that unleaded stuff," he orders. "Only the best for my Miata."

I do all this to try to please him, hoping that he won't yell at me again. It's a sad way, conformity. I neglect my own wants and desires in favor of his passions and pursuits.

But after I cry, he relents, and guiltily allows me to pick an attraction of my choosing. "Want to go up to the graveyard?" I ask, a macabre choice.

"Yeah, why not?" he says.

Driving to the graveyard affords me more practice driving Ian's car. I'm almost driving down the center of the paved line, straddling it. The vehicle feels bulkier than my own, even though it's smaller, and the steering wheel feels stiff and turns slowly, so it's harder to control. *Maybe the extra weight is the lawn ornaments I snagged that are now stuck under the grill*, I think. I do not despair, however. Ian is a talented mechanic so I know if anything goes wrong with the car, he'll be able to fix it. Some guys work in offices and are better at pushing papers than at spatial matters. That is not Ian. The way his brain is wired is very masculine and direct. He's great at problem-solving and critical thinking. There's probably an engine-oriented map permanently etched into some part of his noggin. The Miata was an old 1991 model, but Ian replaced the engine completely using his own two hands, guided by the help of YouTube videos and black-market parts salesmen.

We arrive safely at the graveyard, despite the fact that I was the one behind the wheel. There isn't a lawn to this cemetery. Tombstones are wedged in desert gravel. I hear the wind whistle and watch tumbleweeds roll past the graves, like a scene from some old- time western.

We read off a few headstone engravings. Names, dates, causes of death.

"This is morbid," Ian says, shivering. "Let's go."

I wanted to be with the sort of guy who was into thinking deep thoughts and discussing deep topics. Basically, I wanted to be with the sort of guy who would be comfortable hanging out in a graveyard long enough to think and reflect there, commenting on how quickly time passes, so we had better enjoy it while we're alive. That wasn't Ian. It was a matter of taste. Dropping in on old friends was his idea of fun, not visiting graveyards. Once again, I forsake my own wants, trying to compromise. But I can't force him to stay somewhere he doesn't want to.

Mentioning the time, he says he has one last set of friends to visit. Ian has kept in touch with these people for years as well, despite their lower-class socioeconomic status. His station in life wasn't much higher. But I know that his is not as low as theirs, when I see where they live. I *know* their house will be incredibly dirty by the looks of their lawn. The interior will match the exterior. Junk, old car parts and broken, castoff toys litter the weedy, untrimmed lawn. A sunken couch sits on their porch, its springs and stuffing exposed. When they let us in, I see it looks like hoarders live here. It's as if they've saved every item they've ever owned and every last piece of garbage, too. As if they've saved every McDonald's receipt, every gum wrapper... His friends, husband and wife, are wearing matching wife-beater tanks and cutoffs. They smoke and talk about how the Department of Child and Family Services, DCFS, took their kids away. *Well, no wonder*, I think. *In this unsanitary environment… I bet the kids are better off now, wherever they are…*

This house is too emotionally charged even for Ian. Their saccharine self-pity is misdirected. They lost the children due to their own disorder and slovenliness but refuse to acknowledge this. They hold others accountable.

After listening to a litany of complaints about the state of the world and everything in it, Ian turns to me and whispers that it's time to go. Nearly everything that came out of their mouth in those fifteen minutes was negative, and I can tell it's bringing him down.

"Nice visiting with you guys. I hope everything goes better for you," Ian says, shutting the door behind him before they can protest. "I don't want to stick around and hear their sob stories," he whispers softly to me.

Those people gave me the creeps and make me feel like I need a large bottle of hand sanitizer after visiting their home. But Ian refuses to forget a friend, no matter how hard off they are. A friend of Ian's is a lifelong one. That doesn't mean he wants to share their misery or take on their problems, however.

It's still snowing, but we can't avoid going home any longer; we must go back to our respective residences. There are bills to pay, jobs to work. On the return trip, Ian drives, and I am relieved that he has taken back his car and delivered me from responsibility for his property. Together we see the remnants of a terrible highway accident. The sight is a gore-fest. I am shocked by the metal and carnage, but Ian giggles, delighted at the sight of such a fantastic wreck. His ghoulish glee horrifies me. And Ian had called *me* morbid at the graveyard earlier. After much introspection, I realize it was me as a person that Ian was objecting to, and not my preferences. He probably enjoys dark nights and cemeteries, a thrill and a ghost tale, as much as I do. And he likes *real life* ghost stories more than I do. Much more. Ian snaps photos of the wreck from the driver's seat on his cell phone, acting like an ambulance-chasing rubbernecker.

A Ford Explorer had burst through the metal barrier, completely wrapping itself around it in a 'U' shape, bent in half around the median.

"Gruesome," I say. There isn't a single police cruiser in sight, but we don't see anyone in the Ford Explorer, if there is anything left of them. The car is a total loss and has been abandoned. There is no visible person left behind in need of rescue.

Ian is so awed by the wreck, he calls his brother to tell him about the whopper of an accident he just saw. It's like the accident gave him a rush, a high. I like Ian's brother Robert. I think he is a good influence. Robert is older, more mature, and more responsible than little brother Ian—he has a wife and kids and a stable job as a computer repairman. Robert doesn't smoke marijuana like Ian does—those wild days are long gone for him.

"Marijuana makes you slow," Robert says. Predictably, Robert's reaction to the accident is more conventional than Ian's. Robert doesn't seem to think the accident is hilarious in any sort of way.

Ian sloughs off the reaction, hangs up, and keeps driving. Robert didn't share his enthusiasm, so he changes the subject. "I love winter. It's my favorite season. I'm so glad it's here, aren't you?" he says when he pulls into the parking lot of my apartment.

I nod. "Sure, Christmas will be here soon."

He makes it sound as if he'll be seeing more of me this winter. Do I want to see more of him? We have had a fun and memorable vacation together, minus his mercurial explosions. Cordially, Ian helps me retrieve my suitcase from the trunk and then walks around the car to kiss me. His soft kisses obliterate any competing thoughts of not seeing him again which exist in my brain.

"Sweetheart, don't forget to call me," he says, and drives off with a content half-smile lingering on his face.

The vacation over, it is back to the working world for me. I had signed up for a temp service and was working for a telemarketing company. I hadn't taken any medication since leaving the hospital a year ago, but miraculously found myself still able to function at my job. When I did try the pills, briefly, my work performance was dismal. The pills clouded my thoughts and caused me to make lots of errors on customers' orders, garnering reprimands from my boss.

"I miss you; I'm sad you're not here," says Ian, when he calls me at work. I fall in love with him then, all over again, over the phone, when he says he misses me.

While making dull and repetitive sales calls, I dream of him. And when salesmen stop by my cubicle to flirt and to invite me places, I hardly notice that they exist, so steadfast am I in clinging to my status as a taken woman and attempting to honor my relationship with Ian. I do, however, seek female friendship. I meet another saleswoman there and we become friends. We are still friends to this day, many years later.

The age difference doesn't deter us. I am in my twenties and she's middle-aged, about fifty, and her name is Ellie. She is sophisticated and handsome with a large misshapen beak for a nose. She couldn't be called pretty, but she knows how to groom and accessorize, which lends her an air of glamour which gives her the illusion of beauty. She gets her nails done at the salon regularly, and her hair is curled under and stylish brown with carefully placed honey highlights. She looks like a competent business woman. Ellie has an exotic background. She is Ghanaian. Her family is originally Jewish and from Israel, but they moved to Africa during World War

II. She's a rare leopard, a white lady from Africa. Her diction sounds faintly British and she drops the R's in words in an inflection that sounds oddly like Barbara Walter's. English is, after all, the official language of Ghana, a holdover from its colonial past.

"Great bag," she says. It is our first conversation.

"This old thing? Oh, yes," I say, modestly trying to downplay its attractiveness. I carry a black tote bag with hot pink lips printed on it.

"Could you help me with the sales software?"

I teach her, patiently going over the steps to take in order for it to operate correctly. She doesn't get it, but doesn't think that not understanding how to work the sales software at her *sales* job is concerning. We're a good match because she doesn't worry much and I worry a lot, and her easygoingness counteracts my nervousness. She just assumes that she will understand the software eventually, and leaves it at that. There is no place for rumination in her life—she is too busy living it.

CHAPTER 32

Life at the Law Firm

There are periods when I leave the safety and comfort of temp agency jobs for contractual gigs. My catering job for the temp agency would last two-and-a-half years on and off. I find a contractual job in a downtown law firm. It is the city's oldest, most established firm and one of its most prestigious, established in 1875.

I fancy myself an urban career girl now. The firm's lawyers pretend I don't exist. My position in life is way beneath theirs, so I don't matter to them. The firm itself may be prestigious, but I am not a benefactor of its prestige. After all, I'm not even a lowly paralegal or a law clerk. I'm known as a copy runner and I do all the firm's grunt work, pushing a paper and supply cart. My warehouse office is in the basement, out of sight and out of mind. If the lawyers and paralegals run out of supplies, I'm supposed to conduct inventory control, to mark down how many of what item they need, to order more and then redistribute them. I am the one who provides the paper used to write all those vitriolic, hateful legal briefs. Due to my low status at the firm, I am an easy target, an easy scapegoat. If something goes wrong, the copy runner is blamed. One lawyer even accuses me of having lost his papers, notes on an important case.

"I can't find them anywhere!" he fumes. He then proceeds to

yell at his secretary, "*You* lost them, didn't you?" as he points a finger at her.

The secretary shakes her blonde bob meekly, "No, not me, sir, I haven't seen them," and then shrinks back into her swivel chair and stares at her computer screen, chagrined after having been chastised. The accusatory lawyer is a tyrant. He would later find his papers sitting on his chair at his desk, where he'd accidentally been sitting on them. I wonder if he was ashamed when he sat down, after hearing a crunch and realizing he'd been sitting on them all along.

The secretary who has been demeaned is named Heidi. She has a cautious approach toward life and seems submissive and shy at first, but she has a nice smile and a sunny sense of humor. Heidi has a streaky manicure and highlights. Such upkeep and maintenance seem mandatory for professionals in this city. With her blonde hair, cheerful demeanor, and shy smile, Heidi reminds me of a fragile sunflower. She looks up shyly under feathered blonde bangs. I later find out she has been through a lot of traumatic experiences. She was adopted, then abused, though I'm not sure if she was adopted for the sole purpose of abusing. Heidi says her dad chained her to the washing machine as a child, then left her there to enjoy the rinse cycle.

With her strategic position in reception, Heidi always knows the juiciest tidbits of law firm gossip. The large firm has one hundred employees, but it is really a small, close-knit world when it comes to gossip. Word travels fast, as the paralegals' desks are arranged in a semi-circle on each floor. They can each lean over and spread the word around the office like wildfire. There are no secrets.

"Oh, So-and-So went skiing this weekend and broke his leg" or "Did you know that So-and-So started dating So-and-So?" Heidi would say, as she peppers me with bits of law firm gossip while I restock her paper tray. For someone so humble and shy, she does enjoy gossip. But what else is there to do when the phones aren't ringing?

There aren't many inter-office romances to gossip about though, because of low ratios for potential mates. Out of one hundred lawyers, ninety-nine of them are men and most of them are married. There are quite a few lawyer-and-secretary romances though, and Heidi seems to know the details of all of them. In the paper room it is all testosterone, too; for eight months I'm the only girl until they eventually hire one more.

Nancy works in the firm's hospitality department and she's also a friend of Heidi's. The firm is so large, it has to serve as a veritable hotel to meet the needs of the lawyers, who work such long hours that they occasionally fall sleep in their offices. There's even a gym downstairs and periodically spaced breakfast nooks and coffee stations on each floor. Someone has to refresh each of these stations to ensure that the firm is a comfortable, well-stocked place you could almost live in. A place where you can get also get a bite to eat while working on a long case. But God forbid Nancy should forget the morning coffee. The attorneys would go on the caffeine fritz. Nancy's job duties include folding napkins, counting spoons, the daily delivery of fresh food, beverages, cups, and plates to each floor, and restocking the breakfast nooks according to supply and demand. This is why Nancy is a vital part of the firm's team. She's been there for years, so she gets her own desk and wears a silver nametag reading: *Nancy, Hospitality Services*. I don't get a nametag or a desk. My office, if you could call it that, is really just a storage unit and a place where I can be found if needed, a warehouse where all the office supplies are kept. Nancy's desk is included in the paralegals' semi-circles. She's one of them, an accepted member of their clique. She's also in a strategic location where she can soak up gossip. Nancy pushes a silver cart piled high with treats down the halls of the firm, which is why everyone's always glad to see her and I'm just someone they call when their printer jams, after they've already made several frustrated attempts to fix it while letting out expletives.

Nancy seems to know even juicier pieces of gossip than Heidi somehow, and her mind is much naughtier. Nancy has a saucy streak for sure, and a talent for embellishing stories. She isn't afraid to be edgy, to act younger than she is. Nancy is a fifty-one-year-old cougar dating Stan, who is just thirty-two. When I was introduced to Stan, I just plain didn't like him at first sight. He looked gaudy and tasteless to me, wearing loud print shirts that displayed his plentiful chest hair, and tight leather pants. Stan also spoke too loudly and slurred his words when he drank. Then again, I only had eyes for Ian, so others never measured up. Not that Stan ever came close to meeting my requirements, the first one being a good appearance.

Stan must have tired of dating Nancy, someone nearly his mother's age, so he seemed to latch on to me. He seemed to think I was free and available, which of course I wasn't. At no point had I given him any sort of indication that I reciprocated his feelings. He was a bum, in my opinion. Nancy allowed Stan to live in her apartment rent-free. His excuse was that he was going through a painful divorce and didn't have the money to pay child support. I thought that Nancy was way too lenient. She cheerfully tolerated this unconventional living arrangement in a simple exchange for Stan's youthful company. Stan was a kept man. He was her boy-toy, ready at her disposal, dependent on Nancy.

I soon found out how much Stan liked me when Nancy invited me to her apartment to play cards with them. It wasn't the best of nights to try to find an address for the first time. It was late and mid-winter and snowing hard. Clearly, they weren't considering the weather when they first extended the invitation. And neither was I overly concerned with safety, since I had been promising Nancy at work that I'd come visit for weeks now and didn't want to renege. I would never tell any of my friends about my checkered past, or think of chickening out because I had a poor night's sleep. Full steam ahead was my motto.

The snow was so thick my visibility was nonexistent. My view consisted of one long, white blur. I had to unroll the window and stick my head out in order to be able to see anything at all. Suddenly, a roadside iceberg that seemed to emerge out of nowhere ripped a hole in my tire. I could hear hissing and then a loud thump. I almost gave up and went home, but I didn't. I was bound and determined. Driving on a lumpy, lopsided tire was a horrible way to arrive at a party, but I knew I didn't have much further to go before I could find safety and relief from the cold. I showed up late, just in time to see Stan and Nancy making snow angels on the lawn, both waving their arms to achieve artistic perfection. Already Nancy seemed a bit tipsy and Stan seemed positively goofy, and was slurring his words. Later I'd count the total number of beers he'd consumed at fourteen within a short period of time. I was surprised he was still conscious; that sounded like a lot to me. I was sure their snow angels would come out with horns on top of them instead of halos, knowing Stan and Nancy. I figured I'd worry about the tire later when the weather calmed down.

"Come join us!" said Stan. He looked delighted that I'd arrived, and grabbed me by the back of my neck, dunking my head into the cold powdery snow. I stood and shivered, shaking the snow off me.

"I'll get you back!" I yelled at him, incensed.

"Get me back at a game of cards." Stan and Nancy both laughed and led me inside.

But soon Stan's game of cards became a game of *strip poker*. "I can't play strip poker," I said. I was in a dutiful relationship with Ian. I loved Ian, even if he was mercurial and temperamental. *I should leave*, I thought. How could I think of betraying Ian by playing strip poker with Stan and Nancy?

Thinking quickly, I managed to switch the game to *beer poker*, scrapping Stan's whole strip poker idea. Stan reluctantly agreed to the change of rules. "Okay. If you lose, you take a sip," he said, probably hoping to get me drunk and incapacitated.

I managed to become really adept at the game of cards just then. I became an expert in no time flat. I had no intention of getting wasted with Stan.

Mostly, it was Stan and Nancy who ended up losing and taking sips. They were really tossing back the cans. I felt uncomfortable due to the attention Stan was paying me, and I could tell that Nancy felt uncomfortable as well. I didn't intend it to be this way. She had been so insistent at work that I visit. I wondered if Stan had pressured her to invite me. He was obviously flirting as he tickled me under the chin with his deck of cards and coaxed me to take a sip. Nancy suddenly draped her leg possessively over Stan's.

"Get *off*, Nancy!" he said rudely. "Go get me some more beer!" The incident seemed to sum up their whole relationship and the balance of power between them.

When she disappeared to the 7-Eleven next door, he was more candid. "I love Nancy but I'm not *in love* with her," he said. Then, tossing down his cards, "You lost and you've got to kiss me!"

"No, Stan, those are *not* the rules of the game!" I reminded him.

Nancy reappeared with the beer as if Stan had her on a leash and buzzer system. One thing about young boy-toys and middle-aged women, you knew who had the upper hand.

After the card game I was ready to leave, having outsmarted Stan. This hadn't been hard to accomplish, as he was pretty wasted. Unfortunately, there were blizzard warnings, and the snow showed no signs of stopping. Also, with a flat tire I'd be risking my life to drive in the snow. Circumstances as they were, I was forced to crash at Nancy's.

The next day, Ian rescued me by doing the nicest thing he could have done. I was touched by the gesture because it demonstrated that he cared. He helped me change my tire. He was a mechanic and could have done it blindfolded, of course.

Weeks passed before I spoke to Nancy again, having felt uncomfortable after the whole Card Night Incident. Then she told me she was holding a ladies' night at her apartment. I agreed to go only when I was reassured that Stan would *definitely not* be there and that it would indeed be ladies *only*. I wouldn't have gone had he been there. Nancy extended the invitation to all of the paralegals and secretaries at the firm. I wanted to fit in with my colleagues, worrying that I'd be the odd one out if I didn't attend, and then become the subject of office gossip. When I arrived at Nancy's apartment, I was relieved to see that Stan was nowhere in sight. But as usual, Nancy hadn't told me the whole story. She told me she'd be holding a small soirée with refreshments. I knew how hospitable Nancy was at the law firm. Refreshments were her area of expertise. But Nancy hadn't mentioned that the soirée was to perpetuate a pyramid marketing scheme. Nor that the products available for demonstration and sale were sex toys. Apparently, one of the paralegals worked for a company which sold sex toys through a catalogue. She was eager to sell the products to her coworkers to rid herself of the starter kit she had purchased from the company for several hundred dollars.

I am shocked and embarrassed to see women who were usually office conservative on Mondays, in their tight buns, navy pencil skirts, and tightly buttoned shirts, letting their hair down and dressed in casual wear in Nancy's apartment. The paralegal who worked for the multi-level marketing company, the instigator, is holding up a sample toy, demonstrating its functions. There is a lot of giggling and blushing involved during the toy demonstrations.

The paralegal presses buttons and pulls out creams and lotions. She's a large woman with three chins and the thought of her having sex in the first place grosses me out. Somehow I can't imagine her doing it without smothering her partner, suffocating him. She passes the toys around the room for everyone to look at. I'm freaked out by the whole thing, but I giggle over the pink plastic penises like the others. It seems the right thing to do.

The party goes too far for me when the heavy-set paralegal asks us to excuse ourselves to test out the products on ourselves so we can see how well they work. *Yuck*, I think. I glance at the snack bar, at the cubes of cheese, at the chips and dip, and the diced vegetables. The thought of these women testing out sex toys in the bathroom and then plunging their fingers into the bowls of dip makes me want to puke. *Gross*. I avoid the snack bar for the rest of the night, refusing to eat. I also refuse to try out the products. It's too awkward, not at someone else's place, with others present. I work with these women after all, and whatever occurs here, I will have to live down. To make matters worse, some of the products are masochistic and scary—like whips and bondage chains. I feel obligated to buy something, though, and crave social acceptance. I play it safe and buy a discreet heart-shaped back massager which is advertised as a pain reliever that administers heat to the muscles. The heavy-set paralegal smiles, happy that I've chosen to buy a product. *They should really pay paralegals more if they are forced to start a sex toy business on the side to pay the bills*, I thought.

The law firm is preparing for its annual Christmas party. Nancy, in hospitality, prints up fancy engraved invitations. Just one year ago, I was attending the hospital's Christmas party. No one at work knows this fact, and I'd like to keep it that way. I would experience prejudice, could maybe even lose my job. My survival depends on concealing my past, sadly, despite these modern times. The firm's holiday party will be much better than the hospital's. My attendance will be voluntary this time. The event seems so formal, I realize, as I finger my glossy invitation. A black-tie gala. R.S.V.P. confirmations are required. I feel I should go because my boss from the paper supply department is going and his band is going to be playing. He's only mentioned this fact to us about twenty times. I never knew he was in a band. He seemed so staid and conservative.

The party is held in a fancy dining hall on top of the city, with glass windows on all sides and a view of the urban skyline. The décor is red velvet with white trim. I don't know whom to sit by due to a lack of showing from my peers in the paper department—a complete absence of representation that disappoints me, especially after our boss so strongly encouraged us to attend. The only people left to sit with are lawyers I don't like, including the one who accused me of losing his papers. *Wait, no, there's the new boy in the paper department.* He arrives late, and heads straight for the desert bar. I attempt to strike up a conversation with him.

"Oh, hi... Love the éclairs," he says.

"Oh, yeah, they're good," I say.

"Great band," he says. Our boss is on stage. Based on eye contact, they don't seem to be stirring up much excitement from the crowd. The delicious food upstages them as people block out all thoughts but those of satisfying their hunger. I finish eating and leave the party long before it's over.

I leave the law firm after working there for nine months, a record for me with my sparse job history. It remains one of the best jobs I've ever had. I would have continued to work there longer, but I had signed a nine month contract and preferred to work temp jobs for their variety and ease of obtainment.

CHAPTER 33

A Glimpse at Canadian Socialism

Once again I found my next job through the temp agency, trying on occupations and identities like hats. With my new job, I immediately dropped from white collar to blue collar status. I find work at a U.S./Canadian transnational RV rental company.

During this period, I decided to briefly take psychiatric medications for a few weeks. It would lead to some erratic behavior, as I was prescribed addictive benzodiazepines. It had been deeply ingrained in me at the hospital that I would never be well again and that I would need medication for the rest of my life. So during periods of doubt, I would resume taking them. I suspected mind-altering psychiatric drugs made me worse and clouded my judgment, but I wanted to find out for myself. It was only a few days before I built up a tolerance to the drugs and needed to increase my dose. If I didn't take the drugs, I felt sick and shaky. And it was only a few weeks after taking the benzodiazepines before the damage to my life was done and I became addicted to them.

The manners here at the RV rental company were worse than they had been at the law firm. People were meaner, possibly because they got paid less. The casual, blue collar atmosphere at the RV rental shop was kind of nice, though, because you could let your guard down. I let my guard *way down*, getting loose as a goose and dosing myself with Xanax when I felt like it. My coworkers preferred to roll joints instead. The Xanax led me to doze off at odd times at work, at which I'd try to snap back to attention, and it probably made me seem stoned. My coworkers didn't notice; they were stoned too. The difference was that my drug was legally prescribed. They laughed more than the white-collar types I used to associate with, because they were less afraid of being politically correct. They played more practical jokes because the work was boring and we had to pass the time somehow.

At the end of the summer, I got tired of cleaning out those RVs in the one-hundred-degree heat and took the opportunity to head on up to Canada myself, although not in one of their vehicles. I was curious after tourist reviews. As one of my job duties, I was allowed to drive the twenty-foot vehicles, albeit around the parking lot. I backed them up, honking the horn for fair warning. The job paid the bills and that was my sole evaluation of it. The Mexican manager hit on me, making suggestive comments as he sprayed down the RVs. Trying to win me over, he employed cheesy one-liners, called me "princess," and gave me special privileges, like letting me take more frequent breaks than the others and allowing me to chill out in the RVs with the air conditioning on full blast.

In order to pay my room and board in Canada, I decided to volunteer. My room would then be provided by the worksite, which would also include meals, as long as I contributed. I will be volunteering at a Canadian nursing home. I would witness how the Canucks treat their elderly. So what if I had to tour Canada during my off-hours from work, instead of being on a sightseeing leisure trip purely for pleasure?

My enthusiasm for Canada dampened immediately upon arriving at Vancouver International Airport. Instead of something like a Canadian version of the Statue of Liberty greeting me with open arms (which would have been too much to ask for as an American), I was faced with suspicion and hostility. This was in the post 9/11 era and security was tight. The navy-blue-clad baggage handler told me to leave my luggage on a cart and to come with him. But the bags weren't placed on a conveyer belt or sent through any high- tech electronic equipment. There my bags sat, on a cart in the center of the room, easily accessible to passersby. At one point the baggage handlers went over to the airline desk, abandoning my luggage completely, where anyone could have tampered with the contents. The gloved baggage handlers dumped out my underwear and pawed through my clothing piece by piece, searching for contraband. I wondered if they had found my bottles of benzodiazepines. I wondered what the reason for my lengthy detainment was. The baggage handlers glared at me. *Stupid American smuggler*, I can tell they are thinking.

I wasn't prepared for an interrogation, but that is what happened next. The baggage handler gave me a suspicious look, with a raised eyebrow. "Why would you come to *Canada* just to volunteer?" he asked. "To *Canada,* just to *volunteer*?"

As if visiting his country was the most outrageous thing he had ever heard of. Then he asked me to provide him with my contact info. I was to write down the name and address of the nursing home where I would be volunteering. I had become a person of interest.

He read the name off and asked if what I had written was true.

"Yes, that's true," I said, confused.

He raised an eyebrow again, and shook his head as if I was crazy for wanting to visit the frozen Arctic, instead of British Columbia, which is Coastal Pacific Canada. "Just a minute, please wait here for your bags."

Told to step aside, I heard a barely concealed heated argument going on behind the closed door where the baggage handlers had gone. I felt like I was getting the American runaround and being held back. It was half an hour before they would surrender my bags, and I hadn't brought anything with me but my clothes, passport, and ID. Oh, and a few bottles of benzodiazepines...No big deal, right? But by then I'd had the chance to chat with some nice Australian students, admiring their accents and asking them questions about their homeland. At last my luggage was returned to me.

Vancouver was a multicultural city if there ever was one. One glance into a crowd there was like looking at the attendees of a UN convention. But the cab service left much to be desired. You could wait stranded for an hour or more before being picked up. The Pakistani cab driver who finally pulled up confided that traveling by cab in Vancouver was a less efficient method of travel than traveling by boat and ferry, and that you could get to your destination faster here by sea than by land. Vancouver's motto was, after all: "By Sea, Land, and Air We Prosper." But the cab driver told me to bank on the sea part of the saying. During the ride he also waxed sociopolitical and patriotic, having become a Canadian citizen himself. He talked about Canada being a nation of pacifists who prefer a lesser role on the world stage, leaving their powerful and more populous neighbor to the south as the world's babysitter. He spoke as if he was speaking for all Canadians, and knew their hearts and minds and as well as their consensus opinion. I thanked him for his insights as he stopped in front of the nursing home, neither denying nor agreeing with anything he said, but simply listening. I fumbled for the unfamiliar denominations in my pocket, money I had exchanged at the airport after talking with the Australian girls at the baggage claim. I pulled out a couple of loonies and toonies, the hilarious names Canadians use to refer to their currency, and paid him. Then I remembered that comedian Jim Carrey is from Canada. *How fitting*, I thought.

Upon arrival at the nursing home, I realize that this Canadian volunteer trip might be a little more than I bargained for, might require me to be tough and persevering and to cope or improvise with what I was given. I was shown to the volunteer quarters, and that was the first letdown. They were the size of a janitor's closet—and there were seven of us. So this was the way I would see Canada, from a cramped, dusty closet. I was certain that's exactly what the room had been before it was cleaned out. There was even a drain hole in the center of the floor. I could picture the spot where the mops and cleaning supplies had formerly been. A janitor-closet-sized room for *seven people*! There would be seven co-ed strangers from around the world sharing bunks. I could see that there wasn't any space for individual beds and they had to stack us on top of each other like sardines in order to save space. It seemed like a recipe for disaster, a setup for a reality TV show on house cooperation.

For the volunteers, there was a boy from Madrid, two American girls from San Francisco, a boy and a girl from China, a Slovenian girl, and myself. It was clear we would have to learn how to get along, especially in such limited space, as well as to overcome our cultural barriers. Observing the room, I noticed that the Spanish boy had left his underwear and jeans in a pile on the floor. He was shoving his suitcase under one of the bunks.

"Hi. I'm Diego. Welcome," he said, in a heavy accent.

"Hi. I'm Marilyn." I moved to shake his hand, then thought better of it after seeing the underwear on the ground near his bunk. Instead, I stuffed my hand in my pocket and nodded casually. Natalie, from San Francisco, loudly announced her name and place of origin, then reclined back on her bunk.

"THIS ROOM IS TOO SMALL," she said, practically yelling. She would always speak at top volume.

"I guess we'll have to make do," I said unconvincingly, and shrugged as I looked around the room.

Natalie was messy like Diego, which made the room seem even smaller and more constricting. A Cabbage Patch Kids bag with clothes tumbling out of it sat on her bed. A childish cartoon bag on someone who appeared to be in their mid-twenties? I shuddered inwardly. Sadie was the other American girl. She had come here with Natalie; they were college friends back in San Francisco. Natalie was studying geriatric nursing and Sadie was studying special education. With their related fields, an old folks' home was the perfect place for them to learn more about their professions. I had nothing to gain from being crammed into a small closet, except the avoidance of homelessness and an introduction to Canada.

Sadie looked perpetually angry, with her eyebrows plucked downward. She scowled instead of smiling. She told us of her sophisticated origins, an affair that took place internationally, crossing several lines. Her mother was French and her father British, they met in a café in Paris—it was love at first sight. They decided they couldn't live without each other and went through the necessary cross-boundary red tape and customs paperwork so that they could be together, and had settled on San Francisco, an American city with a European flair. Sadie seemed reserved, the way a British girl might be. I couldn't detect any French influence. She didn't even smile after telling us about her parents' emotionally touching love story, one that defied all odds. I expected Sadie to burst into tears at any moment due to the expression she wore on her face, but she didn't. She simply continued wearing the grim look on her face.

The two San Franciscans asked where I was from, so I told them. Big mistake. They soon dismissed me as "that hick" from that "tiny little state," although I am an educated person with a bachelor's degree and I'm not into pig wrestling and fermenting moonshine. Those minor qualifying factors aside, I am also aware of world geography and current events. When they began inquiring about Donny and Marie and asking me if I had ever even seen a movie and did they even allow movies where I was from, because weren't they banned by the church—I knew that I was experiencing cultural discrimination.

Then the boy from Hong Kong, Hai, pulled out his laptop and started showing us a slideshow of his many vacation photos. There were photos of him in Dubai, London, Cairo, and Vienna. Canada was just the next stop on his list, the photos he took here just another souvenir, another part of his scrapbook. Interesting, but he didn't seem thrilled to be here, as if he'd already seen many more exciting places.

I saw that there was no way I could compete with these seasoned travelers in terms of experience. Those cosmopolitan, urbane kids had been sent by their parents to what essentially amounted to a day care for rich kids—that's what this nursing home was a substitute for, this Canadian worksite. I imagined that their parents thought it would build character and keep them occupied, rather than having them spend the summer working on their tans in Martinique. After they returned, they'd probably hit their country's version of a country club, maybe attend a charity function or a debutante ball and brag about their charitable actions. Their parents probably thought they were doing these Canadian geezers a huge favor by letting their precious children sacrifice so much of their precious time here, shining some publicity on the place. Except for the Spanish boy, their parents had all purchased their tickets for them. Diego had arrived a month earlier than the rest and had been working longer for his room and board. In the course of that month he had familiarized himself with Vancouver and knew its ins and outs, its best cafés and prime beach spots, and had memorized the festival schedules. I still wasn't sure what he was doing there, as his

English was halting and his vocabulary limited. But few of these fine young adults had had to scrub and scour RVs in baking one-hundred-degree weather to pay their way through good old-fashioned hard work. I tried not to let my resentment show. I knew I'd have to work on the nursing home floor with these people, to become one of them, to explore the city of Vancouver with them, and that we'd have to live in a closet-sized room together, which left little room for disagreements.

The Students (as I referred to them in my head) and I set out to see Vancouver that night, following Diego's recommendations since he knew the city best. The Students. I was the only one not currently enrolled in a university. I had already graduated, but was close enough to them in age at twenty-six to seem as if we belonged together as a cohesive peer group. As we strolled the streets that night, we dodged skunks and raccoons on every path. I couldn't believe how many furry creatures were out in the open. They would randomly scurry across our feet, furry black and white blurs. It was as if the woodland inhabitants had suddenly all decided to relocate to the city. Canadians didn't seem shocked as fuzzy, striped tails dodged past. They acted as if it was a common occurrence. Vancouver seemed to have a vermin problem. I'd never seen so many small mammals freely trotting down the street at home, just roadkill. Or maybe they didn't have a vermin problem; maybe Canadians were just more respectful of nature and let it take its natural course, allowing wildlife and humans to cohabitate. Maybe there wasn't a sharp dividing line between city and country here. And, as it was a sparsely populated country in the first place, perhaps there were few distinctions between. It was liberating to see so many animals roaming freely and made me feel that the rights of animals were well protected in Vancouver. I didn't want to think about the raccoon's final destinations, likely a backyard garbage bin, where they would engage in a rummage binge. The Slovenian girl, Darja, mistook a skunk for a small black and white bear and tried to run after it, giving the students a chuckle. I guessed that she hadn't seen many skunks in Slovenia.

The pub that we settled on was dark, like most bars, and had a wooden countertop with shiny liquor bottles gleaming behind it. The yellow overhead lights created reflective pools on the bar's surface. Its clientele was young; no one appeared over thirty-five. It looked like the sort of place where you could find steak and potatoes in addition to booze.

I chatted with Diego in semi-fluent Spanish and we laughed. Only by questioning him in Spanish did I find out what he was doing in Vancouver. His girlfriend was Canadian and he wanted to stay here to be near her. Actually, he had a couple of them. His love life seemed very complicated. We asked the waiter for his recommendations, searching for something quintessentially Canadian. "Try the Poutine," he said. The dish looked like a squat pile of mashed potatoes to me and I've never liked mashed potatoes, never mind fancily-decorated Canadian mashed potatoes, so I declined.

"Your Spanish is quite good," Natalie of Cabbage Patch Kids fame insisted, overhearing our conversation. "Well, actually, I really can't understand Spanish, but it seems as if you were able to speak fluently with Diego. You guys were just chatting away like you're the only two people in the room."

I smiled at her. "Thanks. Sorry, guys, I'll try to include you more. Don't want to be rude."

We returned to the tiny janitor's closet at the nursing home. It was odd falling asleep in a room with so many people in it. I jammed my headphones in my ears and stuck to an early bedtime, though the students stayed up late talking and crawling into bed at 2 A.M. after partying in the clubs all night. I didn't want to jeopardize my success by showing up late for my first day of volunteer work and desired a restful night's sleep. I swallowed a handful of benzos in anticipation of this. I slept a drugged, unnatural, fractured sleep that was not restorative.

The next day we were introduced to the nursing home director. She was young and elegantly dressed in modest, fashionable styles. We were also introduced to the activities director, who looked to be gay, with exaggerated mannerisms. I have no problem with gay people; I accept them completely and believe in equality, but this guy happened to be *both gay and a jerk*. And I *do* have a problem with jerks.

"Hi, everyone! I'm SSSteven. Oh, don't you look ssspecial..." lisped the activities director, with the odd mannerism of licking his pointed finger and raising it to the wind to emphasize what he was saying, despite a complete lack of a breeze indoors.

Steven would mock my hastily thrown-together current events group for the elderly residents. Truthfully, he had just cause to be unimpressed. I had a benzodiazepine drug hangover and I had hastily prepared myself for the group by glancing at a Canadian weekly tabloid. So I instead began talking about the real news of the summer, the birth of Prince George. Canada is a fitting place to hear such news, as the country is part of the commonwealth and George is set to be its new monarch one day. I thought Canada still had a British feel to it, a legacy of its past. They still drank tea every afternoon at the nursing home and from my wanderings around the city, I discovered polo matches being played on green fields, a sport I had never witnessed played before. *But hey, was it really my fault that I, newly arrived from the States, wasn't familiar with Canadian politics?* The nursing home director had given us a five-minute briefing of our duties, then announced that she was very busy and had to attend to the problem of one of the elderly residents being upset with his assigned roommate. The next day would be more regimented, she added.

At 6:30 A.M. our grueling work schedules mysteriously appeared on our bunks, placed there by an unseen hand (likely that of the nursing home director) while we slept. We were to follow them precisely. I had been assigned a floor and a list of elderly charges to care for. Diego was assigned my partner. But Diego overslept most mornings—whether out of a delayed adolescent body clock, depression, or homesickness. Diego resembled a Spanish prince, but he seemed lost in a foreign country. I watched his hygiene deteriorate. His breath smelled stale and his clothes were wrinkled. He was diametrically handsome and dirty at the same time. I had to prod and encourage him to get going each day, begging him to eat some cereal so that we could attend to our patients on the floor, just as Kyle had attended to me. I was the caretaker now, not the recipient of care. It felt good. Though we *were* fifteen minutes late each day (he must have been running on Madrid time), Diego and I hurried up the stairs to see our assigned patients on the third floor. We were required to care for their basic needs, to serve them coffee, to engage them in conversation, and to assist them in activities, games, and puzzles. Down in the common room, we'd lead the elderly residents through morning Jazzercise exercises, set to lively, energetic music. This was somewhat pathetic as some of them could barely lift a finger, they were so weak and frail. They halfheartedly attempted to make some sort of motion that counted as movement, perhaps a slow swirling of the wrist in time to the music—a blank look in their eyes. After that, the schedule said "lunch." These were no high-calorie, fatty, rich American lunches complete with a bag of chips and a brownie. The residents of the Canadian nursing home appeared to eat some variation of what looked like stringy reindeer meat, potatoes, and steamed vegetables every day.

My favorite patient was Shirley, who was blind, because of her resilience, which reminded me of Giancarlo. She had a pure and innocent quality about her. She was placed in the nursing home at a young age, just forty, probably because she'd been too much of a handful for her caretakers. The best part about Shirley was that, like Giancarlo, she had a fighting spirit. And Shirley was too true to herself to conceal the way she really felt and just conform socially. She bluntly stated what was on her mind, and exactly how she felt at the moment. Shirley was too real to pretend otherwise. She was too pure to feign cheerfulness for the benefit of others. I admired that unbending quality in her. Since she couldn't see, I could tell she felt often ignored as there were no visual cues for her to gather to measure if she was being paid attention.

If Shirley felt she had been stonewalled, she would loudly announce, "Well, I hate that old bitch anyway, Gladys. I didn't want to sit next to *her, anyway*. And Catherine's a bitch too. I didn't want to sit next to her, *either*." As a method of coping, Shirley would rather first be the scorner than the scorned. Shirley wore a mask of superiority to make up for years of hurt feelings. Despite turning her over to the nursing home, Shirley's relatives hadn't thrown her to the dogs. They left her with a reasonable monthly charge account for spending items: gum, chips, soda, bingo money, and toiletries.

I watched Steven pop open a can of ginger ale with his pointy, elongated fingernail, which had been painted fuchsia and had a press-on gem stuck to it. I heard the sound of ice tinkling in the bottom of a glass and a gaseous liquid being poured. I noticed that Steven insisted on Canada Dry to exclusivity, as if he was tooting the national horn. I also observed that the nurses allowed the elderly residents to have a glass of wine with their dinners if they wanted, a very liberal, humanistic approach. I thought of the possible interactions between the residents' medications with wine, but the Vancouverites ignored all this, putting pleasure and enjoyment above all. This was Canada, it was dark and cold. Let them have their wine.

The students and I ate what the residents ate and had to wait until they were finished eating before it was our turn. Oddly, the seven of us were given only a ten minute window in which to receive our food by the cafeteria cooks. We were scolded harshly or denied food if late, although we had paid them three hundred dollars each in volunteer fees. Some of the students had volunteered to learn medical policies and procedures. Here we were busting our butts and working for free, yet were treated badly by some of the staff. I couldn't believe it. Welcome to Socialist Work Camp 101. Small people will try to deny people privileges with what little power they have, I suppose. It must have given the cooks an ego boost to tell us no. Perhaps they were simply tired of slaving away at the stove and wanted to go home early.

One day, as I escorted Shirley to her room, her daughter called. She did not want to speak to Shirley, probably having underestimated her mother's capabilities, but to me. "How's mom?" she asked.

"She's fine. I'll let you talk to her if you'd like." I felt as if her daughter needed to acknowledge that her mother was a person too, with feelings.

I handed the phone to Shirley, who was very eager to speak to her daughter. "Janice, I'd like to get me a radio. I'd like to go buy a radio with knobs since I can't even see the other ones and it's a real pain to maneuver them," she said.

Poor Shirley existed in a near constant state of paranoia concerning her surroundings. I couldn't imagine what it would be like living in the dark all the time, suspecting the worst. Yet Shirley and developed a special rapport. She trusted me to be her eyes and allowed me to guide her. Maybe she liked the sound of my voice or that I didn't treat her like a baby like the others did. I was her own personal cheerleader, prodding her to achieve more, and setting the bar higher.

Shirley handed the phone back to me. Her daughter asked if I would take Shirley to complete her requested errands. She wanted me to take Shirley shopping to find a radio with knobs, easier for someone who was vision impaired to access. Shopping trips went above and beyond our call of duty. They were considered extra credit, but Shirley was my favorite patient, so of course I agreed. Shirley wanted to leave at once. She reached into her drawer, fumbling for her purse. She had a systematic way of placing her belongings so that she could find them by touch alone and was able to quickly find it. I wouldn't have dreamed of helping Shirley find the purse, lest she think I was taking advantage of her or that I wanted to control her money. Nor did I want to take away her dignity. Establishing trust with Shirley seemed especially important, considering her condition. Fingers scrambling, she rested her hand on the worn leather purse, then dumped it out and used sensory touch to identify the individual coins. I was impressed that she could tell their worth and amount just by the feel of them. It was one sense compensating for a lost sense.

Shirley did allow me to tie her shoelaces, and then we were off. Progress was slow, as Shirley was always afraid of falling and acted as if her environment was hostile—which, as unfamiliar as it was, must have been. I was new to the city myself and didn't know it well. Vancouver's streets followed complicated, winding old gold mining paths. That was the way the city was formed. It was a difficult city to navigate while sighted, never mind while blind. Shirley was so fearful, she would take only small baby steps. She asked me to constantly update our surroundings for her, as if I were a human GPS or a carrier pigeon.

"We're passing a sandwich shop now. There went a little white dog, that's what *that* was." I did my best to be her eyes and to explain things to her.

Shirley freaked out in the taxi cab. She waved her hands frantically in a state of panic. "Where are we going? Where are we going? Where are you *taking* me?"

"We're going to the store, Shirley, to get the radio," I tried to reassure her.

Unaware that she was blind, the Pakistani cab driver seemed annoyed. "Would you calm down, Lady?"

"Look, she's blind and she doesn't know where she's going," I explained. "Give her a break."

"Well, you didn't have to tell him *that*," Shirley said, embarrassed. "People don't have to make allowances for me."

"Sorry, I was just trying to help," I frowned, feeling insensitive.

The electronics store could only be reached by going up an escalator in a shopping mall, an especially arduous and frightening climb for Shirley. I made sure to never let go of her arm. Every unfamiliar sight seemed a possible threat and a potential panic instigator for her. I kept up a constant descriptive stream of our surroundings. As we finally got off the escalator, I made sure to introduce the objects we passed in the store to her and to let her feel them for herself. She even asked about the clerks and who they were, though we couldn't go around *feeling clerks*. It wasn't polite. If a passerby got too close, I warned her of their impending approach.

"Step, step, step," I'd warn, trying to make sure Shirley wasn't overwhelmed by the strange new environment. She wanted a very specific kind of radio that was hard to find, probably an antique.

I wished we had been able to find a Braille radio, but of course we didn't. After visiting many different stores (which was no easy task with Shirley in tow) and testing many different radios, I at last found a radio that she deemed acceptable. Then I managed to get us both back into the cab with the radio as well, in one piece. I pulled out a handful of loonies and toonies for the driver, unfamiliar with the currency and praying it would be enough. The two of us must have been a vulnerable pair. We were: a foreign American woman exploring new territory and a blind Canadian woman exploring territory that should have been familiar, but wasn't.

Back at the nursing home, Steven was organizing Happy Hour. Shirley had very specific seating requests, of course. Because her ears were her main sensory organ, she preferred that I not seat her next to anyone with a harsh-sounding voice. And when I sang during Choir Hour with her, I realized Shirley proved to have perfect pitch.

"Why, that's a C-flat," she identified, with only one ring of the bell.

But all was not well within the janitor's closet. I made a foolish error by not bothering to ingratiate myself with my roommates during our off-hours from the nursing home. Instead, I had spent most of my time with Shirley. I was, to put it mildly, cash poor, and their parents had paid for their tickets. I was someone to be looked down on and pitied and I lacked the resources to keep up with their outings. I failed to accompany the students on a trip to Vancouver Island. As a result, they had formed established cliques. As they went on ferry trips, I stayed in the city napping on my bunk in the janitor's closet. I failed to partake in the bonding ritual of drinking Wild Moose Canadian Whisky out of a bottle they kept in a paper bag in the sand on English Bay, where they attempted to tan—a somewhat unsuccessful activity in Canada. They thought me odd for wanting to swim in the cold-water bay, but I was accustomed to harsh winters and they had come from sunny California and tropical China. The Slovenian girl equated Canadian waters with polar ice caps and didn't want to swim, either. It's just bad politics not to accompany your volunteer corps roommates on their outings. But I really couldn't afford their expensive day tours and was consequently pushed out of their circle.

Diego appeared to have adapted to Canada well, accepting what it had to offer, particularly its Nordic beauties. He appeared to be running a male bordello and stud farm out of the janitor's closet. A Don Juan character, he would invite one girl over one night and a different one the next. I couldn't keep their names straight. He begged us not to tell the other girl about the "*other girls*."

One night Diego introduced us to his girlfriend Alex. The next night he brought over his other girlfriend Stephania, and began making out with her on his bunk.

The sharing of the small space that was the janitor's closet worked against the formation of a comradeship, and instead fostered competition for limited resources. The San Francisco girls were unforgiving. "So is Donny Osmond still real popular in Utah?" they mocked. And, "Do they even sell *beer* in *Mormon* Utah? Utah, what a hick state! I could never live without my tofu and wasabi pea soup, all organic, of course." Their stereotypes were false, of course, but I couldn't convince them of the truth. Then they would make 'mooing' sounds, mime cows, and giggle, leaving me feeling as if I'd just stepped in a giant vat of cow shit.

Things got worse. I awoke to find my cell phone "accidentally" broken one day.

"Oops," said Natalie, the special education student. "I think I dropped it."

I was furious. It was only a several-hundred-dollar phone. No big deal, right? I should have reported the incident to the nursing home director right away, but I have an intrinsic distrust of authority figures. Some part of me also wanted to believe that dropping the phone really had been an accident. *No one could be that evil, right*?

Sssteven was very picky with his free laborers and wanted to make sure we had culinary expertise. "No mixing ssstrawberry with vanilla. Don't let the flavors touch." Steven then licked his finger, hissed, and pointed it in the air as if to measure the direction of the wind, then tipped his finger downward in a dramatic gesture.

Forget washing the scoop, licking your fingers, that's real hygienic, I thought, as I stared at his manicured nails. Perhaps Steven's polished manicures gave him a fascination with his fingers. But that was why they hired him, right, because he was artsy and knew which flavors tasted good with which? Because he had an eye for matching patterns when the residents made crafts. However, Steven was the boss and I accepted his modus of operandi. What no one bothered to question was: If the ice cream was Neapolitan flavor and therefore already technically mixed, did it matter if we mixed the other flavors, which were chocolate and vanilla?

After accumulating quite a few losses, watching Steven lick his finger one too many times, and lamenting the loss of my phone, I decided to leave the nursing home. I was now without a means of communication, but thought I could find a pay phone. Clutching my broken device, I left the dormitory, a.k.a. Former Janitor's Closet, for greener pastures, giving up on the whole volunteer project. I felt a sense of relief at having done so.

Steven had never liked me (I couldn't get the flavors right) and did not bother to thank me for three weeks of volunteer service for the Canadian medical system, which amounted to a socialist work camp that only served reindeer meat. Nor did he apologize for the cramped seven-persons-to-a-room quarters. I shrugged, having collected another sample of the world's weirdness, and brushed it off.

Dragging my luggage with me, I now had to fend for myself in the city of Vancouver in the province of British Columbia. Vancouver has a laid back, West Coast vibe, as if what dwelt just beneath it, Washington, California and Oregon, had drifted northward and stuck. Vancouver is also one of the top film production centers in North America and is known as Hollywood North.

I was now free to explore one of the world's most liberal, multicultural and accepting cities. Rainbow flags were hung everywhere, the smell of marijuana plentiful. The day I left the nursing home, there was a pride festival going on that allowed gay people to apply for a permit from the city to streak naked for a day through Stanley Park. I'm not sure what such a gesture was supposed to accomplish. The removal of self-consciousness perhaps, or body equality awareness? But what if streaking naked only gave you a look at your own shortcomings when you observed that your own body failed to meet the physical fitness standards of others by comparison?

With my meager budget considerations, my new home was to be the Vancouver Salvation Army. A native woman, my new roommate, told me only that she was from "The Great White North" and that she knew native magic, as if she were some sort of character out of a Jack London book. Ironically, I *did* find a Jack London book on the shelf at "The Salv" and wondered if she had been reading it too much. Better to imagine yourself as an adventurous sled dog master, to hear the call of the wild, than to accept the reality of our situation. I saw a suspicious lot of Jack London's books in Canada. It seemed that Canadians were particularly proud of London as a symbolic national figure and remained thankful for the tourism he promoted, though he was actually American. I saw his books displayed everywhere. He was their national merchandise. I put back *Call of the Wild* because I had read it before, and picked up a biography of London. I was dismayed to find out he had been an abortionist. Canada was bursting all my bubbles. Not that I had many left, nor much innocence left to salvage.

My roommate talked about waving sticks and making smoke signals in some kind of spiritual ritual that she had performed "up North." Our room was unheated, even in this dark, northern country where heat should have been a basic requirement.

After visiting The Salv's library, which consisted of one shelf of mostly Jack London books, I then visited The Salv's damp, shared bathroom with its garish pink tile and showers left running. There I was accosted by a masculine-looking woman with beefy arms lined with tattoos who screamed, "Get your orientation straight!" The woman must have seen too many people streaking at the pride festival. She looked like a lumberjack in her ripped plaid shirt and workman's boots. *My* orientation straight? I wasn't the one who seemed confused. The manly-looking woman then plodded over to the couch and tuned the channel to a French-Canadian women's wrestling contest. It made sense. She seemed like the sort of person to spend time watching wrestling matches on TV. As the program was in French, I gratefully didn't understand a word of it.

Going back to my room with its bare linoleum floors, I quickly excused myself from the conversation with the native woman to lay down on my hard, lumpy bed with its scratchy blanket and its missing tooth-shaped nibble mark that looked as if a Canadian beaver had eaten a chunk out of it. The bed was harder than any bed I'd *ever* experienced in the States before, even in a thirty-dollar-a-night motel. It felt as if it had been made from burlap sacks stuffed with marbles.

The blonde French-Canadian woman across the hall seemed to have a kidney stone, which kept her awake all night and howling in pain. She was eventually transferred to my room. Just my luck. The howling French woman told me that Canadian hospitals had long waiting lists. I took her word for it. *Socialized medicine*, I thought. One could wait at the Salvation Army for a bed at St. Mary's while they also waited for a grave at the cemetery, whichever came first, she said, with the long wait lists.

She told me she had been born in a small village where they spoke only French and that English was her second language. Her howls of pain kept me up at night. I felt compassion for her, but there was nothing I could do except keep her company and try to converse with her to distract her from her misery. I was an American familiarizing myself with the world of the Canadian poor.

I managed to support myself in Canada by writing web articles for online customers on the website Fiverr.com. Not being a Canadian citizen, in this way I could support myself legally. Barely support myself. I was living on crumbs. Sometimes I would sell only a few articles a week, which paid five dollars each, like the website's namesake. This was an impractical way to live, of course, as a near penniless writer, but my only other alternative was starvation. The money took forever to clear and to transfer electronically to my bank account, so I would lord over my meager five dollar checks as if they were gold, budgeting my money down to the dime. Upon one of my trips to a dollar store to spend my thin, inadequate checks, a homeless Canadian beggar woman pulled me off the street to ask me for a toonie. I gave it to her because she was worse off than me, with mossy teeth and greasy hair. I gave it to her because she had a good sales approach and she asked nicely.

As I headed down the street bound for the store, she grabbed my arm, held it in hers and said, "Let's get you off the street first."

In other words, she was a beggar concerned for my welfare, or at least she knew how to tug at the heart strings and she didn't want me to get hit by a car as I handed her the money. Though some might have been disgusted and said, "Get back, you leper!" and inflicted moral judgments upon her, I realized I was a starving artist and that my station in life wasn't much higher than hers. And my current address was the Salvation Army. I also gave the woman a can of soda I'd purchased at the dollar store earlier, which was almost the last of my weekly food and beverage rations. I limited myself to one can a day.

"God bless you," she said when I gave it to her.

I felt accomplished after handing over the money and soda. I had made someone's life slightly less miserable, if only for a little while. I felt myself smile more that day and experienced a warm, glowing feeling. I continued to wander the winding streets of Vancouver, frequently losing my way on the city's hard to navigate streets. For six dollars, I also purchased a lock for my locker at The Salv. At five dollars an article, the relinquishing of the can was a huge sacrifice.

And then one day, karma in the flesh arrived on my scene. As I was walking back to the Salvation Army, a handsome ship's crewman (Vancouver was loaded with them, as it is a coastal city) asked me out. In the States it wasn't customary for me to be asked out directly on the street, but I thought that as a sailor often away at sea, he had long been without female attention and must have been desperate for feminine graces. It gets very cold in Canada, so I chalked up the forwardness of Canadian men to their primary need to have someone warm to curl up with, making friendships ever more vital here, due to the whole-body heat conservation issue. Or maybe the sailor was just so good looking and charismatic and had such high self-confidence that he assumed anyone he asked out would agree to have coffee with him. I was starving and recognized a free meal ticket when I saw one, though I reminded myself I would be considerate of his feelings whilst dining with him. This particular meal ticket was all wrapped up in a six-foot-two, blond, handsome package. His flaxen hair was cut in a Beatle's bowl cut, but did not look childish. He looked like Paul McCartney, minus the brunette part. He had a happy looking face if such a thing is possible (the soft angles of his face were emotional reserves) and dimples, and his blue eyes sparkled. He wore the official red and blue uniform of his cruise line with fancy white piping on the sides and starched white pants. He must have been about forty-one or forty-two, much older than me, but who was counting? He introduced himself as George as we walked along together. I was flattered that this handsome Canadian sailor picked me above all the other girls he could have eaten with, and immediately agreed. I was only agreeing to coffee and a bagel at a café at the Vancouver Public Library, *public* being the keyword. The idea seemed harmless. I was so hungry, that even the thought of a small meal like coffee and a bagel left me eagerly anticipating the treat. I had dressed nicely on a pauper's budget that day, as nicely as possible on the miniscule paychecks of a few-gigs- a-week writer. I even carried a new plastic purse, albeit from the dollar store. No doubt I was dollar store chic that day.

I've seen stranger trends. For example, runway models dress ostentatiously, in ostrich feathers and loud makeup, for emphasis, making art a fashion statement. And remember when clogs were popular? Once, my sister and I urgently needed jackets in a ritzy part of Manhattan because we underestimated the chilliness of a New York spring, yet realized we couldn't afford to buy jackets in the opulent shops. Instead we purchased fleece blankets to wrap ourselves in at a Manhattan K-Mart. It was then that a fashion photographer began following us, asking if this was some sort of new fad, the fleece blanket fad, as we giggled and ran away.

So carrying a plastic purse wasn't all that strange to me; it was better than carrying a plastic bag. I don't think that George asked me out as a matter of pity. I think that perhaps the peace sign emblem on my jacket in the shape of the American flag made me stand out from the crowd. Or maybe I looked slightly different and therefore more mysterious and exotic than the Canadian girls he was used to. Ian and I were not on speaking terms before I left for Canada, so I thought that no harm would come from grabbing coffee with George.

I gave George my phone number and then went back to The Salv to prepare for the date. To avoid the female lumberjack who lived there, I waited until she had finished in the shower and then went in. To dodge her odd questions about my orientation, I cautiously sidled into the bathroom sideways like a crab, making sure she was really, truly gone and not just hiding in a shower stall. I relaxed when I realized she'd left. I applied cheap, flaky dollar store makeup, which I normally don't use, and tried to look presentable. One of the faucets refused to shut off and dripped constantly, giving the room a dank, moldy feel as I spliced on congealed mascara and powdery glitter eyeshadow. I'm positive that men can't tell the difference between dollar store makeup and the top organic brands I normally used, and if they can, that it's probably not an issue as long as the finished product, "pretty," is what they get. When I was finished, I was more than poverty-level presentable. George and I met at the café as promised and ended up hitting it off; we ended up talking for three hours. He told me about his job working for the cruise line. We laughed lots, as we had similar senses of humor, cracking jokes about Canadian-American cultural confusion and the differences between the two countries. George answered my very basic, very naïve questions about Canada, and even gave me a photo he'd taken of a fan memorial site for Canadian-born *Glee* actor Corey Monteith, who'd just OD'd on heroin and alcohol the day before our date. Monteith died at the Vancouver Fairmont Pacific Rim Hotel. The photo depicted dozens of bouquets of flowers, gifts, and other fan mementos in a tribute to their idol. George's photo was a real fresh, current, of-the-moment, memorable, newsworthy photo—a real slice of journalism pie. I wanted to go to the memorial site to snap some of my own. Soon I would, having found the monument using George's directions. He promised to keep in contact when I got back to the States. George bought me coffee and a bagel at a time when I had little change to spare and truly needed it. I was an American trying to get by in a foreign country. I truly thought that George was karma personified—a reward for having given the homeless beggar woman a soda and some CAD.

CHAPTER 34

A Last Hoorah

After my trip to Canada, I began to taper my intake of benzodiazepines and immediately felt my head clear. My sleep became more restful and restorative, the quality of it less artificial. I had built up a tolerance to the drugs and eventually they stopped working. I thought back to the drug hangover I had experienced during Steven's current events group at the nursing home. After taking the benzodiazepines the night before, I had slurred my words while reading the paper and had eventually picked the most obvious headline, which was already common knowledge, to discuss—angering Steven. After much contemplation, I realized that the pills I was taking probably had a lot to do with my intoxicated performance during Steven's group, and my subsequent dismissal. I eventually stopped taking the addictive pills completely and soon stopped feeling spacey and hungover. The idea that I needed these pills to remain well warred with reality, as they seemed to make me dull and stupid. After stopping the drugs, no longer did I fear becoming a park pigeon lady, or feel the need to run off to foreign countries on a whim. My drug-fueled behavior evolved into a state of tame, clear-thinking calm. Taking the pills had been a flirtation with experimentation. I was curious to see if the pills were vital to my success or not. Turns out they weren't, and were even detrimental to it. Other than a few weeks of following my doctor's advice, I would not continue taking the pills and would remain well without them.

My Canadian volunteer adventure was now a fading memory. Life went on as usual for me. George and I *did* keep in contact for a while. He kept me entertained with his witty emails and his humor. Ian and I broke up. Previously, Ian had trouble establishing my identity and my place in his life. Occasionally he would introduce me as a girlfriend, but now I was "just a friend." And being "just a friend" wasn't enough for me. Our relationship eroded after the honeymoon period ended; after over a year together, we didn't have enough in common to keep the fire burning.

Though I indirectly distanced myself from him, Ian still continued to contact me occasionally. Passively, I hadn't exactly gone out of my way to eliminate all traces of him from my life, by changing my phone number or blocking *his* number. A few years later, Ian would be happily married to someone else about whom he felt no ambivalence, someone whose virtues he would champion. He would propose to her after knowing her for only two months, much less time than the year-plus I had spent with him without receiving a rock. Ian had always been critical of my looks and acted as if they were subpar. He reinforced my negative self-image with his comments. I had long, thick hair, and when I woke up it would be tangled and matted until I brushed it. Ian was hypercritical. He would refer to me as "Jungle Queen" on these mornings. I didn't have the self-esteem to dismiss the label, even though by the time I dressed for the day I looked presentable. In high school I had been teased about the glasses I wore and someone had called me "The Librarian." I didn't take the comment as a compliment on my intelligence. Looking at my mousey brown hair in the mirror, I believed them. So without question, I was sure that Ian was right. Ian's future wife had short, fine hair cut in a bob. In truth, she probably had a backbone, where I was permissive, which might have been more important than looks. She would become pregnant soon after their wedding. But before Ian married, we continued to go places together.

Ian once said he would take me to see a *Twilight* movie. He told me he would arrive at eight to pick me up, but didn't call with any sort of explanation for why he arrived at 10 P.M., hours later than the agreed-upon time. I didn't have enough confidence to stand my ground to ask where he'd been. I assumed I was ugly and deserving of such treatment. Pathetically, I had been sobbing on my bed, thinking that he wasn't coming after all, when he tardily breezed in to collect me without an excuse. The movie was an insufferable bore to him, but I liked the emotional, female-audience-targeted dark romance, and there was a song from the movie's soundtrack, Christina Perri's "A Thousand Years" that Ian did like. Aware that Ian took a circuitous route by my apartment to get home, one night I left the window open with my stereo blasting that song. I wasn't surprised when Ian asked if he could come up.

Ian was a very playful person with his spot-on impersonations and talent for mimicry. Once he decided to call me incognito, pretending to be one of his coworkers.

"Hey, Leo here. Can I come in?" he asked.

I played along with the game, but knew it was secretly Ian. I put on a stern voice and tried not to laugh as I spoke. "Well, if it's Leo, and not that Ian character that I despise, then I suppose you can come in."

In the parking lot of my apartment building, I witnessed Ian step out of his shiny black Miata with its convertible top. The car was flashy and sporty. It was the sort of car in which I could picture him driving away and leaving me. He would have no trouble finding a replacement girl behind the wheel of such a vehicle. It is my impression that to instinctively ensure the survival of their offspring, women can be superficial beings who often judge a man by the size of his wallet. Or by the shininess of his car. I was certain that women, as materialists, would fall for Ian easily when they saw him in that little black sports car.

"It is I, Leo," Ian coughed, under the streetlamp.

I pretended to be shocked when it was Ian and not Leo who stepped out of the vehicle.

"You don't *look* like Leo…" I said. Ian in no way resembled his coworker Leo, who had dark hair and a mustache.

"I *am* Leo!" Ian insisted in Leo's voice and then burst out laughing. "Look at me. Can't you tell? Hi, honey."

He wrapped me in his arms and kissed me. His lips were pillow soft and his chin was stubbly and scratchy and he tasted salty like the ocean and smelled strongly of cologne.

"I got you, didn't I? I tricked you," he laughed. "Sweetie, look at all this new stuff I installed in my car."

Ian was always showing me the latest features he'd added to his car. He went on to describe the new engine he'd put in with the aid of his stepdad, a retired Ford diesel mechanic. They'd looked up the parts together and it was the ultimate D.I.Y. project.

"Look at these new speakers." Ian turned on the stereo to demonstrate the new feature.

"That's great," I said, trying to sound enthused about cars and boys' toys.

Only when cars broke down and their glaring need for repair became obvious to me, or when they became inoperable, did I concern myself with them, considering them in existence only to transfer me from point A to point B. I maintained them regularly and then forgot about them, and they did not interest me.

When my car needed repairs, Ian was a very handy person to know, as a mechanic. I had a dented trunk and Ian told me he could find a discount one at a junk shop that matched mine exactly and that he would install it for much less than the usual shop rate, just for me, because I was a special customer as a personal friend. I'd be at work and Ian would call me to tell me of his diligent progress and his search for a trunk that was an exact match. He would tell me how he'd scoured every junkyard in the state because he didn't want to let me down. It was then that I thought he must love me in some absent sort of way, in his own way, to do this favor for me. He finally tracked down the right part in a city an hour away and then drove up there to get it. Ian and his stepdad worked on my car together on Ian's days off in their home garage.

I paid him generously to do this. I didn't know that Ian was scamming me. I thought that he was doing me a favor. He told me that he could get the job done cheaper because I wasn't just any customer, but it was all lies. When I looked up the market cost of the parts myself, I saw that Ian was charging me much more than the repair shop average and I had been foolish to trust him. Ian was scamming me in both life and love. He was stringing me along. Certainly someone who seemed so honest, someone who grew up in the same places I did could be trusted, I thought, foolishly. I was tricked into believing him, tricked by a handsome face and earnest-sounding words.

I remember the last time I saw Ian. He reappeared at Christmas that year, walking back into my life seamlessly, as if he had never left. I shouldn't have allowed him to. I was on a snowmobiling trip with my mom and siblings in rural Idaho when I received a text from him. We were staying in a tacky ski lodge with garish deer antlers and crimson eighties shag carpet. I considered "the return of Ian" an insufficient Christmas present. When he called, I thought that he was just calling to wish me a Merry Christmas and churning up old dirt. I told him we could talk when I got back.

I wasn't confident in my ability to maneuver such a large, expensive piece of equipment as a snowmobile that day. I thought I would hit a tree, and my sister wanted no part in riding with me because she thought I was being a sissy over taking the reins. My younger brother seems to have a soft spot for me. While my sister refused to allow me to ride with her, my brother allowed me to be passenger on his machine. My siblings and I drove snowmobiles for a good eight hours, until the daylight seeped away and our faces were ruddy, wind-burnt, scorched by ice crystals, and numb. The scenery flew by at top speeds, a blur of tall pines, aspens and open white expanses. We covered fifty miles on *snowmobiles* that day! We looked at the mileage gauge when we were done, which confirmed how far we had strayed. I can see covering fifty miles by car, but covering fifty miles by snowmobile is a remarkable feat. My limbs were numb, but I had never slept better due to physically exhausting myself during the day. I felt healthy, natural and vibrant, like a girl in a soap commercial.

Shortly after Christmas, Ian pulled up in a new car, not his prized Miata, but a Bronco. I'd later find out he chose the SUV because it went along with his plans for seating accommodation, which involved a lot of horizontal reclining. And me.

"Oh, sweetie, you look beautiful tonight," he said. I was wearing a brown suede coat and gloves, perfect for the holiday season.

I told him what I'd gotten for Christmas—a portable vintage record player. It was an item that had gone out of widespread use, a rarity, so I treasured it. Ian wanted to park someplace private, so we drove out to the reservoir. Later I'd learn it was the only reason he'd chosen the Bronco instead of the Miata. I had outgrown Ian by then and had matured. Actions that seemed hilarious when we were younger now seemed cheap and adolescent. My need for comfort and clean bedding came before my sense of adventure. I'd brought the record player with me, thinking he might enjoy listening to it.

"I don't know much about music," Ian said, staring absently at his hands as we briefly listened to a Barbara Mandrell record. We were listening to Mandrell's "Sleeping Single in a Double Bed," which was, ironically, the very item we were lacking. It was hard to find newer vinyl for cheap.

As the record turned, Ian told me about the promotion he'd received at work. He had been promoted to manager. He proudly showed me the new sweatshirt he had been given by his boss, which was emblazoned with the company's logo. The shirt was warm and soft as I pressed it to my face and breathed deep and it reminded me of an old green sweatshirt of his that he used to let me sleep in.

"Hey, hon, you're really moving up in the world!" I teased.

I wanted to talk, the way girls often do, to unburden myself and draw closer to him. Talking is a woman's attempt at intimacy. But as usual, Ian was more interested in the physical.

Staring at me intensely, he said, "I really feel like kissing you right now."

The headlights reflected blue on the snow as we looked out the windshield at the lake. We cuddled closely together inside the Bronco for warmth. We had sex and then he said wistfully, entwining my hand in his, "We fit nicely together. That's one thing we've always done right."

But it wasn't enough. There has to be something more, a deeper connection for two people to remain together. And for us there just wasn't. After he drove me home that night, I never saw Ian again. He simply disappeared, a vanishing act into thin air. A few months later I heard he had gotten married to someone who was so unlike me as to be my total opposite. I knew he would marry eventually. He seemed the matrimonial type with a steady job and strong family connections. But I just wasn't his cup of tea, and he wasn't mine.

CHAPTER 35

Some Kind of Love vs. Finding Self-Love

Working for the temp agency gave me the opportunity to work in a different place each night, never getting bored by my surroundings. I preferred working for the agency over utilizing my journalism degree because the jobs didn't require any mental legwork. I had a great fear of being fired—my biggest fear. I imagined disaster, bankruptcy, and homelessness resulting from my termination. Caring so much only made me more anxious and afraid of making the slightest blunder. I should have simply reminded myself that if fired, I would find another job, and repeated the assuring mantra to myself. Of course, self-employment and scheduling my own hours would have been the ideal situation, but that was not possible. The reason I feared getting fired so much was that I sometimes didn't sleep well and this led to performance anxiety. Tiredness and lack of sleep made me prone to error. I was phobic about sleep and these worries made me less likely to drift off. After losing sleep, I worried about getting fired in my impaired state. It was a vicious cycle. Though I had been bombarded with supposed cure-all drugs in the hospital, I had never been given therapy or any sort of analysis. I had never even been asked about my sleep habits or routine.

Being another uniformed worker, one of many who was not

expected to be in one place for long, relieved my anxiety because it allowed me to fade into the background. No one expected a temporary, contractual employee to make a lasting impression, nor to be particularly efficient. That's what the permanent employees were for, to instruct their subordinates. The jobs were a utilitarian means to an end. Open one instant, filled quickly. Mistakes were of little importance at work, then. Unless the mistakes were dramatically noticeable and majorly detrimental to the company, they went unpunished. Stealing and loafing were major sins, a lackadaisical attitude nothing new and commonplace—even expected. Operating under these assumptions and attempting to triumph over my fears, I began to work as a caterer for the temp agency. Though little value was placed on our jobs, of course I still wore the proper uniform—one of many rotating outfits and bow ties we had—tried not to drop any plates, and served guests promptly. There were no white chef's hats and creatively decorated cakes, nor aprons smeared with confectioner's sugar. The food was premade, created by someone with fancy European training—we simply served it. At least twice a week I'd see someone drop a stack of plates and hear the crash of broken porcelain, at which everyone would turn their heads, pausing to stop and stare or mutter their regrets and their expressions of pity for the dropper. I tried to never let it be me. I couldn't bear the shame and I'd wither under the fixed, concentrated group attention. I still struggled with insomnia, and sometimes I'd find my heart pounding as if it intended to beat through my chest. Lack of sleep also left me with a dry, hacking cough at times, as if my lungs hadn't completed their appropriate resting period, nor had the chance to regenerate. Those symptoms were my only noticeable, aberrant ones. But I found I could work around them, accepting assignments from the agency only when I was feeling well, simply not responding to them when I wasn't, and scheduling my own hours. In this way I resolved my insomnia with creative solutions. As the agency allowed us to search for a permanent position in our free time, not accepting every assignment and long periods of silence were fine with them. I couldn't imagine holding down a job with regular, set hours. Certainly holding down a desk job in journalism with its more traditional hours would have been unthinkable for me, as no matter how hard I tried, I was only able to fall asleep at around 3 A.M. I am a night owl to the core. I come alive in the dark, becoming functional only at dusk, working bartender's hours, a vampire's dream schedule. I am fit for the life of an artist.

I met Phil when I was sent to cater at the largest convention center in the state, the night that Train performed there. Of all the men I have ever loved in my entire life thus far, I would love Phil the most. Our relationship was forbidden from the start. He was my "captain," or in the catering world, the section supervisor. He became my captain both at work and at home. I would never sleep with someone to climb the catering career ladder. I didn't associate with Phil so that I could obtain upward mobility and get ahead at work—there wasn't much room to grow anyway in such a job.

As an added bonus, while I worked that night, I would get to catch the Train concert secondhand, by default. Catering *at* the Train concert wasn't as cool as catering *to* the band, of course. But I got to be present for the excitement of it all without being a paying guest; this way I got to skip out on the entrance fee and attend the concert gratis, even if this hadn't been intended and was just a pleasant side effect.

That night, despite being at the Train concert, my attention wasn't on lead singer Patrick Monahan or his music. My attention was on Phil. He fascinated me upon first sight, capturing my attention instantly with a flip of his long, blond ponytail from where he stood at the buffet table. This man was quite literally the handsomest man I had ever seen in my entire life, including all the movie stars I'd seen on-screen put together. He was worlds handsomer than Ian. Phil would make Ian look short and scrawny by comparison.

The concert night décor was straight out of an Ann Rice novel. The place resembled a Parisian vampire theatre draped in elegant black and red silk, the theme "Haunted Circus." The banquet hall was set with floating glow-in-the-dark snack bar islands, and circus performers on stilts in ghoulish clown makeup teetered through the crowd to entertain guests as part of the pre-concert event. Patrick Monahan made all the female caterers swoon as he sang "Drops of Jupiter." It was the perfect, dark, romantic Victorian setting in which to fall in love with someone.

And I would. Phil had a tan which contrasted nicely with his golden hair—he looked warm and inviting like a tropical summer—which was misleading, because he wasn't. I would later find out he had Portuguese blood on his mother's side and that his father was American and that he spoke a little Portuguese, badly. But having been born in the U.S., he was just another member of the melting pot we call America. Phil had the face and body of a Roman statue, with a full, sensuous mouth that often took on a bitter cast, as if he'd tasted sour apples when he was being sarcastic, which he often was. His mouth at rest was a perfectly formed rosebud and he had high, sculpted cheekbones which showed off his striking green eyes. I wanted to kiss that pliable, soft-looking mouth set in a strong, rather angular jaw. As I looked at him from across the room, my heart started to beat very fast and I felt my heated blood rush to my face. I seemed to be using up more oxygen than usual. I had to subtly gasp for breath, pretending that I was coughing to disguise my shallow breaths and to remain collected.

Both Phil's sarcasm and verbosity were legendary at work. "Don't ask Captain Phil for help, he'll go off on a tangent," was the refrain. We would rather figure out a work procedure ourselves than brave his wrath. He spoke in lengthy monologues and would often get into the history behind catering traditions like a college professor delivering a lecture, when his coworkers would have preferred a simple "yes" or "no" answer, especially while carrying a hot plate.

It was just that he was so much smarter than the people he worked with, and he had to deal with the inequality somehow, he would later state, not at all modestly. I found Phil to be a challenge. I thought him arrogant and wanted to break his ego and bring him down to earth. Phil was also a very curious person, I could tell, which made me want to set out bait and play girlish tricks on him. He was always reading books on science, religion and philosophy, trying to discover the meaning of life. I wanted to play curiosity-killed-the-cat sort of tricks on him, snaring him and entangling him in his own quest for wonder. I wanted to engage him in a cat-and-mouse game. I thought he'd probably be unable to help himself from investigating and wind up in my trap, had I tossed him a lead. And he would indeed fall for my ploys later, just as I suspected. After falling in love at first sight, I was already plotting deviously. Other men did not inspire the devilish gears in my head to begin turning. Phil, slightly devious himself, did. I wanted to capture Phil and prey on his vulnerability.

I saw that Phil had a single-minded, autistic focus. I saw that he lived in his own world and seemed unaware of others' discomfort, making him an easy target. He was an absent-minded professor. The complicated subjects he discussed were above his catering coworkers' heads, incomprehensible to them, but he kept trying to keep the explanations basic for the simpletons. His tone of voice would escalate and change pitch as he became more and more enthusiastic about the subject as his audience fell asleep, while he was unaware of their boredom. He had a very distinct and recognizable voice, high and clear for a man's without sounding feminine, a high tenor. I could always tell when Phil was in the room before I turned my head to look, by the sound of his voice. He even appealed to my ears. I admired his passion and his search for answers. Phil seemed better suited to a life of academia.

Our standard catering uniform flattered men more than it did women. The classic black and white penguin look—black tie, black pants, vest and shoes, all looked better on men. Uniforms varied by event and from company to company. While I wore penguin black tie, Phil had on a blue crushed velvet tuxedo that fit him like a valentine. If the ideal figure for a woman is the classic hourglass shape, then Phil had the ideal men's figure. He had broad shoulders and a tapered waist, like a superhero. He was very tall, standing at six-foot-three.

But that night I did not yet know Phil's name, the first step in the process of getting to know someone—that first introductory step, and I was dying to find out. I was new to the company, and didn't know who was who yet, so I gave him one of my own made-up names. I referred to him simply as "King" in my head, because I was sure he would become my personal one. I referred to him as King as I continued to collect people's trays and to watch him from across the room. I noticed that he never smiled, not once. Rather, he sneered. He seemed to employ a lot of sarcasm in his interactions with others. His flippant, rebellious ways turned me on.

At lunch he seemed standoffish. I attempted to sit next to the mystery man on our meal breaks, but he would move to a different table with an arrogant toss of his blond ponytail. I nearly gave up then, thinking that he thought me hideous. I would later find out he behaved conceitedly with everyone, as a protective façade to hide his insecurities.

If not for Amy, I would have given up hope and the beautiful creature would have been forever unknown to me. Amy also worked for the temp agency. She was saving up to move to Virginia to attend military college there. We bonded over the fact that we had both been to Ireland. I had gone there with my family when I was twenty. Amy and I made jokes about the way the Irish say "tree" for the number three and then stated that our phone numbers were "tree tree tree-, tree, tree, tree- tree tree, tree, tree." One night Amy and I were cleaning up after an event and we ran into the angelic being I referred to as King. *Gasp.* Amy and I were bussing tables, telling each other dumb Irish fairytales and clowning around. I felt foolish, as if I'd been caught in a compromising position when he spoke to us. I immediately stopped laughing, trying to behave sensibly and demurely. It was time to get back to work.

"What the hell happened to these wires? They're all tangled. Who did this?" he said in his familiar voice, which was neither deep nor grating. The voice was soft, the sort you'd want whispering in your ear before bed at night. He was often irritated with others, believing he was the only one who could do things right. I turned around. It was King.

"I believe it was the wire rat," I said, shrugging, for lack of a better culprit. I had no idea who'd tangled up the production wires, marring the sound system.

He didn't get it and continued holding the dangling wires. "The wire rat?" he asked. And then, suddenly, a light appeared to have gone on in his brain. "Ah yes, the wire rat," he said, a half-smile dangling off his face.

He never smiled with teeth, but his smile was nevertheless exquisite to me. It was sweet and adorable, like watching a rare flower bloom for a short time, the only time it bloomed, one day a year for just a few hours, observing the magnified fuzz on a bee's knee, or watching a baby kitten yawn. The smile spread throughout his face and lit up his features.

"Ha!" he ejected as he smiled, turning his face downward shyly as if the smile had escaped beyond his will and he had to control it and to suppress it.

Thrilled just to have basked in his light for a bit, due to my shyness around the blindingly handsome, I scurried away. But Amy wouldn't let me off the hook so easily. Knowing of my crush on him, it was she who handed him my card. *My card. How "business lunch,"* I thought. He hadn't exactly shown any signs of encouragement. Set on a black background, featuring a single velvet carnation and emblazoned with my name on it in pink, it looked more like a call girl's digits. *What an awkward thing to do*, I thought. *To give someone your card.* Worse, to have your *friend* hand him your card.

"What did you say to him?" I asked her from a safe distance, like a seventh grader asking for a report.

"I said, 'Here's a phone number, call it.' Simple."

"And why should he call it?" I asked her.

"I told him he'd get great benefits if he called it."

I burst out laughing at that. The whole attempt at contact seemed a fiasco. And Amy hadn't remembered to ask his name. Actually, she thought his name was Bill, having misread his nametag during the brief glance she had given him as she handed him the card. Phil, King, Bill. His true identity remained unknown. No one ever said, "Report to Phil" that night, or we'd have known. There was another acting captain in control that night and Phil was to take the helm on other nights. Our efforts came to a happy conclusion. He did call as Amy instructed, or at least texted (the modern form of calling, I suppose), a week after receiving the card. He saved the number, waiting for a few days, savoring it, probably so he didn't look too eager. Our texts said:

Me: What's your name? Amy told me it was Bill.

Phil: Bill? Not quite. Guess again.

He liked to play cat-and-mouse games, too. To outright tell me his name would have made it too easy and would have taken the fun out of it. He wanted me to struggle.

Me: Is it Brad?

Phil: Nope.

Me: Alan?

Phil: Nope.

Me: Who are you, Rumplestiltskin?

Phil: Alright. My name is Phil. Want to hang out sometime?

He knew of a place, his favorite haunting spot, a bar downtown. Upon arrival, Phil's abrupt nature put me off. He had been standing on the street corner near the bar with a friend, on the lookout for me as I approached. When he saw me, Phil arrogantly turned on his heels, as if I hadn't lived up to his expectations with my entrance, and disappeared into the bar with his drinking buddy. The drinking pal would not resurface that night. I was appalled by Phil's actions. I wondered if he was perhaps a little autistic or lacking in social graces, which was probably partially correct, judging by his behavior at work. *We're off to a promising start*, I thought, debating whether to go home or not. I should have ended things right then and there, and I almost did. Instead, I peeled back the curtains and trailed in after him. I'm a sucker for wanting to find out what's on the other side of a curtain. Curiosity killed the cat. Perhaps Phil had been trying to create an air of mystery about himself. If he had, it worked, and only made me desire him more.

When I peeled back the shimmering curtain, I wondered whether Phil was an exotic male dancer or something. It was obvious he wanted me to trail in his star dust by following after him into the bar. What a narcissist! Yet I ate it up, deeming his actions acceptable. It's common knowledge that women are attracted to bad dudes and rebels.

Our first meeting outside of work fell on July third, a significant date as it was just before the holiday. I'd hoped we'd hit it off and that we'd both see fireworks that Independence Day. Real fireworks exploded in the air around us, in loud, colorful bursts, but Phil and I struggled with our chemistry and fluidity. The conversation lagged, perhaps because we had been drinking. The bar sold artisan beer and I thought my glass of citrus ale tasted like urine. I wished that we'd agreed to meet somewhere else, preferably not a bar.

To start things off, Phil seemed anxious and pushy when we ordered.

"Order, order a beer…" Phil growled out of the side of his mouth as he nervously jiggled his leg, staring straight ahead, refusing to look at me.

I felt ugly, unwanted, and of little importance. It had to be why he wasn't making eye contact. I didn't know what to order as I prefer brandy, not beer, so I just ordered what he ordered.

While I fumbled for the right change, Phil impatiently plopped down a twenty on the register saying, "Too late," handing over the money for me as if I was just too slow and awkward to keep up.

He claimed to be a beer connoisseur the way some men are wine connoisseurs, but I'd later find out he mostly stuck, unadventurously, to Pabst Blue Ribbon. His drinking buddies were present somewhere in the back of the bar that night, but he wouldn't introduce me to any of them. How odd. Either he seemed to enjoy keeping secrets, or he was embarrassed of me. It hurt, but I consoled myself in thinking that he wanted me all to himself and didn't want to divide my time with his friends. I seemed to have a knack for picking the sort of guy who didn't want to get too attached and held me at a distance. Perhaps I was uncomfortable with true intimacy.

Phil was easily bored, and with his fast-moving mind, seemed to feel caged in. This would be reflected even in his seating preferences. He would always seek out the least confining sections of bars, preferring to sit outside on the porch. Once seated, I tried hard not to stare at him, even though he was pure eye candy, deliciously handsome. His eyes were a clear, cat green and close-up, he looked older than he had from across the room at the concert, but not in an aged way—in a mature, distinguished way. He was thirty-four to my twenty-eight. We were a study in contrasts. I was still an overgrown adolescent, he looked adult. He must have been interested in me that night, regardless, because I could see his pupils dilate as he stared at me. Hopefully it wasn't just the alcohol.

I tried, but I couldn't take my eyes off Phil's soft-looking mouth, which resembled pressed pillows or crushed rose petals that I desperately wanted to sleep on. Phil talked on and on about his

Brazilian mother and his American father and how they'd met during his dad's religious mission. There was a Brazil vs. Argentina futbol game on the bar's TV and I noticed that Phil kept sneaking glances at it, checking the score. His father had served an LDS or Mormon mission in Brazil and made a convert of his mother. Phil could trace his patrilineal heritage back to Brigham Young, the polygamist leader of the Mormon Church, although Phil openly denounced such behavior as foolish and disrespectful to women. The practice of polygamy was banned by the church since the late 1800s, anyway. On the day Phil's dad met Phil's mom, the church elders had been desperately praying for divine inspiration to find a badly needed organist to fill the chapel with beautiful music. After fasting and praying diligently, Phil's father had a hunch that he would be able to find who he was looking for behind a particular door. He knocked, and there was Phil's mom behind that door, who just happened to be a talented organist. His prayers had paid off. Phil's dad gave her the Book of Mormon and taught her the principles of the Mormon faith. She would later immigrate to Utah to attend Brigham Young University, which is owned and operated by The Church of Jesus Christ of Latter-day Saints. It's a familiar story for many of the residents of the state of Utah. A Mormon love story involving a conversion and a temple marriage and ending with them being sealed together "for time and all eternity," as doctrine encouraged.

Phil himself was an atheist, though he hadn't started out that way. He attempted to follow in his dad's footsteps and serve a mission, which would leave him scorned and unbelieving. Phil served as a missionary in Northern California when he was nineteen. Although Phil had, at first, a single-minded devotion to his church and to spreading the gospel, that would change once he discovered the hypocrisy of the church hierarchy firsthand and chafed under its strict rules. For example, his mission president kept a forbidden BMW in his garage. Cars weren't allowed on the mission, so Phil snuck around to the president's garage to make sure that what his eyes had seen was accurate. It was true. Parked in the garage was a shiny, taboo BMW.

"President, that BMW, is that a six or an eight?" Phil asked him when he had the chance.

When the president denied any knowledge of the BMW, and said that it had never been in his possession, something in Phil died. Here was a man, supposedly of God, lying to his face. Phil knew the president was lying because he had seen the car with his own eyes. Phil said it was then that he realized that his mission president wasn't some saint, but an ordinary mortal, a flawed human being. It was at that time that Phil began to lose his faith and to doubt everything about the church and what it stood for. Forsaking the 6 A.M. start time designated for scripture reading, Phil began to rise leisurely, whenever he felt like it, and encouraged his mission companion to do the same. And when opportunity struck, Phil answered, rebelling against the church. One day, one of his neighbors in the apartment building where he lived with his mission companion was walking down the stairs carrying a used TV, and he offered to donate it to Phil. Phil gladly embraced the technology, even though watching TV on missions was also forbidden.

As a final division between the church and Phil, he fell in love and his parents didn't condone his choice of partner. Dating is of course forbidden on missions, as the focus is meant to be on God and spreading the gospel. But Phil was besotted by one of his prospective converts, a young, innocent-looking girl who attended his church; he began sneaking into her apartment at night to sleep with her. He found out that she was pregnant two days before his mission ended, two days before he was set to discharge honorably. He almost got by, but didn't.

When the mission president found out about the pregnancy, Phil was excommunicated. It was a lengthy process involving long discussions within the church leadership by committee consensus. Being excommunicated didn't bother Phil's conscience much. In fact, he said he felt liberated, the freest he'd felt in years, after the church shunned him. As a first act after excommunication, Phil immediately discarded his sacred, suffocating Mormon garments, the underwear he was required to wear, and purchased some loose boxer shorts. He said it felt great to wear ordinary boxer shorts again. He said he also felt less guilty about masturbation, something he hadn't done in two years, since before embarking on his mission. "I won that battle with myself for seven hundred days in a row," he said, trailing off in laughter, referring to his abstinence. "And then I didn't have to fight it anymore." He made it sound a huge relief.

Instead, he ironically slept with a member of his church, which carried a much heavier penalty. As for the innocent church girl he'd impregnated, Phil married her. As he told it, he made the story sound romantic, as if he'd sacrificed everything for love, including his faith, no matter the consequences. Risked excommunication for love. He brought her to Utah and lived with his little family, his wife and son, for a year until the marriage turned physically abusive. He said she was always bruising and beating him and that eventually she'd "absconded" with his kid. "Absconded" was the only word Phil would give me when speaking of his family, which he did only on one occasion. He never spoke of them again, even when pressed, making it clear the issue was closed with his one-word placatory statement. This was a lot of information to take in on a first date. But it helped me to understand Phil.

Given his early beginnings, it was no wonder Phil was opinionated cynical. He saw people for who they truly were, with no illusions, after having been deceived by the church. His stories only made me curious to find out more about him.

Throughout our night together at the bar, Phil kept running to the bathroom to pee, interrupting our conversation. He must have done this six times altogether.

"Sorry, bladder problems," he explained. I hoped his dilated pupils and frequent urination meant that he was nervous and titillated by me, and that the anticipatory excitement and the electric tension between us somehow gave him the urge to pee.

After returning from the bathroom yet another time, playing the role of the ponytailed bad boy, he asked a random patron on the bar's porch if she had any cigarettes, then tucked money into the pocket of her dress to reimburse her. He was bumming smokes, *how shocking*. He explained that he was trying to not get addicted by obtaining cigarettes individually and then rationing them out. It was a nice thought, but his plans to cut back weren't working. After smoking one cigarette down to the nub, he soon needed another. Later, he would quit after ten years of smoking and announce the exciting news to me, but not that night. Between his trips to the bathroom and his cigarette runs, I was left alone staring into my glass of beer. I liked Phil too much to protest his actions, enabling him. Looking through the bar's frosted glass, I witnessed him stopping by his friends' table to chat. I wondered what tidbits of gossip he was dropping on them and why he hadn't the manners to introduce me. I felt left in the cold, on the outside looking in. Fireworks exploded around us that July third, but they did not light up Phil's eyes, nor mine.

I decided to call it an early night to demonstrate that the world didn't revolve around him and that I wasn't about to sit around and wait. "I've got to go. I've got an early day tomorrow," I said. That would teach him how to treat me.

"You're leaving? So early? Don't leave yet..." he said, regretfully.

"I have to."

I walked away. I could feel Phil's eyes on me, watching my departure. I tried to put on my sexiest, most feminine swaying walk for his benefit, in my heels and cutoff shorts as I strolled away from him. I ended up nearly tripping in the effort, but I eventually made it to my car. *Ignore me? Take that as a lesson to you*, I thought.

Phil never gave me any obvious indication of whether he liked me or not on that first date, other than his dismay over my early escape, so I was surprised when, later that evening he texted and asked if he could see more of me. I was uncertain. I felt the date had gone badly with his frequent disappearances and my loneliness. I wanted to put some distance between Phil and me in order to make up my mind by evaluating the situation critically, from a distance, before getting attached.

Therefore, without much consideration—even though it wasn't the first idea others trying to flee bad situations would automatically think of—I promptly joined the organic farming organization Willing Workers on Organic Farms, or WWOOF. Only this time I would be volunteering without bringing any prescription pills along, and this time the experience would go more smoothly. I signed up for the organization the way some people join the military to escape. Wwoofing was like temping; I would be trying out yet another non-permanent role without committing myself to any contracts, and I would get to see the countryside as a willing worker on an organic farm. Farming experience wasn't required. It was hands-on experience where one would be expected to learn irrigation and planting techniques. My seasonal work schedule would leave plenty of time for diversions. I told Phil that I had gone on vacation. If things didn't work out, I would likely be seeing Phil at work anyway, making it hard to avoid him. I had better concentrate intensely on my next move so that I would not make a mistake. I figured that Wwoofing was the perfect opportunity and would give me time to reflect. I have a love of spontaneity.

I applied to WOOF on an organic Hare Krishna llama farm in Spanish Fork, Utah. Wwoofing. It sounded like something a dog would do, and truthfully, I would be working like a dog. In other words, I was to become a migrant farm slave, paid in room and board and compensated for my work with organic vegetables, fresh air, and new experiences. The fact that I wasn't a Hare Krishna myself did not deter me nor delay my application. Wwoofing seemed to be another one of those aimless volunteer projects that mostly young people embarked on, young people like myself who had little direction in life and were seeking a healthier lifestyle and to "find themselves." And, like the Canadian volunteer project, it was also another way to travel for free when I couldn't have afforded it otherwise. I would enjoy volunteering in my native country much more than I had in Canada. The American "land of opportunity" motto played itself out, compared to chilly Canadian stinginess. Perhaps being a native in my homeland made me less suspicious to others and therefore more accepted. My Canadian trip had grabbed me by the horns, but I would direct every detail of my Wwoofing trip.

I arrived at the Lotus Temple, the centerpiece of the WWOOF farm, with the Hare Krishnas chanting inside. Their chants echoed off the marble walls. It was a million-dollar temple—literally having cost a million dollars, I would later find out—with pointy, golden eastern domes atop it like steeples. Brilliant turquoise peacocks with sapphire eye-like patterns on their feathers wandered around the temple grounds. Allowing animals to roam free and unharmed was part of Krishna's philosophy. In the temple's kitchen was a vegetarian curry bar. Vegetarianism was another Hare Krishna belief. The cook was a transplant from India who wandered about in colorful saris smelling of spices. Since all of the food on the farm was organic, one of our Wwoofing assignments involved chopping up the fresh vegetables we picked from the garden. We gave the pieces to the cook, who then turned them into dishes like curry zucchini soup. The work was grueling but rewarding. We were encouraged by the Hare Krishna not to eat meat, which they explained was tainted due to the release of pain chemicals in animals at death. The cook served only vegetarian meals.

Behind the temple was a fully functional organic farm. The owners sold produce to the local community and held an annual event called Llama Fest, which charged for admission and was a local spectacle and cause for celebration, like a circus. The farm was also a tourist site in its unusualness—a Krishna temple in the middle of the Utah desert, looking as if it had been transported straight from a foreign, faraway place. I couldn't have found anyplace rarer to Wwoof, and I had looked hard. The place was perfect for my bizarre sense of humor and fulfilled my desire to do good in the world. Inside the temple, below the chapel, one could buy temple T-shirts and souvenirs like saris and llama fur sweaters in the gift shop. Phil texted that he wasn't sure about this place. He thought it sounded like a cult when I eventually told him about it.

"*LOL*," he typed. "Tell me more about this place." Having been duped by the Mormon Church, he was especially wary of religious missions.

I assured him that I was just having fun and wouldn't drink the Kool-Aid stirred by cult leaders, nor buy into any fanatical ideas. Phil, with his intensely curious mind, texted me questions about what I heard, saw, tasted, and smelled on a daily basis and asked me to describe the place for him. I adored his childlike need for exploration. While I had previously been on the fence about Phil, my opinion began to sway toward reuniting with him when I returned.

I found the organic farming lifestyle very wholesome, invigorating and refreshing. Our conditional stay at the farm hinged upon the requirement to work in the garden six days a week and to attend temple services on Sundays. I figured inviting a little spirituality into my life couldn't hurt if I didn't have to take it to heart or become a loyal, devout believer. I could let any new religious information that clashed with my core values and personal mission statement just go in one ear and out the other, disregarding what didn't fit, absorbing only what I wanted from the teachings. In an internet disclaimer on the farm's website, it was clearly stated that attendance at the Sunday service was mandatory but that adoption of their beliefs was not, in case anyone had any qualms about being forced.

My roommates, the other Wwoofers, got along well with me. There was even another girl on the farm with my same name. What were the odds? Sharing a room with her appeared to be an act of fate. We Wwoofers were lodged in a small cabin at the back of the farm, which was much larger than the janitor's closet provided in Vancouver. By day we toiled in the fields, by night we played cards and chatted. Marilyn and I cracked lots of jokes about the similarity of our names, and enjoyed confusing the others when no one could discern precisely which Marilyn was wanted when the name was called out in the fields. Then she told me her name was spelled M-a-y-e-r-l-i-n, but people just left out the 'Y' and the 'R' and called her the more traditional "Marilyn" and she was fine with that. I caught the subtle difference, but our names sounded so much alike as to be indistinguishable when spoken quickly or from a distance in the fields. We worked as a team—we had to in order to complete our daily chores, the planting, picking, fence-mending and the erection of barn siding in the hot sun. We were working in 110-degree weather, so it was best to cooperate to get things done early in the day before the sun was high in the sky and at its most scalding. Our hands were calloused and pierced by wood slivers and there were blisters on our feet, but I didn't hear any complaints. We were a group of peaceful, barefoot hippies anyway. I was happy to be helping to produce an organic food supply for the local community; it was our duty.

As we worked, Hare Krishna monks walked about the temple grounds in their long robes, occasionally stopping to pet and whisper to a llama. As the Hare Krishna believe in reincarnation, they place a lot of value on the heads of animals, believing them to be old souls with the potential to return, so they had better be treated well. The monks meditated a lot, but did not help us in the fields. They spent their days trying to achieve a higher state of consciousness and attending to their spiritual studies; they were above toiling of the flesh.

Sundays were sacred. There were no stiff pews to sit in. We sat cross-legged on pillows for the service on the temple's intricately patterned white marble floor and sang long Hare Krishna chants. We repeated after the monks, who also sat on pillows as they led us in instruction and delivered lessons out of the Bhagavad Gita, sung in song saga-form. We were taught the concept of karma.

We groomed the farm's llamas with brushes that tangled in their matted, wooly coats and adorned them with ribbons to prepare them for Llama Fest, the highlight and grand finale of the Wwoofing experience. Hundreds of locals swarmed over the temple grounds to see the show. A crank handle snow cone machine was rented to churn out treats, and a band hired to keep the attendees entertained during periods of inactivity before the llama show.

The trained llamas were supposed to perform stunts at the festival, but the farm's proprietress didn't have confidence in my ability to guide the creatures through their tricks to dazzle the crowd, so she let one of the male Wwoofers star in the show instead. I'm sure I could have lead a beast through a few hoops had she allowed me to. I felt the stinging injustice of favoritism.

Phil texted me every day of my volunteer experience. With his innate curiosity, he had me describe my daily happenings and goings-on. And my reports were absurd and detailed. Tales of llamas jumping through hoops only piqued his interest, making him want to inquire more. I sent him pictures of the gentle creatures and told him how much fun I was having. By sending him the llama pictures, I was sending him a picture of an animal representative of our shared South American cultural heritage. Phil and I both had South American mothers and North American fathers but were just plain old Americans to ourselves, having been born and raised in Utah. It was a background that united us in shared commonality.

With the culminating event, Llama Fest, over, my Wwoofing

experience came to a close. I resumed catering, determined to include Phil in my life now, after much contemplation. Receiving his texts had been the highlight of my Wwoofing days and I loved the way he craved new information like a newborn gazing at his surroundings with wonder. It wasn't so much of a choice of whether I would *see* Phil or not; of course I would see him at work, as his coworker. The question in my mind was whether I would see him outside of work or not. I didn't mind working with him, though his observations of my effectiveness made me slightly nervous, given our revised relationship to each other—one that went beyond coworker and supervisor. I could feel his eyes on me as we worked, watching me, burning holes in my back. Now that we had gotten involved, he paid more attention to me than he had before when I was an unknown worker, one of about a hundred employees. And his appearance had improved since we became involved. He looked even better now than he had the night I first saw him, as if having a woman in his life gave him cause to dress up and reform. His hair looked longer and more luxurious. His smooth ponytail shone under the stage lights. It was easy to spot him. He was the tallest man in the room with the best body, and he was also the handsomest. When I patrolled the ballroom with a male friend and fellow caterer, bussing tables and chatting with him, I felt Phil's eyes on me. Was Phil envious of the coworker? He was glaring at me with his arms folded across his chest, made uncomfortable by my platonic association with the other man. In truth, Phil was a very jealous person. Once he would show up at my house unannounced after a party, jealously ensuring that I hadn't let anyone from the party sleep over, but of course no one had. Though he had declined to attend himself, somehow he felt his jealously was justified. I didn't see any reason for Phil to feel jealous. The caterer I was talking to was just a friend, and there was no romantic interest at all between us.

Phil and I were afraid our dalliance would become public knowledge and an object of water cooler (or in this case, soda fountain) gossip, so we agreed to play it cool. I didn't want anyone to think that I was hired due to Phil. Our avoidance of each other was a matter of workplace politics and for our own safety. Phil played it cool to extremes. He didn't want anyone to think I was given an unfair advantage. He shrank almost visibly from my presence, and would quickly transport himself to the opposite side of the room when I approached. He would only speak to me if absolutely necessary; if I was reaching for the same cart or plate he was, for example.

Once, I was struggling with a hot pan and needed to set it down immediately. When I asked Phil to help me clear a space he shouted, "No!" and jumped back. He was repelling me like a similarly-charged magnet end, and I was horrified. His attempt at nonchalance wasn't very composed, but it was clear he wanted our activities after hours to remain a secret.

Phil may have been a lowly caterer, but he was also an avowed atheist and activist who exercised his intellectual side, which was well developed. In his spare time, he attended symposiums on religion and philosophy, and was even a guest speaker on a radio podcast called *Mormon Expressions,* which dealt with post-Mormon life. Having been excommunicated from the Mormon Church after devoting two years of his life in service to it, he had a lot of regrets over stolen time and took an interest in mass religious deception. He was especially interested in topics like "Religion and Mind Control." Knowing his love for books, especially on religious matters, I offered to give him some of mine after work.

"Hell, yes!" was his eager response, when asked if he wanted them.

We had previously joked over the phone that "Would you like some books?" was code to him for "Wanna have sex tonight?"

So, as gingham-clad guests started leaving the venue and the catered country hoedown appeared to be winding to a close, I walked over to where Phil was folding a tablecloth and said, "Would you like some books?"

I knew I wouldn't get in trouble for it because no one else knew the meaning of our code, and therefore wouldn't make any perverse interpretations. It wasn't as if talking about literature was going against the mandates of the employee handbook.

Phil seemed to physically jump for joy, perking up like a little kid would, and his green eyes sparkled.

He laughed and said, "Hell, yes! I'd *love* them. I collect those." I wasn't sure if Phil meant he wanted sex or books, but logged his answer in the affirmative. If he wanted one, it might signify he wanted the other as well.

After we finished our catering duties, folding a few hundred more tablecloths and stuffing them into linen bags, I waited for him next to the soda fountain with a coworker, a girl named Bronwyn, a tall, thin, pretty brunette, so that I could give him his books. She was present for reinforcement and emotional support as I was nervous about meeting our handsome boss by myself. As Phil spoke with the manager about next week's schedule, Bronwyn attempted to tell him something.

"Can't you just shut up?" Phil yelled at her. "Can't you see I'm talking to the supervisor here, *okay?*"

I was horrified by Phil's behavior and his treatment of Bronwyn. Work was over and we had officially clocked out so I didn't see any taboo in her speaking to him. Even if she had been interrupting, he didn't have to scream at her.

Phil had been snarky and sharp with Bronwyn, which I found appalling. *How they treat others is how they will end up treating you*, I thought. I had found another abusive man, a regular habit of mine.

Bronwyn's face fell as if she had been slapped, in response to Phil's outburst. But I tried to minimize his behavior. Phil must have been tired, stressed out after a punishing and demanding day at work. I thought that Bronwyn should have waited until he was done talking, but I also thought that Phil was being too hard on her.

Then, as soon as the supervisor left, Bronwyn dumped her supersized Coca-Cola, clinking ice cubes and all, over the top of Phil's head. The cubes bounced off Phil's forehead. A syrupy brown liquid now streamed down Phil's cheeks—as if he was crying Coke. The whole scene looked like a cafeteria movie scene out of "Mean Girls," where the unpopular girl finally gets back at the popular guy for jilting her. I didn't know who was at fault: Bronwyn for interrupting Phil while he was talking to the supervisor about his schedule, or Phil for yelling at her. But I felt it wise to side with Phil if I ever wanted to see him naked.

"Gee, Bronwyn, did you really have to do that? Put that ice back in your mouth where it belongs," I said.

"He's a jerk. Hear that? A *jerk*!" Bronwyn shouted indignantly as she stamped her foot.

Phil, who seemed to have cooled off, ignored Bronwyn and collected his prized books from me. Grabbing a couple of napkins to mop up his face and acting as if the incident had never happened, he said, "These are great! They even have a glossary in them so I can look up the terms."

Phil seemed grateful to me for taking his side in the Bronwyn upheaval and Bronwyn, miffed, stormed off. Phil and I then sat at the tables near the soda fountain and talked. I could see that he was beginning to breathe more heavily and would continue to do so the more that we talked, and that his pupils were dilated as if he was excited by our conversation—just as he had looked in the bar. We decided to leave together, parking-lot bound, in search of our cars. He carried his books on his left side and I walked on his right. We could have passed for a fifties-era couple walking home after school with the boy chivalrously carrying the girl's books after class, if not for his long ponytail and our modern clothing. We couldn't take the chance that someone from work might find out about us, though, so I waited until we were almost to the parking lot before enveloping him in a huge bear hug. His body went limp. Something about his passivity made me feel the aggressor. I wasn't used to this.

"Should I back off?" I asked him, releasing my arms uncertainly.

"No, no…" he said softly, but it was all he would say, offering no explanation.

I enjoyed the warmth of his strong, solid body as I pressed myself close to him. I took his big hand in mind. He didn't push me away, but neither did he squeeze my hand back. Why, if he didn't like me, had he agreed to go out with me in the first place? Was he just toying with me? His hand was dry and warm and so much bigger than my own, his fingers long and graceful. I relished the feeling of holding his heavy limb. He was a good-looking guy by any official measure, with his broad shoulders and his patrician face.

We were just caterers to others, but both of us had our side enthusiasms. He considered himself a podcast announcer and I considered myself an aspiring writer. Catering was just something we did to pay the bills. We both devoured books and stashed them everywhere for easy access. Phil was very verbose for a man, a stereotype defied.

He offered to drive me to my car, because mine was parked elsewhere in the multilevel garage. I agreed, because finding it would give me more time with him.

He pointed to a rust wagon. "My dad gave this old jalopy to me. It's a piece of junk on the outside but not on the inside," he said. Unlike Ian, Phil didn't seem overly concerned with material things. Owning a jazzy car was not on his list of priorities. I admired this quality in him, his lack of need to acquire impressive possessions.

I replied, "Your car is like some people I know. Ugly on the outside with a heart of gold."

Phil didn't bother to get the door for me. I appreciated this missing gesture, deeming such actions unnecessary, a waste of time, and a step backward for women's progress. *He is much too natural and sincere for opening doors*, I thought. I was glad that he had at least offered to drive me to my car, proving he had *some* manners. I tried to forget the Bronwyn incident.

"What's on the outside doesn't always match what's on the inside," I continued, reaching for his right hand from the passenger seat, hoping he was one of those people who was beautiful both inside and out.

Phil didn't bother to elaborate on my comment and kept a poker face. I felt ready for the challenge, the challenge of changing the expression on his face to a smile, and I teased him as he drove me to the south lot using his manly, oriented sense of direction, which was no doubt better than my own. As I glanced at his handsome profile from the passenger seat, I felt the urge to tug his dishwater-blond ponytail and acted upon it.

"This is your kitty tail," I teased, twisting his soft, blond strands around my fingers.

Instead of finding my statement ridiculous, Phil practically purred when I touched his hair. His expression changed, and then he *did* smile. I felt his muscles relax into the seat as he turned into a being the consistency of rubber under my touch.

"Mmm... God, I hurt," he groaned, seeming grateful for the hair caress, and exaggerating his pain now that we were out of our coworkers' line of sight. He was looking for sympathy. "It was a long night, wasn't it?"

Phil stretched his legs felinely as he luxuriated under my touch, cramming his foot down on the gas pedal in ecstasy. Phil had a love for cats and he reminded me of a large, sexy mountain lion with his flashing green eyes and his slow stride. I would later nickname him "Luxury Cat," and he wouldn't object.

"Oh? Where do you hurt, exactly?" I teased, feeling him everywhere, sliding my hand across his knee and then further down his leg. "Do you hurt *here*?" I poked him, gently.

"No. That tickles. Why don't you put your hand *someplace else*," he flirted seductively. *If only our respective bosses from the two different companies knew what we did after work. Cruising around in cars, tickling each other...*

"Thank you for giving me those books," he said. "You know, I'm all alone tonight. House-sitting. *Alone*. Just me and the cat. *Alone*," Phil emphasized. "You gave me these books. Why don't I give *you* something?" he teased back.

Phil was obsessed with his hair and more than a touch narcissistic. After parking, he pulled out a six pack of brightly colored plastic Goody combs. "They're brand new. I keep one in my car and one in my pocket at work in case my hair's ever out of place." *Okay, Elvis*, I thought. "But these are brand new and you can have them." He handed me the pack of plastic combs.

"Thank you," I said. "You're really sweet." I didn't know what else to say.

"But I don't think these combs are an adequate gift. I could give *you* some books. When you come over to my house, where I'm *all alone tonight*." He obviously wanted to keep flirting and keep up the cat-and-mouse game.

"I should go," I said, not wanting to rush things so soon after meeting him.

I liked Phil and I wanted to see him again. I didn't want him to think I was promiscuous. By then Phil had pulled up to my car to deliver Cinderella Caterer safely, to let me out of his carriage, a battered green vehicle. *Now, if I could just be on my way…* I looked down at his big, handsome hand which was resting on the stick shift. There was something irresistible about that hand. The oversized hand looked very manly and appetizing resting there. I didn't want Phil to feel let down about going home alone to a dark, empty house and his cat, and I wanted to show him I cared at the same time, so that he wouldn't lose hope. Suddenly I dreamt up the perfect gesture of chivalry, despite the fact that I'm a girl and it seemed to be etiquette from a different time. But it was just the right touch, barely sexy and still innocent without revealing the goods and leaving much to mystery. I took his hand in mine and raised it to my lips. A happy looking sideways grin slid over his face. *I respect you and your body and I want there to be more to come*, the gesture said, without us ever having to speak the words. At least that is what I imagined he was thinking instead of: *I want sex*. We danced the ritual of some nineteenth-century courtesans with that delicate, old- fashioned back-of-hand kiss.

"Goodbye, Phil," I said, releasing my lips from his hand. He smiled enigmatically and drove off.

Over time, Phil would help me discover what hurt and what

could have dangerous, potentially disastrous consequences. For lurking beneath Phil's Prince Charming façade was a lonely young man who had come from an "emotionally chaotic" family, in his own words. Phil had learned how to abuse from abusive people. From the pros. And those who have been abused are more likely to repeat the pattern.

Though his parents were Mormons, it didn't stop them from being abusive as each category isn't mutually exclusive. Of his family, he would only say, "I was raised by crazy people." There was more to his story. While serving his LDS mission, Phil experienced an insomniac breakdown much like my own. I learned about this from his radio podcast when he spoke openly about his past. Phil liked to talk, perhaps a little too much. I listened in on his spilling of the beans, played out on the radio for thousands of listeners.

I thought that Phil and I could do normal getting-acquainted activities, like going to an amusement park or getting ice cream. Your average boy-meets-girl pasttimes.

"No thanks," he responded.

What Phil *did* agree to was to meet me at a dingy motel downtown. And I was the idiot who said yes to him. It was a real dive. There was a stained, beat-up mattress inexplicably propped against the door to our motel room—a filthy reject on its way to the dumpster. Ignoring the flea dump, I stepped past it into the room. I scrubbed the room with a bottle of hand sanitizer that Phil bought for me after I told him I refused to stay there unless we sterilized the place. We were meeting at the motel because both of us had found roommates and needed privacy. Though we were meeting in shady surroundings, Phil looked very handsome and the germ-ridden background didn't detract from his looks. He had a tired look to his puffy, heavily bagged eyes, but he still looked stunning. His green eyes flashed, catching the light. His long, dishwater blond hair was pulled back, his tresses smooth and polished. There were touches of gray-gold at his temples, as if he had been kissed there by the color gods. His Heinz 57 ancestry gave him hair as individualistically varied as mine, woven with several different colors.

He plopped down on the faded comforter. When he turned over, I noticed that his teeth were blindingly white when he smiled. They were a small, even row of pearls. Phil said that half the people in his family were dentists and that they had given him free work. Free cosmetic dentistry. He said that he thought of himself as a screwup and probably could have become a dentist as well, if it wasn't for his insomnia. His ambitions had been curtailed by health problems, just as mine had. I had been through similar troubles and had learned to work around them, for the most part. I cautiously peeled back the dirty comforter and we snuggled on the lumpy mattress together. His skin felt very hot, as if he was running a fever. I rubbed his back in circular motions in a tender gesture. I felt deeply attracted to him and based on his tales of woe, protective of him. I wanted to be near him, to watch his chest rise, to immerse myself in all things Phil.

There were faint scars on his chin "From a car accident," he said. I kissed the barely visible scars on his chin, lovingly. I knew I was falling for him when I was raving over his scars.

"You're still dressed," he said. "Don't be." He began tearing my clothes off.

He wanted me to complete a sexual act with him that seemed rather risqué and adventurous to me. Ian had always acted like sex was a shameful act, but Phil was completely open; a brave, entranced heterosexual charging full steam ahead. Sex was nothing to be embarrassed of with Phil. He viewed it as a natural function like eating. Nothing about my body disgusted him, but when it came to himself he became suddenly self-conscious.

"It's nothing," he said, referring to himself. "I'm nothing."

But the last thing I wanted was for someone I was in love with to feel bad about himself. I wanted him to have high self-esteem, to feel confident and loved. I would boost his ego by complimenting him. He had nothing to worry about with me. I already accepted and approved of him. His insecurities were largely imaginary and self-imposed. I thought he was perfect. I wanted to acquaint myself with every inch of his flawless body. His testicles felt full, round and heavy in in my hand.

"I love these things," I said, wistfully cupping his treasures, in awe of him.

Phil scowled. "It's just a scrotum," he said, blushing, as if he was uncomfortable with his maleness, while appreciating my femaleness. "Buttocks. Ischium," he said, tossing out official medical terms, which made me laugh.

Phil always referred to body parts in scientific rather than crude, slang terms. He usually sounded clinical and detached, like a doctor, when referring to them. Because I nicknamed him Big Kitty (due to his ponytail which I thought resemble a cat's tail), he purred for me happily as we made love, to humor me. He was so eager that night that if I tried to slide the least bit away from him on the bed, he would pin me down on my stomach with his strong arms, holding me there and pressing his weight down on me, trapping me.

"You're not going anywhere," he growled. I loved his display of strength. He seemed so strong, so masculine.

After, he said, "I'm going to take a shower."

"Can I join you?" I asked.

I was about to glimpse a bit of his abusive nature.

"That's too much closeness for me… It's not like we're in a relationship or anything," he said.

I felt as if he had slapped me in the face. With Phil it sometimes seemed that I could do nothing right. I had assumed that we *were* in a relationship. Phil stared straight ahead at the plastic curtain.

I bit my lip and drew in a deep breath out of shock. I imagined myself sliding off of him like a water droplet in the shower.

"Fine," he relented, noticing my sad face. "Jump in," he added half-heartedly.

"I brought shampoo," I said, squeezing it out of the bottle and showing it to him. "It smells like candy…" I coaxed.

I tried to shampoo his hair for him and began eagerly kneading the bubbly, white foam on his head, but he stopped me. "Don't be weird," he said, though I doubted there would be anything weird about washing his hair, had he cared for me.

He seemed afraid of closeness, afraid washing his ponytail was too intimate a move. His fears were Biblical in scale and reminiscent of Samson and Delilah. He never did tell me what had happened to his ex-wife or kid. "Absconded" was all he would say in reference to them.

"This shower is too small for two people. I don't fit under many showerheads, anyway," he huffed, referring to his six-foot-three frame. Phil hopped out of the shower, grabbed his towel and left me under the water. I continued to shower solo. The droplets pelting my face made me feel as if I had been abandoned in the rain. I felt painfully stung by his rejection. I watched the water swirl down the drain, the whirlpool foreclosing on our time together.

"Big Kitty, can you bring me my heels?" I called out to him.

Of course this was a favor that was too much to ask of him. "God! Can't you get your own shoes?" he barked, tossing them down on the tile.

"Thanks, Kitty," I said, ignoring his less than enthusiastic response. He really did look sexily feline with those bewitching green eyes. I was noticing his handsome features and not paying any attention to the way he was treating me, which I should have been, first and foremost.

Our next interactions set off a long chain of events in which I could not please him, no matter what I attempted. I noticed that Phil was already dressed when I finished with my shower. I sat down on the bed, and he complained that my hair was wet. That I was soaking him. I then attempted to do *everything* he asked, engaging in behavior that no self-respecting person ever should.

"I don't like damp hair," Phil said.

"It's okay, I'll dry it!" I said cheerfully. I grabbed a towel and the hair dryer and turned it on full blast.

"God, you only dried your hair for five minutes. You didn't do a good job. A hair dryer? What's up with that?" Phil complained. "Hair dryers fry your hair. Don't you know that?" Glancing at his lengthy, luxurious ponytail, I thought that he might be right.

I didn't understand what he wanted from me. I had wet hair, he didn't want it wet, so I dried it. But when it was dry, that didn't satisfy him either. In truth, Phil couldn't be pleased. I was with someone who was unappeasable when it concerned me, just like Ian. And then I did the unthinkable. I *kept* trying to please him. I tried harder.

"Alright honey, I'll fix it!" I said, in a cheerful, upbeat, Stepford Wife tone. I then proceeded to attempt to towel dry my hair, lock by lock, acting like a complete robot.

"Sloppy," said Phil when I lay the finished product on his arm.

Now he was just being absurd. It's impossible to please someone who can't be pacified. I was quickly realizing that.

"Here, I'll just put this towel on your arm so you won't get wet." I was far too accommodating. Who was I, Superwoman? Was I expected to read his mind? I set the towel down, spreading it on the bed.

Finally, he stopped objecting. Dressed in our pajamas, he cuddled me for the rest of the night as I snuggled under his chin. But I did not hear from him for a long time after that. He chose to distance himself. He wasn't interested, I thought. I was preoccupied by work and tried to forget him. I should have. It was the logical, intelligent route.

I don't always follow my own advice. Three weeks later, I received a text from him.

Phil: We could get another motel room.

Me: No way! I'm not doing that again. You don't seem to like me.

Phil: I want to have sex with you. But as far as a boyfriend goes, find someone who actually cares about you.

Me: Okay. I will! Your loss. I made you (I mentioned the acts he performed in the hotel room). Ha ha. That must have been awful.

Phil: Not really, it wasn't that bad, ha ha. Let's get another room.

Me: I'm not going to. Bye.

I would see Phil again at work. Circumstances bound us together. We shared the same place of employment and there would be no escaping after a bad night together. There, he looked better than ever. The catering tuxedo fit him perfectly and brought out his muscular stature. His hair cascaded down his back as he pushed a heavy cart along, gaining leverage with the swing of his powerful haunches. A hunk in motion. He seemed mostly unaffected by what happened between us and I watched him fold napkins and crack jokes with coworkers. At the end of the night, I felt very depressed.

Valentine's Day is hard on singles. Hallmark cards and red roses are a painful reminder that you are alone and won't be receiving any. The sight of couples holding hands in parks lets you know that you aren't one half of any whole. After Phil's rejection, I hit the bottle on the love holiday. I almost never drink, and when I do it's a single glass, but there I was downing the liquor in large gulps. *And there he was, probably completely unaffected,* I thought, while I would spend Valentine's Day by myself. I washed my beer down with a Benadryl. That's when I promptly had a seizure. My body shook, twitching involuntarily. Alarmed, I went to see a doctor. I was given a diagnosis of myoclonus and told I had mild epileptic-like activity of the brain, due to the combination of alcohol and Benadryl lowering the seizure threshold in my brain. I had seen enough problems. I didn't need to compound them, yet there I was drinking away my sorrows.

CHAPTER 36

Recovery: and Who Is Most Likely to Recover?

Lying there in bed after the seizure, I realized that I had hit rock bottom and needed to make some major lifestyle changes. I asked my boss for a work reassignment, expressing a preference to work with a different company. Eventually I stopped working at the convention center at all and found a new job. I no longer see Phil on a regular, required basis at work. Removing myself from a stressful environment was a successful strategy. It was easier to forget Phil when he was out of view. I began exercising and taking vitamins. I started with baby steps. Instead of running, I first had to walk. I began walking out of the darkness.

Exercise was the most significant resolution I made. It helped my mood and sleep patterns the most. I wish that when I had first become sick, I'd been given a simple prescription—told to exercise three times a week so that I could exhaust myself and get tired instead of being fed pills, especially as my final diagnosis was "medical malpractice." My sleep problems began to dissipate with proper exercise. I hiked various trails to change up the scenery so that I wouldn't get bored with the same old landscape. Running a mile a day and keeping a regular bedtime helped me to obtain deep sleep without the use of medication. For sleeping pills—and I tried numerous ones—were never completely effective for me. The pills robbed me of my personality and made me accident prone and forgetful. Ironically, they worsened the very problems they were supposed to fix.

Sleep, in the modern world, is a precious, limited commodity with our busy schedules, traffic jams, and constant access to digital communication, leaving little time for rest. Our ancestors, prior to the advent of electricity, exercised more than we do (think hunting and gathering) and slept longer. With the advent of the light bulb, schedules changed. It goes against human nature to be up at night under artificial electric lights.

Glen Harrold, author of *Sleep Well Every Night*, wrote about how people used to follow the natural rhythms of the earth and therefore slept better than we do today. "Long ago our ancestors would rise when it was light, work and play during daylight hours, wind down as the night approached and sleep when it became dark. The only source of illumination after dark was fire. Consequently, they followed the natural rhythms of the sun, and probably slept very well because of it. Humans, along with most animals, are biologically hard-wired to sleep at the onset of darkness. So responsive are our bodies to differences in light and dark that our circadian rhythms, or internal biological clocks, are even programmed to reset with each change of season. Now in today's 24/7 world, we are able to watch TV at all hours, work late into the night and be entertained in a multitude of ways long after it gets dark. Shops and bars stay open all night in our 24-hour consumer driven society. As a result of having so many night-time options, the importance of sleep has slowly been eroded. In our technologically advanced society we are sleeping less than at any time in our history."

Now I knew why my Wwoofing trip to the organic farm made me feel so healthy. I was exposed to the natural daylight hours of the earth, rising with the sun, which in turn affected my own internal circadian rhythms, triggering sleep at the onset of darkness. I rose with the sun and went to bed with the moon. And that is how I set my internal clock naturally and also why I slept so well.

Attempting to drink myself to sleep compounded my problems, and after the seizure I stopped trying to alter my consciousness with drugs of any kind.

Today I am especially glad that I continue to choose the non-drug route, exercising and taking magnesium instead, because statistics show that those who choose conventional pharmaceuticals aren't progressing as much as you might think. They are even *regressing*. A study by Harvard Medical School in 1994 announced that outcomes for people with sleep and mood disorders had *worsened* in the past two decades and were no better than they had been a century earlier. And the outcomes for disorders such as manic-depressive illness and schizophrenia were actually *better* for those living in *third world countries*, such as India, than they were for those in developed nations such as the United States. A study found that after a five-year follow-up, India had the *most* success in treating mood disorders, with 42 percent of cases reporting 'best' outcomes, followed by Nigeria, with 33 percent of cases reporting best outcomes. Poorer, less industrialized nations like India and

Nigeria are least likely to use drugs to treat mood disorders. By contrast, the rich countries which are more likely to use drugs as treatment performed poorest: best outcomes were seen in only 17 percent of cases of mood disorders in the U.S., and in fewer than 10 percent in other wealthy, industrialized nations. Thus, the nations who used drugs *the least* had *the best* outcomes, in contrast to the nations with the best technology and most advanced available research.

Certainly, psychotropic drugs made *me* feel worse. I would be slow to catch on to what people were saying, or simply not hear them at all, under the influence of the pills. They also made me feel less sociable, groggy, and less likely to consider myself "recovered." On them, my sleep was fractured.

One would think that psychiatric pills would help people to lead more stable lives. Yet the number of people disabled by mental conditions has risen dramatically since 1955, after the advent of the first psychiatric drug, Thorazine. At Boston Psychopathic Hospital, just after World War II, it was found by doctors Bockoven and Solomon that 76 percent of the patients treated and released from the hospital in 1947 were successfully living in the community. Yet after 1967, when antipsychotic drugs came into widespread use, only 31 percent of the patients remained relapse-free, and as a group they were much more "socially dependent" on welfare as well as needing other forms of support. The conclusion of the Bockoven study was for the selective use of antipsychotics only when absolutely necessary. (Whitaker n.d.)

Further emphasizing the destructiveness of psychiatric drugs, The *Journal of American Psychiatry* (2011) listed the results of a study that had been performed to measure the effect of antipsychotics on brain tissue volumes. They wrote that: "Greater intensity of antipsychotic treatment was associated with indicators of generalized and specific brain tissue reduction... More antipsychotic treatment was associated with smaller [brain] gray matter volumes. Progressive reduction in white matter volume was most evident among patients who received more antipsychotic treatment. Great reductions in brain matter after long-term antipsychotic use were seen in the frontal lobes which is the part of the brain that is the seat of higher thinking and creativity."

Taking psychiatric drugs can cause lasting changes in the brain that, when withdrawn, can cause a withdrawal process that may mimic symptoms of mood disorders despite actually being just symptoms of the sudden cessation of the drugs and the body's need for more pills. When withdrawn from psychiatric drugs, patients appear restless and ill. They appear worse until their withdrawal is complete, as happened to me. Some psychiatric drugs such as Xanax, a benzodiazapene, are *physically addictive*, just as alcohol is. Remember the Mother's Little Helper heyday of the 1960s when it was believed Librium was a cure-all? Just like when the tobacco companies insisted smoking wasn't bad for you? Or when lobotomies were a form of treatment because they *didn't* damage the brain? Drugs like Xanax and Librium work by increasing the amount of a neurotransmitter called GABA, or Gamma Aminobutyric Acid in the brain, which has a calming effect. When removed, the brain lacks the ability to calm itself down after having relied on the drug as a crutch. When high-dose benzodiazepines are abruptly discontinued, this "down-regulated" state of brain inhibitory transmission is unmasked, leading to characteristic withdrawal symptoms such as anxiety, insomnia, autonomic hyperactivity and, possibly, seizures. The observed withdrawal symptoms from these addictive psychiatric drugs mimic symptoms of mood disorders. After witnessing them, doctors encourage patients to go back on their medications, insisting that they can't function without them. With long-term high-dose use of benzodiazepines, just as with alcohol, tolerance develops and the pills are no longer effective. So more must be taken to achieve the same effect.

(www.aafp.org/afp/2000/0401/p2121.html)

Long-term use of antipsychotic drugs may cause a permanent, repetitive movement disorder called tardive dyskinesia, which is thought to occur due to damage to parts of the brain which control movement. Tardive dyskinesia involves permanent involuntary movements of the tongue, lips, face, trunk, and extremities. The incidence of the syndrome rises with the dose and duration of drug treatment. The treatment for tardive dyskinesia is usually to stop or minimize the use of the offending drug if possible, but it still may not always resolve.

(medline.net n.d.)

For me, the permanent and disabling risks of psychiatric drugs were too great, and I was able to get by, even thrive, without them. I'd rather not be stuck with permanent, disfiguring movements, no thank you, or even the risk of that occurring. It is too bad that people are still being forced to take such drugs against their will.

One may ask why people are still being given drugs that are known to be harmful. The answer is probably for profit. Would a psychiatrist ever have any business if all of their patients recovered, never to return again to seek more help? Of course not, so there is little motivation behind psychiatric wellness. It is found that every year the pharmaceutical industry spends more than $12 billion dollars on drug advertisements and invests an estimated $8,000 to $13,000 per U.S. physician. This may include free gifts, samples, trips, and cruises sponsored by the drug companies. There is a Western mindset desire for a magic pill, a cure-all that is easier than conducting therapy sessions.

(Null n.d.)

The National Alliance on Mental Illness, or NAMI, which is supposedly in place to improve the health of the mood-disordered, and whose edicts include advice to "stay on your medication," was reported by the *New York Times* to receive 75 percent of its funding from the pharmaceutical industry. *The Diagnostic and Statistical Manual of Mental Disorders* has been linked to the drug industry. Tufts University researchers in 2006 reported that 95—or 56 percent—of 170 experts who worked on the 1994 edition of the manual had at least one monetary relationship with a drug maker.

Cultural interpretations of mood disorders and the ethics behind the consumption of drugs of course affect outcomes for recovery. Third world nations are often more permissive in their acceptance of people with mood disorders. In *Crazy Like Us: The Globalization of the American Psyche*, Juli McGruder, PhD, of the University of Washington Puget Sound, went to Zanzibar where she sought to find an answer to the question: Why do people diagnosed with schizophrenia in poor, developing nations have a better prognosis over time than those living in the most industrialized countries in the world? She found that ideas of mood disorders springing from brain chemical imbalances had not yet been accepted by the population of Zanzibar and that mental illnesses were attributed to spiritual possession, not thought to be permanent and incurable. Therefore it was assumed by the Zanzibaris that their afflicted loved one would eventually heal. McGruder found that it was the remarkable *tolerance* toward the mood-disordered that Zanzibaris showed which made a difference in their recovery and the way they were treated. Researchers found that those who adopted biomedical and genetic illness beliefs were most often those who wanted less contact with the mood-disordered and thought them dangerous. Those in industrialized nations were more likely to blame biology, while poorer nations attributed the illness to external factors such as a "crowded home" or "spiritual possession." Maybe less knowledge is more. Thus, the already ill person was not inflicted with additional guilt, such as the blame of incurring their disorder or bringing it upon themselves.

McGruder made a specific study of a Zanzibari girl named Kimwana to see how her mood disorder was handled within her culture. First, she was hospitalized for a week and then given antimalarial pills, as doctors thought that malaria could have made her sick. Kimwana returned to work on Monday but still continued to hear voices. Interested in her long-term outcome, researcher Juli McGruder returned years later. Kimwana's family agreed that her auditory hallucinations were made worse by their noisy household. They lived across from a Muslim girls' school and an Islamic school for boys, so the chorus of hundreds of children chanting in Arabic could often be heard, as well as the sound of the children playing at any given moment. They also lived across from a noisy city square where bicycle repairmen could often be heard passing. Interestingly enough, Kimwana's voices were those of persecutory bicycle repairmen, a reflection on where she lived. Kimwana was a modest Muslim and the voices of the bicycle repairmen she heard would often tell her to be more modest or to cover up. Another theory her family believed was that Kimwana could have a bad spirit following her. Yet in Muslim culture, unlike Christianity, spirits are not given an exorcism. Instead, spirits are catered to with song, food and dance in the hope of appeasement. Also, as part of Kimwana's treatment for what we Westerners see as a mood disorder, her family encouraged her to write messages from the Koran on teacups and then to dissolve them in saffron. Kimwana found such exercises calming and encouraging of healing. The tolerance displayed by Kimwana's Zanzibari family made the difference in her outcome for recovery, McGruder thought.

"It was not the popularly believed Western notion that life is simpler in third world countries, then, that made recovery more possible. In fact, Kimwana's family had a lot of mouths to feed under one roof and experienced a lot of stress. Instead Kimwana's behavior and deficits were well-tolerated and she was never pressured by the family into displaying "normal" behavior. Kimwana was encouraged to participate in household chores and her triumphs, such as having swept the house, were reported with delight. When Kimwana wasn't doing so well, her family encouraged her to withdraw and rest. Kimwana's family did not consider their sacrifice in caring for Kimwana remarkable. They were used to such hardships. For the most part, Kimwana was allowed to drift back and forth between periods of health and sickness without much comment from her family. Thus, Kimwana felt little pressure to develop an identity as a permanently ill person," wrote McGruder.

It seems that one's culture can *vastly* affect even the *type* of delusions one experiences and also the outcome for recovery within a society. "Delusional guilt is most often associated with Judeo-Christian cultures, as are hallucinations such as hearing the voice of God. Such hallucinations are rarer in Islamic, Hindu, and Buddhist populations. Schizophrenic patients from Pakistan are more likely to have visual hallucinations of ghosts and spirits than are British schizophrenics, who are more prone to "hearing voices." In traditional Southeast Asian villages, where it is often frowned upon to strive willfully for personal status, delusions of grandeur are rare. In the United States where celebrity, wealth and power are popular fetishes, people with mood disorders often say that they believe they are famous or all powerful." (*Crazy Like Us: The Globalization of the American Psyche*, pgs. 135-184)

Outcomes for recovery are also influenced by the way families view mood disorders. Researchers found that a family's level of something called "expressed emotion"—their reaction to illness—affected the outcome of an afflicted family member.

Global levels of expressed emotion were as follows:

- Among British families-48 percent
- Among Chinese families-42 percent
- Among American families of Mexican descent-41 percent
- Among British Sikh families-30 percent
- Among Indian families-23 percent

Hispanic families, who actually had lower levels of expressed emotion than Anglo-American families, referred to schizophrenia as an "ataque de los nervios" or an attack of the nerves. Just a simple case of shaken nerves, no big deal. It was assumed the afflicted family member would recover, as they deemed bad nerves a temporary condition, much like dizziness. It was in the cultures which minimized illness that higher rates of recovery were seen. The families which accepted poor, old nervous Juan as another member of the family, like the family pet, expressing empathy for him, fared better and saw higher rates of recovery than in those families who saw him as biologically ill, incurable Juan.

Race affects the recovery outcome of those with mood disorders as well. In my particular situation, I was told by the social worker Jeff that because my mom was Peruvian, I needed to accept the standard treatment practices of the United States, despite the fact that I had been born in the U.S. and have lived here since the day I was born.

"We'll have none of this Peruvian Shamanism," he said, insensitively.

I am American-born with a Peruvian mother and an American father. Jeff spoke to me as if I'd just stepped off a boat. Such statements notified me that race had indeed affected my treatment. Statistical studies show that psychiatrists diagnose African-American males as having schizophrenia at up to 1,500 percent more than they do whites. One study carried out in both 1984 and 1990 in Tennessee found that although African-Americans represented only 16 percent of the Tennessee population, 48 percent of the almost 3,000 involuntarily committed patients were African-Americans with the diagnosis of schizophrenia. Black patients were *consistently* diagnosed with more severe disorders than whites, subjecting them to heavier doses of drugs and longer hospital stays. (Null, *7 Steps to Overcoming Depression and Anxiety* n.d.)

Such singling out and labeling can be damaging because it can cause one to give up hope of recovery. Or, after being given Social Security Disability payments, as could happen to the mood-disordered in the U.S., one could lose his desire to rise above his poverty level circumstances. It's typical to be afraid of losing the automatic, guaranteed $450 or $700-a-month government checks if one makes over the income limits, disqualifying him as disabled. Therefore, recovery comes with a price, one that is often too high with too many hoops to jump through, and ambitions are often abandoned.

Robert Whitaker, author of *Anatomy of an Epidemic*, wrote about how the very drugs used to treat mood disorders can be an impediment to recovery. He interviewed Cathy Levin, a former college student who is now on SSDI payments and taking Risperdal, an antipsychotic drug. "The very drug that has helped her so much nevertheless has proven to be a barrier to full-time work. Although she is usually energetic, by the early afternoon, Risperdal makes her so sleepy that she has trouble getting up in the morning. (Whitaker n.d.)

He continues: The other problem is that she has always had trouble getting along with other people, and Risperdal exacerbates that problem. Levin said, "The meds isolate you. They interfere with your empathy. There is a flatness to you, and so you are uncomfortable with people all the time. They make it hard for you to get along. The drugs may take care of aggression and anxiety and some paranoia, those sorts of symptoms, but they do not help with the empathy that helps you get along with other people."

Joining the patient rights organization Mind Freedom was another aspect of my recovery. Mind Freedom emphasizes personal choice in psychiatric treatment and fights against abuses of the system. I actually had the chance to meet Robert Whitaker, the author of *Anatomy of an Epidemic*, in person in Connecticut, and listened to him speak at a Mind Freedom conference. Whitaker is a Harvard trained health journalist and reporter for the *Boston Globe* who has written several books on the destructiveness of psychiatric drugs. I traveled to the conference with my mom, who is supportive of helping me heal with less harmful methods. Family support was central to my recovery. So was meeting peers at the Mind Freedom convention, who shared with me their experiences and their stories of healing without the use of psychiatric drugs.

CHAPTER 37

Therapy

As part of my recovery, I also joined the organization CoDA or Co-Dependents Anonymous. CoDA is a twelve-step program based in the tradition of Alcoholics Anonymous, only the focus is on recovery from relationship addiction. Obsessive worry over the state of my personal relationships sometimes kept me up at night, worsening my insomnia, along with exacerbating my overactive mind. Social abandonment was one of my biggest fears. My family's departure on a fishing trip had sent me into a downward spiral of destruction.

Soon after I embarked on my own imposed health regime: incorporating more exercise into my day, eating healthier, getting more sleep, attending therapy groups, and sticking to a regular routine, I would receive a message from Phil: *Let's get a motel tonight.*

Change was harder than I thought it would be. I had made some progress by then, but wasn't completely ready to say no to him. I hadn't yet incorporated the CoDA-advised idea of accepting that abuse has occurred and labeling it for what it is. I hadn't worked the first step: "Admitting we are powerless over others—that our lives have become unmanageable."

I was also attending individualized therapy, in addition to my CoDA group. Therapy would be instrumental in my recovery and came with few side effects. I foresaw no damage in talking to someone about my life for an hour a week. I had several different therapists but did not find all of them effective. Some of them had widely different backgrounds from mine, and we couldn't find common ground, so there were long silences in our conversations as I sat on their couch idling and they stared at the clock, willing the time to pass. I switched therapists after incidents like these, and eventually found one who was compatible. After all, therapists are people too, with differing personalities, and you won't find a perfect match with all of them, just as you won't like every person you meet.

Jean *was* a good match. She was the therapist who would banish my phobia of sleep forever. Because I was traumatized by the insomnia I experienced on antidepressants, my sleep patterns were ruined for a long time afterward. Jean insisted that I call her by her first name. She had many years of experience. Her specialty was actually child psychiatry, which appealed to the kid in me. Her office was filled with toys and stuffed animals. *What a cheery environment,* I thought. It was Jean's talk therapy and advice that helped me heal most, more than any drug ever could.

"Don't worry about sleep, just don't worry about it! It's a natural inclination of the human body to fall asleep on its own. It will happen automatically. Everyone will fall asleep when their body gets tired enough. Look, you're either going to sleep or drop dead, and it's much more likely that you'll fall asleep first," Jean said.

I hadn't considered such blatant common sense previously. My preoccupying, blinding fears had obscured such basic logic from me. Falling into a deep sleep was much more likely to occur than death, especially at the tender age of twenty-eight, Jean said. I wondered why I had never looked at sleep that way before. After speaking with her, I simply stopped worrying about my sleep. I went to bed when I felt tired (usually around 3 A.M.) and I scheduled my work whenever I woke up. I took on freelance writing projects and worked the swing shift. Some people just have delayed circadian rhythms, and a natural-feeling bedtime will come later for them than it will for others, Jean explained in one of my therapy sessions, as if it was the most natural thing in the world.

Jean was able to help me gradually withdraw from my sleeping pills and embrace more natural treatments, a rarity for therapists to encourage. Nowhere could I find a clinician willing to take me off drugs due to his or her fear of being sued, except for Jean. None of them wanted to carry the responsibility should any harm befall their patient. They were not willing to risk their reputations on it. It is all too easy to get started on psychiatric pills, but it is hard to find a doctor willing to take one off of them. Doctors greatly fear repercussions. But I think Jean understood me and perceived that the pills I had taken had only made me worse. Jean was the first therapist who *asked for my feedback right away.* She told me that I would never follow through with a treatment plan I didn't agree with. So we constructed an individualized one together ourselves, whose terms I found agreeable and I could stick with. Open to my input, Jean even accepted my use of the handbook the *Harm Reduction Guide to Coming off Psychiatric Drugs*, written by Will Hall, as part of my treatment plan. I had failed in my previous attempts to withdraw from sleeping pills by quitting them all at once. Successful withdrawal involves a slow taper. Withdrawal effects can be dangerous, causing seizures and worsening your problems at first, the guidebook warns. I already knew about seizures. Seizures and Benadryl, and I was cautious. Jean was on board with this plan, lowering my dosages in small increments each week. The slow taper method to stopping psychiatric drugs, as recommended in the manual, was key. *The Harm Reduction Guide* recommends a 10 percent reduction in dosage every two to three weeks. Using this program, I was able to come off the mind-numbing pills. Trusting in my natural instincts and never forcing sleep, going to sleep only when I was tired, finding Jean and *The Harm Reduction Guide*—all assisted in my recovery. Obtaining adequate sleep was a pivotal factor in my healing process. Sound sleep made my life run more smoothly, improving my mood and energy levels. My problems dissipated after a night's deep rest.

Every once in a while, a physical illness such as a cold will precipitate a bout of insomnia in me. It happens when my energy reserves are running low, if I'm busy, stressed, my time and resources are stretched to the limit, or if I take a cough medicine for a cold which happens to have a stimulant in it, such as the decongestant pseudoephedrine. I now make sure to keep track of everything I consume, because I know that whatever I ingest will influence my mental state. I make sure to take in the proper nutrients and to keep well rested, checking for interactions from other medications.

But there was one thing I just couldn't figure out—my love life and my attraction to bad men. And by bad, I meant mutually destructive. I meant Phil. That's where going to CoDA meetings came into play.

I seemed to jump from one bad relationship to the next. *The CoDA Bluebook reads*, "Codependents... are extremely loyal, remaining in harmful situations too long. [They] Place a higher value on others' opinions and feelings and are afraid to express differing viewpoints or feelings. Codependents... accept sex as a substitute for love." The phrase explained my life with Phil.

In a brief hiatus from Phil, I hadn't found anyone new to replace him. I was vulnerable to the next loser, and in a strategic spot for an old loser to reappear in my life. I had not yet learned to apply the principles of detachment and boundary setting that CoDA literature advises. I missed Phil, or rather was codependent on him, and I liked him even more than I liked Ian. Ian was loud and funny and wore his emotions on his sleeve, but Phil wore a cloak of mystery at all times, making him seem more unobtainable, and therefore more desirable. Because Phil rarely revealed his thoughts, I was always left curious and attributed mysticism to his every action. Phil left me wondering with the monosyllabic speech he used where I was concerned, although he was quite wordy at his radio gigs. I responded to Phil's sleazy messages as if they were an invitation to some grand ball: *Sure. I'd love to.* Phil's simple, short messages continued: *A Motel, where?*

Phil was either scamming me, or had the communications skills of a Neanderthal. Foolishly respondent, I arrived first. Greeting him, I teased, "Hey there, handsome, remember me?"

CHAPTER 38

Walking out of the Dark

I certainly hadn't solved all my problems, but at least I was drug free at this point, attending therapy, and feeling healthier than ever. Most of all, I was sleeping. I felt ready to play. I thought I could handle Phil. I was in denial.

"Gee, I don't know if I remember you. Remind me," Phil returned, stepping into the room and closing the door behind him. He looked especially delicious in a form-fitting T-shirt with a beer company logo on it, showing off his bronzed arms. His blond ponytail cascaded down his back in a neat waterfall effect. Despite having a ponytail, there was nothing feminine about Phil.

Men don't usually go to hotel rooms to talk, I found out. That was not what Phil had in mind. As usual, I wanted to know more about him and was left full of questions, but talking was not on his agenda. I curled up on the bed with him and poked his rock-solid chest with my finger, tugging at his T-shirt.

"California Beer Co.?" I asked.

"Shh, it's just a silly logo," he said, silencing me.

He enjoyed playing the part of the matter-of-fact older guy. "Guys don't do that," he said. "It's gross. It's okay for girls to do, but not guys," he explained in a serious tone, as we fooled around and flirted and traded cheesy romance novel lines.

I tried to put on a sophisticated, worldly mistress act. "We're anatomically different," I explained. "Therefore, you must do what's necessary." I hoped my dominatrix persona was believable, but I kept bursting out laughing.

"I don't want anyone else to play with you. *I* want to play with you," Phil said. Then he shrugged. "I'm a bread-and-butter kind of guy, a former church missionary. Maybe not."

After our flirtatious volleying, we pulled the covers over our heads, but it was baking hot in the room and Phil was sweating profusely. His soft, fine hair clung to his forehead damply, the strands more adherent than usual.

"I didn't sleep well last night," he apologized. I seemed to attract this type. Phil had his own problems with insomnia, the ones I had just overcome. Due to a need to nurture and my own experiences, I could definitely sympathize. *Oh*, could I *ever* sympathize!

"It's okay, Kitty," I said, my nickname for him because he walked the way a panther prowls, was aloof, and had catlike eyes as well as his ponytail that reminded me of a cat's tail. Phil was a total sex kitten. So I made allowances for him. *Safety first. Don't drive when you haven't slept. You can go home if you want, to take a nap.*

At least that's what the *old me* would have done. I suppressed my own wants and desires like a true codependent. I never mentioned that I felt lonely myself, and would have gladly slept next to him.

"I've got to go… I'll let you know when *and if* I *might* be back.

I'll call you around eleven," he said coldly, as he stepped out the door.

"Goodbye, Phil," I said.

"Goodbye." He closed the door behind him.

I stayed in the motel room in his absence, anticipating his return. I tried to read a little but my head throbbed, so I decided to lie down. It was long after eleven, when he promised he would call, and I still hadn't heard from him. I decided to phone him to see if he was coming back. There was no answer. He was treating me the way Ian had. Ignoring me. And I was letting it pass. *Wait, I knew this kind of behavior was wrong.* CoDA taught me that this wasn't normal. Somewhere, deep within me, I mustered some strength.

Me: *I'm leaving*, I texted him, and began packing my things.

Phil: *Wait, I was going to come back and give you some money.*

I was unforgiving. He had broken his promise and stretched me to the limits of leniency. (Phil later apologized by mailing me the money, a conciliatory attempt. His gift showed up in my mailbox, a tightly packed wad of cash. Phil could be a jerk, but at least he was an honest jerk. He was a former missionary, after all, even if he was now a proclaimed atheist. He had once answered to a Higher Power.) CoDA advises the setting of boundaries in relationships. I set boundaries with Phil by refusing to hang around the motel and wait for him. Maybe setting boundaries actually worked and could produce results, I realized. I wondered what would have happened if I also set boundaries with Ian, long ago, but it was too late.

"God, grant me the Serenity to
Accept the things I cannot change;
Courage to change the things I can;
and Wisdom to know the difference,"
read the Serenity Prayer.

By leaving Phil that night I had begun practicing detachment, which the *CoDA Bluebook* lists as necessary to healing from co-dependency. Melody Beattie, author of *Codependent No More*, writes: "Ideally, detachment is releasing, or detaching from a person or problem in love. We mentally, emotionally and sometimes physically disengage ourselves from unhealthy (and frequently painful) entanglements with another person's life and responsibilities, and from problems we cannot solve. Detachment is based on the premises that each person is responsible for himself, that we can't solve problems that aren't ours to solve, and that worrying doesn't help. We adopt a policy of keeping our hands off other people's responsibilities and tend to our own instead. We practice present-moment living."

After improving some aspects of my relationship with Phil using CoDA principles, I finally realized that complete detachment from him was best. He came to the same realization himself. I continue to exercise regularly and eat healthy foods. I am not afraid to ask for help from others when I need it. It has been seven years since I consumed a psychiatric drug. I continue to maintain employment and an apartment without the use of psychiatric drugs. Today I have completed my walk through the dark. I am well again.